A PARENT'S GUIDE
TO
CHILDREN'S READING

A PARENT'S GUIDE
TO
CHILDREN'S READING

by Nancy Larrick

Fifth Edition
Completely Revised

With illustrations
from favorite children's books

THE WESTMINSTER PRESS
Philadelphia

Copyright © 1982 by Nancy Larrick.
Cover art copyright © 1982 by Bill Cadge.
Bantam fifth edition / December 1982

BOOK DESIGNED BY CATHY MARINACCIO AND MIERRE

Published by The Westminster Press®
Philadelphia, Pennsylvania

PRINTED IN THE UNITED STATES OF AMERICA
9 8 7 6 5 4 3 2 1

Library of Congress Cataloging in Publication Data

Larrick, Nancy
  A parent's guide to children's reading.

  Includes index.
  1. Reading (Preschool)—Handbooks, manuals, etc.
  2. Language arts (Preschool)—Handbooks, manuals, etc.
  3. Children—Books and reading—Handbooks, manuals, etc.
  I. Title.
  LB1140.5.R4L37 1983   372.4   82-24702
  ISBN 0-664-32705-2

COPYRIGHT NOTICES AND ACKNOWLEDGMENTS

  *The copyright notices are listed below and on the pages following,
(p.v & p.vi), which constitute an extension of this copyright page.*
  *Grateful acknowledgment is made to the following for permission to
use copyrighted material:*
  Excerpt from "Weather" from CATCH A LITTLE RHYME *by Eve
Merriam. Copyright © 1966 by Eve Merriam. Excerpt from "How to Eat
a Poem" from* IT DOESN'T ALWAYS HAVE TO RHYME *by Eve
Merriam. Copyright © 1962 by Eve Merriam. Reprinted by permission
of the author.*
  Atheneum Publishers, Inc.: Four lines from N. M. Bodecker, LET'S
MARRY SAID THE CHERRY. *Copyright © 1974 by N. M. Bodecker.
A Margaret K. McElderry book (New York: Atheneum, 1974). Reprinted
with the permission of Atheneum Publishers.*

To These, My Special Thanks

Since 1956, *A Parent's Guide to Children's Reading* has been a part of my life—first as a dream and later as work in progress. In preparing the first edition (1958) and through subsequent editions, I have had the encouragement and practical suggestions of literally hundreds of people. Many of these are parents and teachers who have written to tell me how they have used the book and how their children have responded.

In the first and second editions, representatives of eighteen national organizations read the manuscript at various stages and gave from their wealth of experience. Their suggestions and their continuing interest have contributed enormously to the book as a whole.

In addition, many friends have served as unofficial consultants whose help is deeply appreciated. Chief among these are the teachers and librarians who have been among my students in the School of Education at Lehigh University. Recently I have met with groups of classroom teachers in the Winchester Public Schools to hear their comments about the changing ways and tastes of children, the kind of books they respond to positively, and ways of getting children involved in reading.

These day-by-day anecdotes about children's interests and their reading at home and at school have provided a living documentary about today's children for which I am very grateful.

My special thanks go to Bessa Fitzgerald, librarian at the John Kerr School, Winchester, Virginia; Carolyn Parr, Children's Librarian of the Arlington, Virginia, Public Library;

and Lanita Kemezis, kindergarten teacher, parent, and teacher at the Northampton Community College, Bethlehem, Pennsylvania. All three offered valuable suggestions as the manuscript was being written and edited.

And for flawless typing with a smile, I am grateful to Jeni Fox.

NANCY LARRICK

Winchester, Virginia
February 1982

Contents

A Parent's Guide to Children's Reading—Fifth Edition

In 1958 the first edition of *A Parent's Guide to Children's Reading* was published under the sponsorship of the National Book Committee. The first and second editions were prepared with the assistance of consultants from eighteen national organizations representing youth, parents, teachers, librarians, and others concerned with children's reading.

The enthusiastic response to the first edition led to a second in 1964, a third in 1969, and the fourth in 1975.

By this time there are hundreds of thousands of young parents and teacher whose childhood reading was influenced by *A Parent's Guide to Children's Reading*.

Each year new children's books are published, and some of the old ones drop by the wayside. Our way of life changes and with it children's interests and needs. The concern about children's reading continues unabated as parents and teachers endeavor to keep abreast of new reading possibilities and new juvenile interests.

The continued plea for guidance in developing children's love of reading in today's scene has led to this fifth edition of *A Parent's Guide to Children's Reading*. It has been completely rewritten to include notes about the ways of children today as well as the new print material which they find appealing.

I

HOW YOU CAN HELP DAY IN AND DAY OUT

1

You Are the Major Influence

"I can always spot the children who have been read to," said one kindergarten teacher. "They come in full of talk. They are eager to read because they have learned that books and reading bring delight."

Innumerable research studies arrive at the same conclusion; five-year-olds who have been read to continuously speak with confidence and seek answers to questions. Often they are ready to plunge into independent reading. In fact, some are already reading on their own.

A story from New Zealand dramatically illustrates what reading aloud can do for a child. It tells of the almost miraculous development of a little girl born with multiple physical disabilities. Doctors hinted that she might be mentally retarded as well.

As a time-filler, her parents began reading day and night to their fretful, wakeful infant. She responded with growing pleasure. Favorite books were read hundreds of times, and the fragile little girl began to blossom in mind and spirit. By the age of six she was an avid reader even though she had not been taught to read in the accepted sense. Instead, she had become so immersed in language and story that she seemed to achieve reading as naturally as a normal child learns to walk and talk.

Dorothy Butler of the University of Aukland tells this true story in *Cushla and Her Books*, a remarkable testimony of the power of books and reading in a child's life. "But," she writes, "there must be another human being, prepared to intercede, before anything can happen." Al-

3

though Cushla's parents were only twenty and twenty-one when she was born, they were "prepared to intercede." They gave their child untold hours of time, affection, and books. Cushla flourished.

If conversation, print, and pictures could transform the life of this little girl, think what they can do for the child with normal capabilities!

BABIES BEGIN TO LEARN AT BIRTH

By the time children enter kindergarten, they have achieved fifty percent of the intelligence they will have as adults. These first four years of life are called the peak learning years.

A major accomplishment in this period is the development of language skills. Babies soon learn to distinguish one person's voice from another's. With practice they learn to respond with smiles and arm waving, then with sounds that imitate speech. Soon they can say whole words, then phrases and sentences. Even at this early stage children are preparing for reading, which depends on verbal ability. This means recognizing words by ear, speaking them easily and correctly, using words in sentences that are coherent, understanding the meaning and implications of words and sentences, and raising questions about stories, songs, and poems.

Illustration by Anne Rockwell in *Gray Goose and Gander*

A child doesn't acquire these skills alone. He needs someone who knows the language better than he does and who is willing to play a pleasant game of conversation. Someone who will read aloud and stop to raise questions about pictures and text. Someone who will sing to the child and then sing again. This shouldn't be a word drill, just fun with words at bath time, at playtime, at bedtime. Talk about anything is good so long as you are drawing the child into the game with words happily.

Parents have the major responsibility to develop a child's oral language skills, but baby-sitters, older brothers and sisters, grandparents, and day-care aides play a part as well. Whether they are good teachers will depend largely upon the guidance you give and the example you set. Without happy experiences with oral language and books, children may have a struggle with reading when they get to school.

NEW DEMANDS IN THE MODERN HOME

The modern home is very different from the one that Grandmother knew as a child. More and more mothers are working outside the home. An increasing number of children are growing up in one-parent homes. Schedules are tight, and parents are torn by growing responsibilities.

Reports indicate that parents are spending less and less time with their children. One study showed that some fathers spend less than half a minute a day interacting with their infants.

Ninety-eight percent of the homes in the United States have at least one television set which is turned on six and a half hours a day. In many of these homes, the TV set becomes the baby-sitter, or, as someone put it, "the third parent." Often the television provides the only voice a child can count on when he or she comes in from school.

On the average, children of two to five watch more than four hours a day or close to 6,000 hours before they enter first grade. During their school years, they spend more time watching television than they spend in their classrooms.

They hear millions of words with their television viewing, but they remain silent all the while. To develop verbal skills, children need to use words in conversation with another person, asking questions and hearing the answers directed to them personally. They need self-assurance to venture into conversation and later into print.

Teachers report that heavy TV viewers are likely to remain inarticulate in the classroom, waiting to be entertained. As one teacher put it, "They expect me to be Big Bird all day long."

If you question a child about the TV program he or she has been watching, you may get the response one youngster gave me: "I don't know. I was just watching." Another responded to such a query with still another question: "Do I have to say it with *words*?" Both of them seem to be well on their way to becoming language cripples.

Heavy television viewing devours time children could be using to develop language skills through talking, singing, and exploring the words and pictures of beautiful books.

PARENTS MAKE THE DIFFERENCE

In several communities, projects have been set up to help preschool children develop language skills and the self-assurance to speak up and ask questions on their own. Those in which the greatest and most lasting gains have been made are home-based and involve parents.

On one project teacher-demonstrators make visits in the homes of preschool children twice a week over a period of months. During this time they show parents how to talk to their children at play, how to read to them and draw them into conversation, and how to build a child's self-confidence in the mastery of language.

The IQ scores and verbal ability scores of these preschoolers have increased considerably. Toddlers and in-school children of the same family begin to make progress as well because of the greater companionship of parents and children and the greater emphasis on oral language, reading aloud, and books of all kinds.

2
Listening, Singing, and Talking
Prepare for Reading

Children who learn to read quickly and easily are usually those who speak fluently. As infants and toddlers they have heard the singing and speaking voices of others. Gradually they have experimented with their own voices until they can express themselves with assurance.

In a few short years they become familiar with literally thousands of words, and the rhythm of oral language is on the tips of their tongues. With this beginning, reading seems to come easily and naturally.

Thus the foundation for reading begins long before a child is old enough for nursery school or kindergarten.

YOU CAN'T START TOO SOON!

In a number of community hospitals, parents of newborn babies receive information about preparing their infants for reading. "Now is the time to begin," says one Letter to Fathers and Mothers. "Talking, singing and reading to your baby now will help him or her become a good reader later on." A list of books for babies accompanies the letter.

An infant is aware of sound and can soon distinguish one voice from another. A four-week-old baby may respond to your voice by smiling and cooing. If you encourage this recognition, you may soon find your baby is waving arms and legs, even gurgling and babbling, with pleasure over the sound of language.

At eight months a baby may develop a jargon that sounds like a real language of questions and demands. The more you talk, sing, and read to the young child, the sooner the child will be drawn into responding.

Your first play with your baby should include lots of oral language—your own spontaneous commentary, for example, during a bath or at feeding time. When you bring a teddy bear or rattle to your baby, talk about it. Your voice—tender and soothing—brings reassurance and security which will encourage your baby to respond.

One of my friends begins the day for her little one by singing "Good morning to you" when she first comes into the room. It is a lyric she made up for the tune of "Happy Birthday," which she varies as the notion strikes her. Andy responds by smiling and jiggling the side of the crib as she approaches. I think he will soon be chiming in with some of the words as he beats time.

Even very young children experiment with their voices in response to voices directed to them. As you read or sing the old nursery rhymes, the baby is hearing words that rhyme and lines that repeat themselves. These rhythmical phrases invite imitation. Babies soon realize they can have a part in all of this and gleefully express their joy—right to the tips of their toes.

A baby should have the opportunity for conversation even in playpen days. At first you may feel you are doing all of the talking. But through smiles and sounds, the infant becomes part of the act, interrupting and giving as well as receiving.

This is a time when you can introduce nursery rhymes and songs. Many of them fit easily and naturally into the small child's daily routine: "Rub-dub-dub" at bath time, for example, and "One, two, buckle my shoe" as small shoes are pulled on. Don't forget such old favorites as "Ride a cockhorse" and "This little pig went to market."

Even before a baby can repeat whole lines, he or she likes to participate in nursery rhymes and songs. Take time to make a game out of "This little pig went to market," touching each tiny toe as the words suggest. Show the baby how to clap to "Pat-a-cake, pat-a-cake" as you repeat words and phrases.

Many Mother Goose rhymes include invented words which seem to invite repetition. Remember "goosey, goosey gander,"

Illustration by Gyo Fujikawa in *Mother Goose*

for example, and "hey diddle diddle." When you repeat the words "hickety, pickety, my black hen," you may get an echo from the child saying "hickety, pickety" with almost mischievous glee. Children repeat such words and phrases again and again as though savoring the sounds.

Or they may try new combinations of sounds. Sometimes a child will begin a chain of words, one seeming to grow out of the other. *Clickety-clack* may suggest *clackety-clack* and then a long string of *clack, clack, clack, clack.* This is a period of experimenting and testing sounds and combinations of sounds. How soon it begins and how deeply your child becomes involved will depend, in large measure, on the experiences you provide.

SINGING WITH CHILDREN

Singing with children is a beautiful way to draw them into participation in language. Many of the old folk songs for children have extended repetition which appeals to the very young. As a start, try "The Muffin Man":

Oh, do you know the muffin man, muffin man,
  muffin man?
Oh, do you know the muffin man,
  who lives on Drury Lane?

The second stanza substitutes "Yes, I know" for "Do you know" but otherwise is identical to the first, so toddlers can join in easily. This simple pattern and tune invite new lines which you can invent to fit your child and family. For example,

Do you remember Uncle Jack, Uncle Jack, Uncle Jack
Do you remember Uncle Jack who lives in Baltimore?

The more inventive you become, the more the child is likely to experiment with words and ideas. This is basic to good reading.

If you are somewhat hazy on the words and tunes of such songs, consult some of the song books listed at the end of this chapter under "Books for Young Children." There you will find everything from getting-up songs to lullabies, from songs about animals to rounds and singing games.

Traditional folk songs are another delightful way to introduce your young child to new words. A Kentucky mountain folk song that is always popular begins:

Bought me a cat and my cat pleased me
I fed my cat under yonder tree
Cat goes fiddle–i–fee, fiddle–i–fee.

Every stanza tells of another acquisition—a hen, a duck, and a goose, for example—each with sounds: "Duck goes quack quack," and "Goose goes swishy swashy." And each verse repeats the voices of the previous animals. Very young children will chime in on the "quack quack" and "swishy swashy" while older brothers and sisters revel in mastery of the whole tongue-twisting sequence. This is a song for all ages.

One folk singer who transforms listeners into participants is Ella Jenkins on the recording *You'll Sing a Song and I'll Sing a Song* (FC 7662, Folkways Records, 43 W. 61 St., New York, NY 10023). With the simple words of the title song, she sings a few lines and then invites you to sing a line until finally: "We'll sing a song together."

One of her most popular songs is an old, old one which begins:

> *Miss Mary Mack, Mack, Mack*
> *All dressed in black, black, black*
> *With silver buttons, buttons, buttons*
> *All down her back, back, back.*

Even children of three and four will echo the repeated words. Older ones soon master the fourteen-line song and go all out.

For all ages, singing brings pleasure and self-assurance. Those who may hesitate to speak out on their own are drawn into singing along with others. Furthermore, the strongly accented syllables of a song demand careful enunciation which is good preparation for reading.

Sing a few lines of "Mary Had a Little Lamb," and you will soon realize the rhythm demands that you pronounce every syllable:

Mar-y had a lit-tle lamb, lit-tle lamb, lit-tle lamb.

So when you sing with your little one, you are providing the basis for good enunciation which is important in learning to read.

DRAWING CHILDREN INTO CONVERSATION

In 1980 children of two to five averaged more than four hours each day watching television. Because much of this is unsupervised, solitary viewing, many children sit silent and motionless, watching the run-of-the-screen: cartoons, sports, soaps, crime-time thrillers, give-away shows, and thousands of commercials.

When these television children arrive in kindergarten, many remain silent, waiting for the show to go on. They are starting school with a handicap because they do not talk easily and comfortably.

Dr. Benjamin Bloom of the University of Chicago reports that some children enter school with a vocabulary of 4,000 words while others the same age are familiar with as many as 32,000 words. The high-vocabulary child usually moves ahead quickly and easily in schoolwork. Even with time and extra coaching, the low-vocabulary child is apt to fall behind.

Children who have grown up as partners in conversation, may be steady talkers by age three. They talk to everybody, even the cat. Some may even talk to themselves or to an imaginary playmate. They raise questions, indeed ask them over and over, until they get satisfactory answers. These children are on the way to being good readers simply because they are at home with language and are curious about everything around them.

Their skill in conversation results from experience in the give-and-take of words. But conversation requires another person—father, mother, older brother or sister, the baby sitter or day-care aide, for example, who will draw the child into listening, then talking.

When you understand how important talking is to a child's intellectual growth, you see your role as a parent. You turn off radio and television so you and your child have time to go on your own air waves. Without electronic competition, a satisfying conversation can take place, and children respond to the opportunity.

With a young child, conversation can begin with almost any topic—with toys and pets, the weather, food, picture magazines, older brothers and sisters, and on and on. It can continue along with other activities—while the child is getting dressed or eating breakfast, in the car, building with blocks, rolling a ball back and forth, or just looking out the window.

When you go for a walk with the child, talk about interesting sights along the way: a boy riding a racing bike, an Irish setter barking from a Peugeot in the parking lot, and the purple Honda that roars past. This is the time to use the exact word—"Irish setter" not simply "dog," for example.

As you retrace your steps toward home, talk about the familiar sights: "Here's the little girl we saw when we came along this street before." "This is where we turn to go home."

It seems only natural to talk to a child on walks and on the playground. Yet I have seen some day-care aides, even some parents, who walk the children as they would walk a dog, pulling them along with little conversation beyond, "Let's go" and "Come on." A no-talk walk becomes a lost opportunity for informal education and just plain fun.

When you get home, talk about the experiences you have had together. What was the best part of the walk? Where shall we go on the next walk? What shall we look for then?

Asking questions and finding answers should always be encouraged. At the supermarket, for example, take time to identify fruits and vegetables and question their origin. In the woods or park, gather leaves and note their similarities and differences. Speculate about such things, and your child may soon be asking questions too.

Since you want to get a two-way conversation going, try to avoid the questions which bring only yes or no answers. These are called "closed questions" because each one brings an answer which seems to close the conversation.

"Open questions" are those which keep the conversation open by drawing longer, more individual answers. Note this example:

Parent: The jack-o'-lantern seems to be grinning.
       I wonder why.
Child: Maybe he's getting ready to scare us.
Parent: Why would he want to scare you and me?
Child: Because it's Halloween and that's a spooky time.

It takes time for this kind of conversation, of course, but it is an excellent way to stimulate the child's thinking and give practice in oral language—both prerequisites to successful reading.

ADDING NEW WORDS

To be a good reader one must have a good vocabulary. Children learn new words and their meanings from hearing them and using them. Television introduces thousands of words to TV viewers, but until a child actually uses these words, they may never become part of his or her daily working vocabulary.

Parents should help children acquire new words and learn to use them comfortably. Remember that each word you use becomes a model for children to imitate and question. If you call every sea gull and goldfinch a "pretty birdie," you are establishing the habit of deliberately holding your children back. If you point out the difference and use the correct name for each, children have a chance to learn new words.

Unfortunately some adults persist in talking down to children in a special language they would never use with their peers. I recall one four-year-old's reply to the query, "What is your puppy dog's name?" "He's no puppy dog," he countered. "He's my Doberman pinscher."

This youngster was used to hearing and learning the exact word, not the meaningless umbrella term. He recognized the various makes of cars and could name each model correctly. Like his parents, he spoke of weather changes in terms of temperature readings or storm warnings. Later on, when he meets these terms in print, his experience will help him recognize and understand them more clearly than the reader who has not had such experience.

READING ALOUD TO YOUNG CHILDREN

Innumerable surveys have shown that the young child who has been read to continuously and who has learned to talk about stories and pictures is likely to grow up to be a steady reader.

The time to begin is in infancy when the reassuring voice of father or mother, even older brother or sister, attracts the infant's attention and gets him or her interested in verbal communication.

One mother tells of propping up a picture book to entertain her three-month-old baby, who by that time would respond eagerly to various pictures in her favorite Mother Goose book. In another six months, the little girl was chiming in on single words—*down* in "Jack and Jill" and "London Bridge," for example. Soon she could repeat whole phrases and verses.

When you have read aloud to a child a great deal, you will understand what delight it gives him or her. And if you are completely honest, you will admit you have enjoyed it just about as much.

Reading aloud to a child can be the highlight of the child's day. To be most effective, it should be at the same time each day—just after lunch or dinner, for example, or at bedtime.

For the best results, do some advance planning. Choose

a time when there will be no interruptions from telephone and TV. Select a place apart from the turmoil of the rest of the family—behind the closed door of your bedroom, or under a tree in the yard. Usually a child likes to sit close enough to see the pictures as well as to have the warm assurance of your lap or arm.

Before the story hour select several books you think will be appealing. For the best results, practice reading some of the nursery rhymes and stories aloud so there will be no fumbles when the child is listening.

Many of us read too fast for any listener to follow, much less a young child. Or we are guilty of a singsong which quickly grows monotonous. Although it is sometimes discouraging to hear the sound of one's own voice, there is a great advantage in making a tape recording and then listening. Almost certainly you will discover how to improve your reading voice and manner.

Don't forget that today's children—even the very young—are accustomed to the trained voices of television. They like to hear dramatic language. Mother Goose provides the script for many a minidrama.

Once comfortably settled for reading aloud, I like to begin with the familiar, maybe a nursery song or a Mother Goose rhyme. As soon as the child is old enough to make a choice, by all means honor the suggestion. At the same time, encourage her or him to repeat familiar lines, or join in singing the chorus.

Pace your reading so that the child can see the illustrations and explore intriguing details. Pause at intervals to study the pictures. At first, this may require your help.

When I read *Mr. Gumpy's Outing*, by John Burningham, to three-year-old Kate, she listened as though deeply interested but said not a word. Had she really understood the story—the scary part as well as the happy ending? Had she found details in the pictures which added to the story?

On the next go-round, I paused for a few questions: "Kate, can you show me the children in Mr. Gumpy's boat?" Then, after turning the page, "Where is the rabbit?"

As a *Sesame Street* fan, Kate responded easily when I said, "Let's count the passengers in the boat." Later, after the grand upset, I said, "Let's see if we can find Mr. Gumpy and all of his friends." So we pointed and counted again. At the picture of the little group walking home single file, I asked, "Kate, can you find the rabbit?" That took some looking, but by this time we were in a puzzle-solving mood, and Kate squealed with delight when she found the boy carrying the rabbit by his ears.

Sometime later I asked about the last picture in the book: "Why is the picture of Mr. Gumpy's house so dark?" We talked about that picture and then looked at the first one in the book. The contrast tells much about the time lapse in this little drama.

Illustration by John Burningham in *Mr. Gumpy's Outing*

At the beginning, Kate responded with hesitation, as though she had not been used to looking for details in the pictures and talking about them. Gradually she became more sure of herself. The very tone of her voice showed mounting interest and enthusiasm. She had become an active participant in reading and liked the role.

Don't be surprised, however, if a child wants to get on with a story instead of stopping for your questions and comments. If the book is a familiar one, he or she may give you the same advice a three-year-old gave his young aunt: "You can just read the words."

Usually young children like to take part in reading aloud by chiming in on repeated lines or speaking the part of a familiar character.

A number of books for young children provide for two-part reading. The adult reads the words and the youngster gets clues from the pictures or from memory to chime in with certain lines.

A favorite book inviting children's participation is *This Can Lick a Lollipop* by Joel Rothman and Argentina Palacios. Each page poses a body riddle in rhyme that is answered on the next page. Photographs show black, white, and Asian children; the text is in both English and Spanish.

A good book may start children talking about their experiences, real or imagined. Or, after hearing a book read many times, a child may want to tell the story from looking at the pictures. For a four-year-old this may be quite an accomplishment.

There is no guarantee that you will always be lucky in bringing child and book together. Sometimes the young listener seems restless and tired. Maybe the book is not right or the time is not right. If the child wants to get on to another book or to go out to play, by all means honor the request. Let reading wait until you can be sure it is a pleasure for both of you.

LET THEM HANDLE THE BOOKS

For young children one of the great pleasures in life is touching things, so they will want to touch the books you introduce. They see you turn the pages so they want to turn pages too.

But their hands are sticky, you say, and their fingers are clumsy. They'll tear the pages! And with that reasoning many a parent has put books away or said, "No! No!" to a curious youngster.

No one learns to love and respect a book that is protected by "No! No!" And no one learns to turn pages carefully without some practice.

For the very young child who is eager to learn about everything by touching and tasting, you may want to purchase several of the so-called board books. Each has full-color illustrations on six or eight pages of heavy board that is washable and almost indestructible. Two beauties illustrated by Gyo Fujikawa are *Mother Goose* (ten familiar rhymes) and *Come Out and Play* (eight four-line rhymes from old games and songs). If you introduce such a book, take time to start a conversation about the pictures. Then even the youngest toddler with sticky fingers can experiment with the book, turn the pages back and forth, and have a beautiful time.

Before your next read-aloud session with a "real" book, be sure that hands are clean. Then when you turn a page, explain that you do it slowly and carefully so the paper is not torn. Gradually show the child how to turn a page with care. Give practice and give encouragement. If a page is torn (that can happen even with adults, you know), get out your transparent mending tape while the child can watch you put the parts together again. Next time I think you will find pages are handled more carefully, and everybody will be happy.

BOOKS FOR YOUNG CHILDREN

No book can be recommended with absolute certainty for any age. Sometimes a book that is right for one three-year-old seems too advanced or too babyish for another. A book that is adored at four may remain the child's favorite at eight or nine.

The following books have been popular with many children. Notice the artwork in these books. The drawings are simple, and the colors are clear. The pages avoid the cluttered, busy look that sometimes confuses young children.

Mother Goose rhymes are available in books of all sizes and prices. Be sure you have at least one book of nursery rhymes that is a thing of beauty. Children sense the quality of such a book and quickly learn to handle it with care. Because the jumbo Mother Goose books include ballads of interest to older readers—even teen-agers—such a volume may be used for years.

The Tall Book of Mother Goose gets its name from its shape (5" x 12"). It contains 102 well-loved rhymes, illustrated by Feodor Rojankovsky with humorous pictures in bold colors. In every library I have visited, this is the most battered children's book on the shelves; its smudged pages are evidence of its appeal.

The Mother Goose Treasury, illustrated by Raymond Briggs, is a large brilliant book containing over 400 rhymes and twice as many drawings and full-color paintings. The illustrations are as robust and vigorous as English villagers at a country fair.

Brian Wildsmith's Mother Goose is a collection of eighty-six traditional rhymes, illustrated with imaginative full-color paintings by the British artist.

Often young children are more comfortable with a less bulky book of nursery rhymes. One very simple collection is *Hi Diddle Diddle*, a paperback illustrated by Nola Langner. James Marshall's *Mother Goose* includes thirty-five of the funniest rhymes with comical illustrations in full color. *Gregory Griggs and Other Nursery Rhyme People*, illustrated by Arnold Lobel, is a winner.

Song books can be a valuable aid to reading. Probably no other books bring more delight into oral language and at the same time relate to literature. Many of those for children are made up of traditional nursery songs, Mother Goose jingles, and folk songs. They have lilting melodies which are easy to remember and lines that repeat or vary slightly. They abound in the humor and tenderness that children relish.

The Baby's Song Book, selected and arranged by Elizabeth Poston, includes eighty traditional nursery tunes with piano arrangement, plus beautiful full-color art by William Stobbs.

The Fireside Book of Children's Songs, collected and edited by Marie Winn and Allan Miller, contains words and music of more than 100 songs, with bold illustrations by John Alcorn.

The Great Song Book, edited by Timothy John, presents over sixty of the best-loved songs for all ages with stunning pictures by Tomi Ungerer.

Eye Winker, Tom Tinker, Chin Chopper, compiled by balladeer Tom Glazer, is a delightful collection of fifty favorites with musical arrangements and directions for fingerplay.

Sing Together Children is an inexpensive little booklet of 125 songs and singing games for all ages, many for the very young.

Bedtime songs and stories are always welcomed by young children. Almost any song, story, or poem can be read at bedtime, of course, but some seem especially fitting.

Oh What a Noise! illustrated by Uri Shulevitz, makes a good starter, telling of the wonderful noises a small boy hears at bedtime—from yowling cats to roaring lions and snoring giants.

Bedtime for Frances by Russell Hoban is a quiet story, picturing an engaging little badger's maneuvers to postpone bedtime. The illustrations by Garth Williams make Frances irresistible.

Goodnight Moon by Margaret Wise Brown is a lovely bedtime story for the very young. Even children of only twelve or fourteen months like the simple pictures of familiar things and the gentle repetition:

> *Goodnight bears*
> *Goodnight chairs*
> *Goodnight mittens*
> *Goodnight kittens.*

One little girl I know liked to add her own good nights: "Good night, dolly," she would say, "and good night, Mommy." Each evening she added more and more, as though trying to prolong the story and her own pleasure.

A Child's Good Night Book, by Margaret Wise Brown, shows one group of animals after another at bedtime—birds, wild monkeys, squirrels, and kangaroos, among many others. At the end children, too, "say their prayers, get under the covers and go to sleep."

For a good-night song to add to the bedtime hour, turn to *The Fireside Book of Children's Songs* which includes several charming ones. Be sure to consider the French cradle song, "The Old Grey Hen," into which you can slip your own child's name as part of each stanza.

Nursery tales, which have been handed down for generations, are like the nursery rhymes in providing quick action with much repetition. Each one is an uncluttered anecdote,

Illustration by Paul Galdone in *The Three Bears*

usually with lots of conversation. The stories are easy to tell, easy to chime in on, and easy to remember.

Established favorites are "The Little Red Hen," "Chicken Licken," "The Three Bears," and "The Three Little Pigs." Each is a real story with characters and plot. Repetition adds to the familiarity and helps build suspense. Thus, in "The Three Little Pigs," the greedy wolf makes the same demand to each one:

> *Little pig, little pig,*
> *Let me in, let me in!*

and to each he makes the same threat:

> *I'll huff and I'll puff*
> *and I'll blow your house in!*

But despite his great size, the wolf is defeated, for he jumps down the chimney into a kettle of boiling water set up by a peace-loving pig. This is a typical nursery story ending, and I think it explains, in part, why children love these tales. Young listeners revel in a smashup at the end of a story—just as they enjoy knocking down a tower of blocks. The old nursery rhymes are certainly full of smashups.

Note, too, that the little fellow usually gets the better of the big one: a plain little hen outwits a fox, a humble pig exterminates a wolf, a modest tortoise defeats a hare. Nursery fiction presents the triumph of the weaker one, an auspicious example for every child who feels dominated by parent or older sibling.

The Fairy Tale Treasury selected by Virginia Haviland and illustrated by Raymond Briggs is a brilliant collection of thirty-two of the best-loved stories for every age. "The Gingerbread Boy," "Henny Penny," "The Story of the Three Pigs," and "The Old Woman and Her Pig" are favorites of the very young.

The Tall Book of Nursery Tales illustrated by Feodor Rojankovsky includes twenty-four favorite tales with delightfully lifelike illustrations. In *The Old Woman and Her Pig and 10 Other Stories* Anne Rockwell retells the old tales simply with bright modern illustrations.

For some children the picture book which presents just one nursery story is particularly inviting. Among the popular books of this kind: *The Story of the Three Little Pigs* illustrated by Lorinda Bryan Cauley, *Henny-Penny* illustrated by Paul Galdone, and *Three Little Pigs* illustrated by Erik Blegvad.

Wordless picture books can bring great pleasure once a child learns how to use them. With some help and encouragement, a child can "read" the story from the picture sequence and thus get a great feeling of accomplishment: "It's my book because I made up the story." The story may vary from one telling to another and will surely take on different meaning with different readers. But the child's sense of involvement and feeling of confidence are tremendous as mastery of language grows.

Do You Want to Be My Friend? by Eric Carle is a favorite among the picture books without words. It begins with the seven words of the title asked by a tiny gray mouse who leads the reader through bold, brilliant pictures to the final answer: "Yes." Each page turned is another episode in the picture story, and as one librarian reports, "Children love it."

More very simple picture books without words: *Changes, Changes* by Pat Hutchins (with bright pictures to make a house, then a boat, then a truck); *Frog, Where Are You?* and *Ah-Choo* by Mercer Mayer; and *Deep in the Forest* by Brinton Turkle.

Somewhat more sophisticated are the wordless picture books by John S. Goodall, which include *Shrewbettina's Birthday, The Adventures of Paddy Pork,* and *The Midnight Adventures of Kelly, Dot, and Esmeralda.* Even older children who are well launched as independent readers enjoy speculating on the dramatic detail and sly humor of the Goodall illustrations.

Modern animal stories have great appeal, even for city children who have no pets and have never visited the zoo. Penguins, bears, elephants, and tigers are easily recognized and accepted without question, as are the most modern illustrations, although these may be more fantastic than real. The young child's imagination seems equal to the artist's.

Several of the most popular books for children show a young animal—a child, as it were—with the behavior, concerns, and happy endings a child knows.

A top favorite is *Whose Mouse Are You?* by Robert Kraus, a very simple story in rhythmical lines. The story moves from the wistful opening question to the reassurance of family love and support.

The Tale of Peter Rabbit, written and illustrated by Beatrix Potter, was first published in 1903 in England, but it continues to be a favorite of American children. They seem to identify with the mischievous Peter and take him to their hearts.

Another beloved animal character is the little lost duckling in *The Story About Ping* by Marjorie Flack, with charming illustrations by Kurt Wiese. For fifty years Ping has won friends among young children who admire his adventurous spirit and rejoice in his safe return home.

Harry the Dirty Dog by Gene Zion, with illustrations by

Margaret Bloy Graham, is another winner. Because Harry hates to have a bath, he gets so dirty no one knows him. Thus he becomes a hero to the child who says, "He's just like me." Harry's story is continued in several equally delightful books.

And surely one of the most popular storybook characters is the monkey whose curiosity gets him in and out of a peck of trouble: *Curious George, Curious George Gets a Medal,* and *Curious George Rides a Bike,* among them. All were written and illustrated by H. A. Rey.

Stories about other children are always popular, especially when the focus is on just one or two children whose adventures have a familiar ring. *The Snowy Day* and *Whistle for Willie,* both written and illustrated by Ezra Jack Keats, are gentle, warm, and real with brilliant collages as illustrations.

Ira Sleeps Over, written and illustrated by Bernard Waber, tells of the first time a small boy spends a night away from home and how he answers the big question: Should he take his teddy bear with him? This is an ideal bedtime story.

A city park and city streets are the scene for the hilariously noisy story entitled *All the Way Home* by Lore Segal with illustrations by James Marshall. When little Juliet announces in the park that she is going to keep on screaming, her mother decides it is time to go home. Juliet screams, the cat, the dog, and the crow who join them howl, and the little parade goes around block after block before the doorman will admit them to their apartment house. Even small-towners will see themselves in this story.

Funny stories, funny rhymes, and funny songs are as welcome as ice cream to young children. Sometimes it is a mild humor as in *The Snowy Day* when Peter puts a snowball in his pocket for safekeeping at home. Sometimes it is a noisy kind of humor as in *All the Way Home.*

Sometimes the exaggerated illustrations make the story irresistibly funny. Take time to examine the absurdities in James Marshall's pictures for *All the Way Home* and have another round of laughs.

For utter nonsense few author-illustrators can equal Dr. Seuss. His drawings are slapstick cartoons; his words are sometimes created from nonsense syllables. He repeats his

Illustration by James Marshall in *All the Way Home*

jawbreakers and rhyming lines with a straight face. Even three-year-olds crack up in mirth.

If I Ran the Circus by Dr. Seuss tells how young Morris McGurk lets his imagination run wild in dreaming up the Circus McGurkus with its Drum-Tummied Snumm, the wink-hooded Hoodwinks, and a Juggling Jot. (After hearing this story read aloud many times, one four-year-old announced that in her circus she would have a "Blooker-Blooker;" another proposed "Nutty Nutter Peanut Butter.")

Be on the lookout for Dr. Seuss books. Some you will have to read aloud; some of them are easy enough for beginning readers. All have great child appeal.

Poetry sings its way into the hearts of children of all ages. For this reason comments about using poetry with children and suggestions about poetry books are in one chapter, "Poetry Is for Everyone" (Chapter 7).

3

From Talk to Print

Children in our society become aware of written language at an early age. They see printed words all around them: on cereal boxes, newspapers, billboards, neon signs, the television screen. They soon recognize familiar words much as they recognize familiar pictures or faces.

Product names seen and heard on television are easily identified and read by children of three and four. In the supermarket, they pick out their favorite cereal by noting familiar words and pictures on the boxes. They have heard and spoken those words many times; thus their experience with oral language prepares them for the same words in print.

Sylvia Ashton-Warner, an extraordinary teacher in New Zealand, used this bridge from spoken words to written words to introduce children to reading. Every morning she would ask each child to name the word he or she would like to see on paper. And out they would come—words of fear and love, of hate and desire—each of them vivid, dramatic, and deeply personal. As a word was spoken, Miss Ashton-Warner printed it on a large tough card: *mummy, truck, ghost, kiss, knife, beer, police, frightened*—and gave it to the child to keep. These were words spoken from the heart, words now in print to read and reread, to show to family and friends.

In her remarkable book, *Teacher*, Miss Ashton-Warner reports that children had no trouble learning to read their own word cards although they floundered for weeks over such preprimer words as *come*, *look*, and *oh*. In two years of observation, she reports, "the two most powerful words" in the children's vocabulary were *ghost* and *kiss*. "Any child, brown or white, on the first day, remembers these words from one look."

Our children are very different from those Maori young-sters, who knew little about printed materials and nothing about television. Yet every child must make the discovery that written language is simply spoken language recorded for the eye to read. As one child from Appalachia put it, "It's just talk wrote down!"

Any steps that will help your child grasp this fact will be a positive aid to his or her reading. Maybe you want to begin with word cards. The first might be the child's name; the next should be a word the child asks for.

FROM ORAL LANGUAGE TO WRITTEN LANGUAGE

Many four-year-olds are intrigued when they see their spoken words transformed to print.

Signs and labels make a good start: a sign for the bridge or airport built of blocks or the one- or two-word title the child selects for a drawing. Also you can label important points in the child's room: "Bed," "Door," "Blocks," "Trucks and Cars," "Books." Most welcome of all is the sign on the door giving the child's name. With a magic marker, sign-making is very easy.

An "experience chart" is a story which a child dictates. It is so named because it tells of the child's experiences in his or her own words. To make an experience chart, you only need a magic marker, large sheets of newsprint, and the warm encouraging personality which will persuade a child to talk freely and vividly. Remember that pressure, threats, and coercion are sure-fire deterrents to creativity.

A good time to begin is when the child is full of talk. Even though it is only a phrase about something the child has seen or done, you can write it down and read it back. Show your child these words so that he or she can begin to understand that this is "talk wrote down."

Perhaps the boy next door has a new bike, and your child comes bursting in to tell about it. After the first excitement, suggest a slow-down so you can record some of the story.

Or, suppose you have just read *The Snowy Day* and the

child begins to tell about fun in the snow. Try to record a line or two for the child to "read" and illustrate. You may be surprised to see how fast interest in reading begins to grow.

One time a group of five-year-olds in Bethlehem, Pennsylvania, walked across the bridge to look down on the steel mill. It was an exciting scene, and they were full of talk. Here are some of the lines they dictated for a wall chart:

> *The steel mill is like a big bear*
> *behind steel bars.*
> *High, high buildings*
> *and smoke.*
> *As big as a Ferris wheel going round*
> *Like an apartment house smoking.*

After dictating this story, the children wanted to have it read. Soon they interrupted with "Let me." After some faltering, they mastered the lines, probably by memory, and then read and reread with pride. A few days later they wanted to dictate another story and then another.

If you do record such stories, use the manuscript writing of the early grades, making the letters at least an inch high:

a b c d e f g h i j k l m n
o p q r s t u v w x y z

These letters are very much like the printing a child sees in books—yet they have the same basic form as the cursive writing of adults.

WHAT ABOUT THE ABCS?

The four-year-old who recognizes STOP and SLOW on traffic signs may not know one letter from another. That child is using what is called "sight reading," or "whole word recognition." It is a first step that many children take on their own.

To go beyond sight reading, it is necessary to recognize

the letters of the alphabet and become familiar with the sounds of individual letters and combinations of letters.

One objective of the *Sesame Street* program is to teach children the names of letters, what each looks like, and what sound it generally represents. One *Sesame Street* fan of my acquaintance recognized all of the letters at age three. Indeed, he seemed to find letter shapes all around him. A Christmas cookie in the shape of a wreath was the letter O to him; the one shaped like a Christmas stocking looked like the letter J. Obviously he was enjoying his *Sesame Street* lessons and doing very well.

Follow-up research by *Sesame Street* producers shows that the children who know their ABCs move more quickly into reading than those who do not. You can help.

As you record your child's name, let him or her watch. If you say the name of each letter as you write, the child can start to recognize those letters and their sounds.

When a child learns to recognize a word by sight—STOP, for example—you have the opportunity to help him identify each letter. You can go on to find words beginning with the same letter and sound: *snow, soap, soup,* and many more. As you find an S word, print it on a poster list in large letters with the initial S in red. Together you and the child can pronounce the words and note the initial S sound.

Or start with the child's first name and find words that begin with the same letter.

Peter learned about the first letter of his name by collecting pictures of words beginning with the letter P: *pansies* from the flower catalogue, a *panda* from the newspaper, *pots* and *pans* cut from a magazine ad, *pears* taken from the label on a tin can, *park* from another newspaper headline, and so on. These were pasted in a homemade booklet with his name and picture on the cover.

You can assemble an ABC book with each page marked for one letter. As your child meets and identifies a word, print that word and add a picture. On the A page: *airplane, apple, ape, accordion.* On the B page: *bread, balloon, black bear,* and so on. I think you will find that this will be one of the most used books in your library for a while.

At this stage a child savors an ABC book. Those with brilliant pictures—*Bruno Munari's ABC* and *Celestino Piatti's Animal ABC*, for example—can stimulate endless conversation along with repetition of the familiar letters.

Illustration by Jane Breskin Zalben in *All in the Woodland Early*

For just plain fun, take a look at *ABC of Monsters* written and illustrated by Deborah Niland.

Anno's Alphabet: An Adventure in Imagination illustrated by Mitsumasa Anno is an intriguing book to pore over and talk about. And in *All in the Woodland Early* Jane Yolen has created an animal ABC in lilting verse with joyous illustrations by Jane Breskin Zalben.

More advanced in concept, and therefore needing more from an adult, is *A Peaceable Kingdom: The Shaker Abecedarius* illustrated by Alice and Martin Provensen. The rhyming lines have a lilt; the animals have great charm;

and the quaint people and Shaker artifacts spur questions and conversation.

WORD GAMES FOR LETTER SOUNDS AND SYLLABLES

Young children quickly learn to enjoy word games that deal with letter sounds and syllables. Often such games can be played while the dishes are being washed or on an automobile trip. Games of this kind are easy to invent. In fact, once children begin to see the possibilities, they will make up their own. Here are a few to get you started:

Words beginning with the same sound. How many can we name that begin with the same *D* sound as Diane? Or the *M* in Maria?

Words that end with the same sound. Start with a familiar word, *cake*, for example, and list words that rhyme: *lake, make, rake, take,* etc.

Words that imitate sounds. Such words as *bang, pop, whir,* and *rustle,* are fun to compile and to create.

Words of one syllable that can be changed to words of two or more syllables. Start with *walk*, for example, and add a second syllable to make *walking*. This game helps to sharpen enunciation.

Words made by combining two or more words. Often these are a surprise to the beginner and all the more fun because of that. Easy examples: *airplane, cookbook, firefly, baseball, milkshake,* and *gumdrop.*

At this stage, many children enjoy meeting single words in print with an illustration for each. Richard Scarry has an intriguing way of combining single words with little pictures. For a sample of his style, see *Richard Scarry's ABC Word Book* and *Richard Scarry's Best Word Book Ever.* With a little adult guidance as a starter, children find them fascinating.

Two picture dictionaries also provide great entertainment: *Richard Scarry's Storybook Dictionary* and *The Cat in the Hat Beginner Book Dictionary*. Both define words through humorous drawings and situations.

Don't worry if your child shows no real interest in words and word games now. Children grow and develop at different rates. Those who seem slow at first will soon catch up. Give your child time and a warm feeling that what he or she does is fine with you. There is only one hard-and-fast rule: don't push, lest you slow down the child's interest and inclination to learn.

THE EVENTS OF A STORY IN SEQUENCE

Reading individual words is not enough for good reading. The reader has to be able to note the order of events, how one thing leads to another, and, in the case of a story, how suspense builds up to a satisfactory ending. Long before children can read the words, they may like to retell a story by following the pictures from page to page.

The sequence in a picture book without words gives a splendid opportunity for the child to create a story that parallels the illustrations. In addition to those mentioned in the previous chapter, hunt up *Bobo's Dream* by Martha Alexander, the picture story of a small boy and his dachshund, Bobo.

Somewhat more advanced is *The Snowman* created by Raymond Briggs, which tells a longer story with 167 pictures in filmstrip sequence. *Noah's Ark* by Peter Spier is a fascinating picture story of life on Noah's Ark with mice, raccoons, giraffes, snakes, and all the rest in exquisite detail. These longer and more detailed books are for children who have had experience in noting tiny differences and interpreting them.

With all of the wordless picture books, children seem to need an adult to get them going. When Mother or Dad shares the fun, many children are ready to talk about the pictures and tell the story of a wordless book.

The same retelling of a story can spring from almost any picture book. For example, the four-year-old who has heard you read such a picture-book story as *Are You My Mother?* by P. D. Eastman, may enjoy "reading" the tale to you or to a younger sibling, following the pictures as clues. Often this child will identify certain words in print and associate the spoken word with the printed word. This is the beginning of reading. (See also Chapter 4, "As a Child Begins to Read.")

BOOKS FOR READING ALOUD

While children are becoming interested in printed language, it is important that they hear stories and poems read aloud. The time they spend looking at picture books without words and familiar books which they can almost recite by heart should not crowd into your daily read-aloud time.

As an experienced reader, you can introduce your child to books with text that is longer and more detailed than the simple books he or she is "reading" from the pictures. Most important, you can bring in new subjects, new scenes, new problems. You may be able to raise questions which will sharpen curiosity and ultimately understanding.

A child enjoys the good feeling of sharing a story. Reading and books become more significant because you are part of the experience. If both parents become involved as readers, the good effect is more than doubled.

Almost all of the books suggested in the previous chapter continue to appeal to five- and six-year-olds. They love to sing the old songs with plenty of repetition. Nursery rhymes and nursery tales continue to be very popular. Poetry brings great delight when the child is drawn in as a participant on repeated lines and phrases. (For more on this subject, turn to Chapter 7, "Poetry Is for Everyone.")

In searching for the books, keep in mind elements which appeal to children of this age and subjects of great interest to them.

As long as it's funny, children seem delighted with almost any story, song, or poem. And if it is downright wacky, they can't get enough.

Dr. Seuss delivers the right combination of exaggeration, nonsense words, and surprises to please all ages. Children love *The 500 Hats of Bartholomew Cubbins*, chuckling over poor Bartholomew's puzzlement as he tries to remove his hat before the king, only to find it replaced by another and another and another. The pictures add to the fun, of course.

Dr. Seuss has also created a number of shorter books, easy enough for the beginning reader, but they are also great for reading aloud to younger children. Even the titles bring delight: *Hop on Pop* and *Green Eggs and Ham* are popular examples.

For more humor and exaggeration, turn to two books by Phyllis Krasilovsky: *The Man Who Didn't Wash His Dishes,* illustrated by Barbara Cooney, and *The Cow Who Fell in the Canal*, illustrated by Peter Spier.

Anne Rockwell has created several humorous books which are very appealing. A prime example is *Gray Goose & Gander & Other Mother Goose Rhymes*. The short comical rhymes are presented one to a page with cheerful colored drawings. *Granfa' Grig Had a Pig and Other Rhymes Without Reason From Mother Goose*, compiled and illustrated by Wallace Tripp, presents old favorites with brilliant illustrations that include hilarious side remarks.

With all of these books, take time to note the humorous details in the pictures and talk about them. Often it is exaggeration that makes an illustration funny. Sometimes the colors make a picture more ridiculous. Children will enjoy all illustrations more when they learn to look for such details.

Monsters, witches, and "anything scary" are in great demand among all children, even those as young as four and five. Several librarians report "absolute infatuation with monsters, even among preschoolers."

The perfect children's book and probably the number one favorite of all children is Maurice Sendak's *Where the Wild Things Are*. When Max is sent to bed for behaving like a wild thing, he lets his imagination soar and the wild things of his dreams get bigger and bolder—not to frighten Max, but to increase his feeling of power and ultimate greatness. Adults who thought Sendak's monsters would induce nightmares in the young missed the point of Max's growing self-assurance and utter delight in being master of the situation.

Not so dramatic, but very intriguing to children, is *Clyde Monster* by Robert L. Crowe. Clyde is a child monster who is afraid of the dark and the people who might get him at night. His monster parents are reassuring to Clyde and to children who may also have bedtime fears.

A troll family is on center stage in *Tim and Trisha*, written and illustrated by Otto S. Svend. Trisha meets Tim, a troll child, and goes home with him to play. When she returns to her own home, it's hard for her parents to believe her tale even though they see the footprints of Father Troll.

Illustration by Maurice Sendak in *Where the Wild Things Are*

Big Bad Bruce, written and illustrated by Bill Peet, tells how a foxy little witch gets the best of Bruce, the bear who is a bully.

Rhythm and repetition in poems, songs, and stories have great appeal for the young. Children enjoy hearing familiar lines which give a surprise as they change a bit from stanza to stanza. Chiming in becomes almost inevitable.

This may explain the continuing popularity of "The Old Woman and Her Pig" which is included in a number of Mother Goose and fairy tale books. A slim picture book illustrated by Paul Galdone is given over entirely to the ridiculous developments of this popular tale.

A number of modern writers have created stories with the rhythm and repetition of old folk songs and stories. One of these is *Catch a Little Fox* by Beatrice Schenk de Regniers, which echoes the old song, "A-hunting we will go." Each turn of the page brings another surprise.

Millions of Cats by Wanda Gág is an established favorite

with children, primarily because of the repeated "millions and billions and trillions of cats."

Many of the old nursery rhymes and folk songs achieve humor and rhythm by adding something new each time a line is repeated. "The House That Jack Built" is a perfect example of the cumulative rhyme or story. It is a pattern employed very effectively by modern authors as well.

Ellen Raskin uses this scheme in *Who, Said Sue, Said Whoo?* As tiny Sue in her tiny car asks "Who said moo?" a huge polka-dot cow comes into the picture and almost envelops her. Sue's rhyming query grows with each new sound; the scene becomes more crowded with one more creature added each time until the surprise ending sends everyone running. It has lots of wonderful sound words: *chitter-chitter-chatter, quitter-quatter, spitter-spatter,* and more.

Many of the folk tales have the elements and the style that make them just right to read aloud to four- and five-year-olds. Many are very funny; many have scary elements; and almost all of them have repeated lines and incidents.

One of the children's favorites is *The Teeny Tiny Woman,* an old tale retold and illustrated by Barbara Seuling. It is a teeny tiny tale which repeats the words "teeny tiny" so often that before long everyone is joining in. *How the Rooster Saved the Day* by Arnold Lobel is a modern tale patterned after the old with enchanting illustrations.

Animal stories continue to appeal to preschoolers. With many children the gentle, friendly animals get top rating. *Little Bear* by Else Holmelund Minarik has an old-fashioned look, but a devoted following among modern children, who enjoy Little Bear's birthday party, his trip to the moon, and the adventures that continue in *Little Bear's Friend, Little Bear's Visit,* and *Father Bear Comes Home.*

Arnold Lobel has written and illustrated a number of gently humorous stories that young children enjoy. His *Frog and Toad Are Friends* and *Frog and Toad Together* are very popular. Each consists of several ministories with an element of suspense in every one. Perhaps because children are used to the short segments of television programming, they like the quick satisfaction of finishing each tiny chapter, even in a very short and simple book.

There are two ministories in the thirty-two page book, *Mother Rabbit's Son Tom*, written and illustrated by Dick Gackenbach. They repeat two demands of the average American child: "I want a hamburger" and "I want a pet."

George and Martha, written and illustrated by James Marshall, is a five-part picture story of two friendly hippos whose very size and shape create comedy. Their rather mild adventures are continued in several books.

For sheer nonsense children delight in Mary Rayner's *Garth Pig and the Ice Cream Lady*, a story of kidnapping and revenge in the animal world.

An even more exciting story is told by William Steig in *Amos and Boris*, which is about a mouse and a whale who become fast friends.

Another Steig book that is a read-aloud favorite is *Sylvester and the Magic Pebble*, the picture story of a donkey whose magic pebble saves him and then threatens his life.

Other children, their adventures, and their problems are told about in excellent books for preschoolers. Those with rhythm and repetition and some sort of emotional pull make a hit with young listeners.

The Shopping Basket, written and illustrated by John Burningham, is one of the winners. What might have been a routine shopping trip grows into a series of exciting encounters, and each time young Steven comes through a hero.

Many of these books tell of the incidents children have to face themselves. For example, there is *Stevie* by John Steptoe, which reports the resentment Robert builds up toward a younger boy living in the family temporarily; *Nothing Ever Happens on My Block* by Ellen Raskin gives the dreary complaint of a small boy sitting on the curb while cops-and-robbers excitement goes on behind his back; *Nobody Asked Me If I Wanted a Baby Sister* by Martha Alexander recounts the familiar situation of an older child's jealousy over the new baby; *George the Babysitter* by Shirley Hughes shows how a teenage boy manages a family of three small children while their mother is at work; *The Terrible Thing That Happened at Our House*, by Marge Blaine, tells what happens when Mother gets a job.

Busybody Nora by Johanna Hurwitz and *A Big Fat Enor-*

mous Lie by Marjorie Weinman Sharmat are heartwarming stories about children as real as your own.

Several poetic tales about a lovable little black boy who lives in a city project have been written by Lucille Clifton. They include *Everett Anderson's 1-2-3* and *Everett Anderson's Nine Month Long*.

Solutions are arrived at in all of these stories; cooperation and friendship spring up and flourish. Unlike earlier books for children, these reflect some of the tough situations today's children encounter, such as crowded living conditions, low family income, and mothers working outside the home. Such books seem to meet the need often heard from preschool children, "I like it if it's real."

Informational books are appealing to many children at this stage, particularly if they include photographs. Perhaps the photos give evidence that "It's real," and this wins today's children.

Photographer Tana Hoban has created a number of wordless informational books that are very popular. One of the best is *Dig, Drill, Dump, Fill*, a photographic essay on heavy duty machines with a pictorial glossary giving exact identifications. This book gives much to talk about.

There are many well-illustrated informational books about animals, rocks and minerals, plants, weather, and simple science experiments and projects to do at home. With adult help, children enjoy these books tremendously. (For more about books on this kind, read Chapter 8, "Build on Their Interests.")

Several well-written children's magazines have dramatically beautiful photo features about such topics as animals, weather, volcanoes, the sea, motion, and gravity. While some of these are designed for older children, the pictures and subject matter appeal to younger ones as well. One issue can start off innumerable read-aloud-and-look sessions that everyone will enjoy. But a nonreader needs the help of some older person, explaining, questioning, and encouraging at every step. (For more about recommended magazines for children, see Chapter 17, "Magazines for Children.")

FINDING GOOD BOOKS FOR CHILDREN

If you have a public library in your community, count yourself lucky. Four- and five-year-olds enjoy a visit to the children's room where you can locate the picture-book section and sit down to enjoy a sampling together. (See Chapter 12, "Using the Public Library and the School Library.")

A visit to a bookstore can be a rich experience too. Let your child look through the books and help make a selection. Also, you may wish to consider a children's book club through which you receive books on a regular schedule. (See Chapter 14, "Buying Books for Children.")

The children who become good readers are usually those who have books to go back to again and again.

4

As a Child Begins to Read

Thirty years ago, few children were taught to read before age six or six-and-a-half. Some schools had a firm rule that reading should not be taught in kindergarten.

Yet there were children who learned to read at home before entering first grade. How did these children learn? What experiences did they have at home?

Studies of such children showed that they expressed interest in written language by four years of age. Often they asked about words in print or how to write a letter or word. They came from homes where at least one parent was a steady reader. All early readers had been read to regularly.

These parents enjoyed their children, took them to interesting places, and spent time discussing and questioning what they had seen. They had also furnished the children with books and materials for writing.

These parents had not made a deliberate effort to teach their preschoolers in any formal way, but they had provided rich experiences in oral and written language. In this stimulating setting children succeeded in becoming readers and writers and enjoyed it.

READING AT SCHOOL

Today some aspects of reading are taught in most kindergartens. Where the school system does not provide kindergarten classes, reading lessons begin in first grade. What is taught and how depend on the experiences children have had and the skills they have acquired before coming to school.

For some children the first weeks at school may be a period of preparing to read, or developing "reading readiness," as the teacher may call it. Children who speak with great hesitation and who enunciate poorly may need time to improve their oral language before they tackle printed language. Those who do not know the letters of the alphabet and the sounds they represent may need time for their ABCs. Many children need practice in listening and then talking about what they have heard. In the same class there may be children who have mastered these skills and are clearly ready to read or are actually reading on their own.

For beginners the first reading materials may be the printed labels and signs around the classroom: each child's name on his or her coat hook, the name of the day and the month on the blackboard, the sign over the fish bowl, the label on the box of colored crayons.

On the blackboard the teacher may record words, even sentences, which children have dictated about some activity they have had together. Reading lessons sometimes begin with just such dictated materials. They are appealing to children who recognize these words as their own which tell of experiences important to them. Such dictated stories always have child appeal.

Printed materials for beginners are likely to be the preprimers and primers which are part of a series of readers used throughout the elementary school. Ninety-five percent of the schools of the United States teach reading with a series of basal readers. The preprimers and primers introduce letter sounds as well as words which are so common that children quickly learn them by sight, much as they learn "Stop" and "Go" on traffic signs.

As children master the sounds of letters and combinations of letters, they learn to pronounce whole words in print. At the same time, they must learn to derive meaning from the words and sentences they have sounded out. After all, the prime purpose of reading is understanding.

In some schools very successful reading programs are carried out without using a series of basal readers. In their place, teachers use children's dictated comments and stories along with very simple trade books or library books.

Thus, the children meet a greater variety of books and avoid the slow-paced language and stories of the preprimers and primers.

With or without preprimers and primers, the teacher should be reading aloud to the children from beautiful picture books, drawing them into conversation about the stories and illustrations and giving them the opportunity to explore the books on their own. Impromptu dramatization of a simple nursery rhyme or picture-book story may sharpen children's interest in going back to that same book again. And those who have repeated such a familiar line as "Little pig! Little pig! Let me in! Let me in!" may easily read the same lines when they find them in print. With such experiences they are eager to read on. Thus, the good teacher whets the children's appetite for books while developing basic skills.

Illustration by Peter Spier in *Noah's Ark*

THE TEACHER MUST PROVIDE FOR DIFFERENCES

The one thing we know about children is that each one is unique. Those entering kindergarten or first grade have

had widely varied experiences and have developed different skills.

At one extreme may be a child who is reading independently. At the other may be a child who has never even
seen a picture book. Yet both may be sitting side by side in
the same kindergarten or first grade class. The teacher
must provide for all children, helping each to move forward
from his own starting point.

The child who can read should be helped to zoom ahead.
Those with less experience should be given the foundation
they need.

How does a teacher handle so many differences in one
class? Frequently the children are divided into small groups
for reading lessons. The teacher works with one group at a
time, giving the experiences and the printed materials
appropriate for those children. Even within one small group,
children differ greatly. So the teacher must vary his or her
approach accordingly.

More than anything else, the beginning reader needs
practice with a partner who will listen, encourage, and
help with puzzling words. With twenty to thirty children in
a class, the teacher can be a one-to-one partner with each
child only a few minutes each day. Children need more
than that, and they can get it at home with the help of
parents, grandparents, and older siblings.

Have the child show you his book and tell about the
pictures. Invite the child to read to you—even though it
may be only a few words or lines at first. Perhaps you will
take your turn and read the next few lines. Help the child
find picture details that add to the story. Make this a time
of mutual sharing and fun, rather than prodding and scold-
ing. Your help at home will strengthen the teacher's help
at school.

PARENTS AS PARTNERS

It is a big step when a child starts to school. Some take
this step when they enter nursery school at three or four.
Others begin with kindergarten at five or first grade at
six.

Often children's attitudes toward school are shaped in
advance by their parents. Those who have had positive

reports of new friends and new experiences at school are likely to take the first days in their stride and move ahead with confidence.

As you and your child talk over the day's experiences at school, try to build on the good things that happened: praise for the child's finger painting, interest in the classroom puppet show, delight over hearing the song that started the school day.

Sometimes parents are so interested in a child's reading that they cause embarrassment. For example, "Haven't you learned to read yet?" is a question that implies criticism. The child who has to say "No" may feel a failure from the start.

From the beginning, parents should help to build a feeling of success and then make that success a triumph.

As a start get acquainted with the teacher. He or she can tell you about the school program and why things are done a certain way. You can tell the teacher about your child: what he or she is especially interested in, why shyness takes over at times, what favorite stories you have been reading at home.

The teacher needs this kind of information and much more that you can give. Later he or she may be able to give you a new slant on the child's ways and concerns.

At this stage there are many ways parents can help at home:

1. By providing the child with rich experiences as well as opportunities for oral language. (See Chapter 2, "Listening, Singing, and Talking Prepare for Reading.")

2. By reading aloud from appealing books. (See suggested titles at the end of this chapter and in Chapter 16, "Books They Like.")

3. By creating reading materials dictated by the child about his or her experiences. (See Chapter 3, "From Talk to Print.")

4. By helping children identify the letters of the alphabet. (See Chapter 3, "From Talk to Print.")

5. By providing some of the easy-to-read books that a beginner can handle successfully. (See below.)

6. By listening to the child read aloud, however slow the pace.

7. By fostering the child's self-assurance so that he or she feels free to speak up, to ask questions, and to take chances with new experiences and new ideas.

FINDING BOOKS FOR BEGINNERS

It is not easy to find library books which both fascinate the beginner and are simple enough to be read alone. This is due in part to the fact that children know many more words by ear—often very advanced words—than they can possibly read in the beginning.

Radio and television bring hundreds of thousands of words into our homes today. Children listening to a weather report may hear such words as *humidity*, *temperature*, and *wind velocity*, which may be too difficult for a beginner to read. On the TV screen children see trade names of products while the words are being pronounced, but these words may be complicated to read and write. Yet in conversation some children show they have picked up a large and grown-up vocabulary.

The books easy enough for the beginner can use only a few simple words at first. As a result the language of these books is less colorful than the speaking vocabulary of the average child. To some children such books seem hopelessly dull. This can be a disappointing period for certain children who want as much drama and excitement in what they read as they get from television.

Many teachers provide variety by having children dictate their own stories to be read in class. Some of these stories tell about pets, holidays, and school experiences. However, teachers tell me that more and more of these dictated stories deal with family problems and the situations seen on television: earthquake and volcano disasters, the latest plane crash, or a satellite launching.

At this stage, the most important thing parents can do is to demonstrate that reading is fun. This means continuing to read aloud from the most appealing books you can find, providing books children can begin to read independently, and listening as they read aloud.

To find appealing books that a beginner might read independently, turn to the child's teacher and the school librarian for suggestions. Then make a search of school library, public library, and local book stores. (See Chapter

12, "Using the Public Library and the School Library," and Chapter 14, "Buying Books for Children.")

You will note certain marks of the good easy-to-read books in the library or bookstore:

- The type is large and clear.
- The vocabulary is simple.
- Sentences are short and follow the rhythmical pattern of conversation.
- Printed lines are short, with the line break coming at natural pauses in conversation.
- Pages are uncluttered, and white space is plentiful.
- Pictures give clues that make reading easier and more interesting.

As you read one of these simple stories aloud, you will find it is more pleasing when the words flow smoothly and rhythmically. Rhyming lines may help the child identify new words. Frequent repetition gives reassurance to the young reader. When an author provides language that sings, children seem to be more at ease, even when their own reading is halting.

By first or second grade, many children know what they want in a book. For the most part, they seem to expect a fast-paced story and situations with emotional pull.

Children won't use the term "emotional pull," of course, but they will say the story has to be "really funny" or "so scary." Although they never admit it, they don't mind shedding a few tears along with the laughter.

If you can find a book that ties in with a recent television program, you probably have a winner.

Humor appeals to almost all children—the more exaggerated the better.

Several of the easiest and funniest books are from the inimitable Dr. Seuss. *One Fish, Two Fish, Red Fish, Blue Fish* fills the bill with lots of repetition, easy words that rhyme, and utter nonsense on every page.

Another funny book for the child who is just beginning to read is *Inside, Outside, Upside Down* by Stan and Jan Berenstain. It is complete nonsense about a bearlike creature with a winning personality.

On the list of easiest and funniest is *Albert the Albatross* by Syd Hoff, an author-illustrator who specializes in incongruous creatures and situations. *Julius,* the story of a circus gorilla, is another popular Syd Hoff book that earns a first-grade rating.

Another author-illustrator to look for is P. D. Eastman, who has created several ridiculous stories that are easy enough for beginners: *Go, Dog, Go!* (utterly zany) and *Sam and the Firefly* (an owl meets a skywriting firefly).

Among the most amusing easy-to-read books are the Clifford books by Norman Bridwell (*Clifford the Big Red Dog* and *Clifford Takes a Trip,* among others). All are best-selling paperbacks.

A shade more difficult—but still on the list for first graders—is *The Cat in the Hat,* also by Dr. Seuss. Published as a book for beginners, it is a sure hit with children just starting to read as well as those who can read. All of them seem to welcome the smash-bang, topsy-turvy humor of the cat who tore up the house while Mother was away and then whisked everything in place in the nick of time. There is hilarious confusion in the sequel, *The Cat in the Hat Comes Back.*

Jokes and riddles are in a class by themselves, but for children of five to seven they mean endless fun and little effort. Changing times bring in fresh or warmed-over jokes, but the question-and-answer pattern is the same. The child asks "What did the pig say when the farmer grabbed its tail?" If you hesitate a split second, out comes the punch line: "That's the end of me." The child is triumphant.

Many easy joke books are just right for the beginner. *Syd Hoff's Best Jokes Ever* and *Stoo Hample's Silly Joke Book* are always in demand. Joseph Low is the creator of two that kids go for: *Five Men Under One Umbrella* and *Mad Wet Hen and Other Riddles.* For fun with rhyme, try William Cole's *Give Up? Cartoon Riddle Rhymes,* illustrated by Mike Thaler.

And if your youngster is on a riddle jag, it may be a good time to make a book of riddles collected or concocted by the child. It will be a good book to take to school some rainy morning.

Monsters and mysteries are favorites even at this age, and—believe it or not—there are monster stories and mystery stories easy enough for first and second graders to read on their own.

One of the easiest and most popular of the mystery stories is *Nate the Great and the Sticky Case* by Marjorie Weinman Sharmat. In this story the boy detective and his dog Sludge solve the baffling case of a missing stegosaurus. Their detective work continues in several books.

A bit more difficult, but suited to many second graders, are the stories written and illustrated by Crosby Bonsall: *The Case of the Cat's Meow*, *The Case of the Double Cross*, and many more. All are blessed with a hint of mystery and the fine relationship of the young detectives. *The Homework Caper* and *Rooftop Mystery*, written by Joan M. Lexau and illustrated by Syd Hoff, are also popular titles in the I Can Read Mystery series published by Harper & Row.

There are stories about monsters, trolls, witches, and goblins which are easy enough for first and second graders to read independently. Sue Alexander has created a winner in *Witch, Goblin, and Sometimes Ghost* illustrated by Jeanette Winter. The fifty-nine page book consists of six "read-alone stories." These are continued in a second volume, *More Witch, Goblin, and Ghost Stories*.

Animals have great appeal for most children of five to seven. While they chortle over the mad antics of such an animal as the Cat in the Hat, they like the gentle stories too. Surely the Frog and Toad books, written and illustrated by Arnold Lobel, are among the most loved by children. *Benny Rabbit and the Owl* by Joseph Low is a reassuring goodnight story for a child to read or for you to read aloud at bedtime.

Several of the most popular of the books about animals are nonfiction—easy to read, scientifically accurate, sometimes illustrated with photographs, sometimes with full-color art. Two that are irresistible are *How Kittens Grow* and *How Puppies Grow* by Millicent E. Selsam with sparkling black-and-white photographs by Esther Bubley.

Illustration by Arnold Lobel in *Frog and Toad Together*

BOOKS TO READ ALOUD

Even when young children can read simple books at home and at school, their choices are limited. They may read in a halting fashion that makes the best story sound dull. This is one more reason why parents should continue reading aloud. The swinging vigor of your reading will give the child a model. And the colorful language of poetry and stories too difficult for the child to read independently gives promise of the treasures ahead.

Select some of the simple books that a beginning reader can soon read alone. Be sure also to read aloud some of those books that may well be out of reach for several years.

Animal stories are abundant and very popular. One of the most amusing of the picture book animal heroes is the debonair crocodile who lives with the Pimm family in New York City. *Lyle, Lyle Crocodile* and *Lyle and the Birthday Party* are among the books Bernard Waber has written and illustrated about the daffy doings of Lyle.

Another book which is an enduring favorite is *Caps for Sale* written and illustrated by Esphyr Slobodkina, an amusing story about a very special kind of monkey business.

And by all means give your family the treat of meeting *The Story of Ferdinand* by Munro Leaf with amusing illustrations by Robert Lawson. Never has a young Spanish bull won such an admiring audience without winning a bull fight.

Several animal stories stir children's sympathy. One of these is *The Biggest Bear*, written and illustrated by Lynd Ward. It is the picture story of a cuddly bear cub which grows and grows until Johnny, his owner, is forced to make a tough decision.

More advanced and completely different is an exquisite book entitled *The Wounded Wolf* by Jean Craighead George with illustrations by John Schoenherr. Through rhythmical text and starkly dramatic black-and-white drawings, we learn how a wounded wolf is saved from a fox, a snowy owl, and a grizzly bear crowding in for a kill. This is a true story to read on a very special occasion when the mood is right.

Anything mysterious is intriguing to most children. There's a touch of mystery and suspense, but mostly humor, in *Ghost in a Four-Room Apartment*, written and illustrated by Ellen Raskin. This is billed as a "two-voice" book—first the ghost and then the narrator. One creates havoc during the family reunion in the four-room apartment, and the other tries to explain the confusion, the noises, and the surprises.

And prize of all prizes is a story full of scary possibilities: *My Mama Says There Aren't Any Zombies, Ghosts, Vampires, Creatures, Demons, Monsters, Fiends, Goblins, or Things* by Judith Viorst with illustrations by Kay Chorao.

Real children are at the center of many good read-aloud stories appealing to the five-to-sevens. Several seem to fit right into the child's school life. *When Will I Read?*, *Will I*

Have a Friend? and *Best Friends*, written by Miriam Cohen and illustrated by Lillian Hoban, are gently reassuring with enough suspense to hold the listener's attention.

More rambunctious is the hero of *Alexander and the Terrible, Horrible, No Good, Very Bad Day*, written by Judith Viorst and illustrated by Ray Cruz. The recital of the day's tragedies gets more hilarious as Alexander's complaints continue.

SCREEEEEEEE!

Illustration by Mordicai Gerstein in *Something Queer Is Going On*

Until recent years most of the picture-book stories for children have been about boys—Johnny in *The Biggest Bear*, Max in *Where the Wild Things Are*, and Peter in *The Snowy Day*, for example. Or they have had male animals in the spotlight—Milton, Leo, Lyle, Clifford, Harry the dirty dog, curious George, and many more.

One notable exception is *Madeline*, written and illustrated by Ludwig Bemelmans more than forty years ago. By this time it is a classic that should be on your list of books too good to miss. Madeline, the stalwart leader of the little girls in a French boarding school, continues her leadership role even when she has an appendectomy in a Paris hospital.

Now we are getting more picture-book stories which break the old stereotype of the male as sole doer and thinker. Some of these newer books have an urban setting, which is also a departure.

Two of the newer books which spotlight little girls in the city are *Tell Me a Mitzi* by Lore Segal, which is made up of three family yarns about city children, and *Meet M and M* by Pat Ross, which recounts the ups and downs of the friendship of two apartment neighbors.

A bit jazzier are the books of Elizabeth Levy about Jill and Gwen, two young sleuths who solve intriguing but not too difficult cases: *Something Queer Is Going On* and *Something Queer on Vacation* are two titles in this ongoing series. The large format, cartoonlike illustrations, and wealth of visual clues attract younger boys as well as girls.

Children of long ago and far away are important for modern youngsters to meet as well. You can make the introduction by reading aloud from the really fine books in this field.

One of these is *The Bears on Hemlock Mountain* by Alice Dalgliesh. This is a little tall tale of a small boy and the threat of bears when he crosses Hemlock Mountain.

A more recent book is *Wagon Wheels* by Barbara Brenner, which tells of the Muldie family's trip to Kansas by wagon and their struggle to survive a bitter winter. Another appealing to this age level is *Old Blue* by Sybil Hancock, which is about a cattle drive in the 1870s.

Two tales of children of other lands are among the books too good to miss. *Gilberto and the Wind* by Marie Hall Ets gives us a simple story and exquisite pictures of a small Mexican boy and his struggle to fly a kite. *Crow Boy*, written and illustrated by Taro Yashima, is the gentle tale of a shy first grader in Japan, whose one achievement is to imitate the voice of a crow.

Folk tales, old and new, have the easy rhythm that makes them ideal for reading aloud. The repetition and cumulative pattern of many of the tales enable children to join in as chorus or sound-effects crew.

For family reading, you will find it helpful to have a big book of folk tales from which to read time after time. For this I suggest *The Fairy Tale Treasury*, made up of thirty-two of the best-loved tales from around the world, selected

by Virginia Haviland and with brilliant illustrations by Raymond Briggs.

There are delightful small collections as well—often selected for their similarity in theme (tales about cats or tales
about ghosts), or grouped by national origin. If you are of
Irish extraction—or Italian or Puerto Rican or Swedish, for
example—you can find the titles of several collections of
folk tales from your mother country by checking in your
local library.

Often children prefer a book with just one fairy tale and
its illustrations, and there are many of these. For example,
The Three Wishes, an old folk tale from the Joseph Jacobs
collection, illustrated by Paul Galdone; and *Stone Soup*,
retold and illustrated by Marcia Brown. A number of the
single folk tale books are available in paperback editions.

American tall tales are increasingly popular with children today. Perhaps this is because they relate the tall-tale
heroes to history and what is "real." A good collection of
these stories to read aloud is *American Tall Tales* retold by
Adrien Stoutenburg. These are fresh stories of American
work heroes—Paul Bunyan, John Henry, Mike Fink, etc.
—and are full of humor, exaggeration, and believe-it-or-
nots.

There are also slim, extensively illustrated books of just
one tall tale each. One of these is *Ol' Paul, the Mighty
Logger*, retold and illustrated by Glen Rounds.

Another which is adapted from a black American folk
tale is *Wiley and the Hairy Man*, written and illustrated by
Molly Garrett Bang. It's scary enough to hold your listener
and easy enough for the good second-grade reader to tackle
independently.

Information books make good read-aloud books too, particularly if they relate to a child's current interest. (For further
information about this, turn to Chapter 8, "Build on Their
Interests.")

A number of the newer informational books are illustrated with photographs, which children seem to like as
evidence that the book is "real," meaning "accurate." Perhaps one of the important lessons you can teach a young
reader is that an artist's drawings may be more revealing
and just as accurate as any photograph. Indeed photos can
be staged and altered for a purpose.

The Let's-Read-and-Find-Out Science Books have simple text and artists' drawings in color which give scientifically accurate information appealing to young children. Two popular books in this series were written by Dr. Franklyn M. Branley of the Hayden Planetarium: *The Planets in Our Solar System* and *Eclipse: Darkness in Daytime*. Children who have watched the television report of an eclipse or the rings of Saturn will welcome such books. Obviously the TV programs and the books will mean more when an adult raises questions and can fill in with further details.

Several excellent children's magazines present intriguing information with stunning color photos and drawings or paintings. These are splendid for reading aloud to the child and for talking things over. (Also see Chapter 17, "Magazines for Children.")

Poetry and Song are winners with children of five-to-seven, provided you choose the right poems and songs and bring the children in as participants. Funny songs and poems make a good beginning. Maybe you would like to start with "I Know an Old Lady Who Swallowed a Fly," a song all children love. (You will find words and music in Tom Glazer's *Eye Winker, Tom Tinker, Chin Chopper*.) Then try some of the shorter poems in *Oh, That's Ridiculous!*, an anthology compiled by William Cole, and go on from there. (For more suggestions about poetry and song, turn to Chapter 7.)

5
Independence in the Third and Fourth Grades

In the early sixties, a university professor declared, "If Booth Tarkington were to write *Seventeen* today, he would have to call it *Twelve.*" It was the educational wisecrack of the year. Twenty years later I heard a new version of the old gag: "If Booth Tarkington were to write *Seventeen* today, he would have to call it *Eight-and-a-Half.*"

Today some of the children who are eight-and-a-half are reaching for the books with the content that appealed to the seventeen-year-old of 1916, the year *Seventeen* was published. Others, not so grown-up, may assume the same pose so as to keep up with the crowd.

When you observe the books that many third and fourth graders choose in the library, you see evidence of this new sense of maturity. They want books about sports—not a story about Joey and the Little League but about professional teams and players. They are keen on mysteries and detective stories. They go for anything that is funny, but it has to be what someone called "laugh-track funny."

In 1980 the average American child of six to eleven watched over twenty-five hours of television each week. It is no wonder that television has a strong influence on children's reading habits and reading choices.

To find appealing books for children of this age level, it is important to know each as an individual and to become aware of the ways and choices of his or her peers.

EIGHT TO TEN, THE VIGOROUS YEARS

Children of this age have boundless energy and great endurance. Those not glued to the TV set may spend hours building a racing car or practicing basketball shots.

It is a time when children begin to assert greater independence. One teacher refers to fourth grade as "the unpredictable year" because a child is likely to swing from a heady independence to what she calls "the sweetness of his first-grade personality" and back again. Such a child may make the same swing in reading—at one time being anxious to read challenging books, at the next, relaxing with picture books.

Above all, children want the approval of their peers. Everything must be done the way other children do it, and woe betide the parent who tries to buck this need for group approval. Neighborhood clubs are springing up. Members show remarkable uniformity in haircuts (or lack of them), designer jeans, and brand-name jogging sneakers. Youngsters are active in Boy Scouts, Girl Scouts, Boys' Clubs, 4-H Clubs, and church groups. The programs of these national organizations usually offer guidance for children's reading activities.

For children of this age the world is rapidly expanding beyond home and school. They are experimenting with new sports and hobbies. Those who have several different collections underway like to identify and classify: "What kind of rock is this? Can it be called a sedimentary rock?"

Third and fourth graders are constantly challenging. "How come?" and "How do you know?" test the good humor of parents every day. Yet these questions are heartening, for they show eagerness to reason things out and verify information. Both are good leads to reading. (For more about capitalizing on children's questions, turn to Chapter 8, "Build on Their Interests.")

ON THEIR OWN IN READING

It is usually in third grade or early fourth that children find their stride in reading. They can read simple material with little outside help and enjoy their independence.

This is a crucial time in children's development as readers. If they find books that are easy enough without being too elementary, they are more likely to become steady readers. If the books seem too babyish, many children become lukewarm. On the other hand, a child who is pushed into reading books beyond his or her capacity may give up entirely, unless there is sympathetic support at home and at school.

Some third and fourth graders have an insatiable appetite for books. They explore new subjects and new kinds of stories. Often they go back to a favorite book and reread it or its sequel four or five times. However, many third and fourth graders cling to the easy picture books they met in second grade.

Some children do not become ardent readers until the fifth or sixth grade, and still others may never read anything they don't have to read. All are more likely to become persistent readers if they get encouragement and guidance at home during these critical years.

READING LESSONS AT SCHOOL

Although the third or fourth grader can usually read independently, reading lessons at school are continued to sharpen and extend reading skills. At this stage, the emphasis is on what is called "reading comprehension;" that is, helping a child to understand what has been read. The child learns to answer such questions as: What does the author say about a certain subject or question? What does the author really mean or suggest by that? How does the author know this is right or logical?

Children's tendency to raise questions and verify information should help them improve their reading comprehension, but this does not happen automatically. Thoughtful reading and questioning are more likely to occur when an adult is helping.

Children's curiosity also makes them good candidates for magazines, the dictionary, the almanac, and the encyclopedia. At school third and fourth graders are introduced to reference books and are learning when and how to use them, but they need help in finding out which reference materials to use. Further practice at home can strengthen interests and skills. (For suggestions, see Chapter 9, "Let's Look It Up!")

Perhaps you wonder how well your child is using these new reading skills. One teacher lists four test questions:

1. Does the child turn voluntarily to reading for information and for pleasure?
2. Does he or she find material related to current interests?
3. Does the child try to help himself or herself with reading?
4. Is the child beginning to vary the manner of reading according to the material and the reasons for reading it?

If the answer is yes for each question, you can be sure progess is being made.

But suppose a child prefers to read the very easy books read last year and the year before? Shouldn't he or she be reading the harder, longer books on the third- or fourth-grade level? Not necessarily. Even though reading tests show a youngster can read at a fourth-grade level, there is no reason for him or her to miss the sheer pleasure of coasting along on an easier level sometimes.

By continuous reading and rereading of very simple books and stories, a child may gain confidence and strengthen reading skills. The more one reads—child or adult—the more fluent one becomes as a reader.

Remember that most adults elect to read at a level much lower than they are capable of. *Reader's Digest* is written on an eighth-grade level, and millions of high school and college graduates read it continuously with no apology and no regrets. The banker who reads the *Digest* one evening has no trouble shifting to technical financial reports the next day. He knows that easy pleasure reading does not undermine the ability to read more advanced material.

HOW PARENTS CAN HELP

There are at least five important ways in which parents can influence a child's reading positively:

1. *Encourage the child to speak freely and fully* so he or she uses oral language easily and effectively.
2. *Provide the child with first-hand experiences* which present new ideas and add new vocabulary words.

3. *Read aloud every day*, letting the child choose stories and poems whenever possible. As the child becomes more proficient, encourage him or her to read to you sometimes.
4. *Help the child find books and stories that match current interests.* The one who loves monsters, will welcome a book about monsters even though you generally avoid them.
5. *Raise informal questions* about the books read, not to test but to stimulate critical thinking.
6. *Continue to build up your child's self-esteem and self-reliance.* Give praise generously. Make it clear that you have confidence in the child's ability to succeed. Remember, the one who is self-assured is likely to risk asking questions, trying a new book, or exploring a new subject. Thus, self-assurance can lead to learning.

THERE MUST BE MANY BOOKS

Since a typical classroom may have children reading on several grade levels, there should be reading materials on many levels. A third-grade class may need books for grades one through seven. A fourth-grade group may have even wider needs.

Furthermore, children's interests are different. One boy is absorbed in space travel, another in dogs. If each can read about a favorite subject, there is likely to be greater progress.

When a child reads on a comfortable level, about a subject dear to his or her heart, reading becomes a pleasure instead of a punishment. This can happen only when there are many attractive books from which children may choose. If reading is to be taught effectively, there must be a good library in each school with plenty of books on many subjects and of differing levels of difficulty.

In addition to library books, every class should have access to such reference materials as dictionaries, an atlas, an almanac, and an encyclopedia. (See Chapter 9, "Let's Look It Up!") Annotated book lists for the students can suggest further reading in library books. (See Chapter 15, "Tools for Book Selection.")

Illustration by Rachel Isadora in *Max*

Each child should be encouraged to read widely in connection with various lessons, as well as for sheer pleasure. If the class is studying early explorers, youngsters can find stories, biographies, maps, and magazine articles to supplement the textbook. Science lessons suggest an equally attractive array of good books.

When children are free to choose the books they are interested in, they show remarkable skill in finding what they can read.

THE FAMILY THAT READS

Children are imitative. They are more likely to seek out books if they grow up in a family where everybody reads. If Mother and Dad turn off the television in order to read, children are apt to do likewise.

If parents buy books, children know that books are important to them. If you borrow regularly from the library, your children will soon have library cards and borrow also.

Of course, not all parents are confirmed readers and book lovers. Unless you grew up enjoying books, you may turn your back on reading as an adult. The children are apt to pick up your attitude and follow your pattern.

You can help establish a child's positive attitude and set an example by reading aloud in the family and encouraging friendly talk about books the children have been reading or want to read. And if you are like me, you will find that good children's books make refreshing reading for all ages.

BOOKS THEY LIKE AND CAN READ

It is almost impossible to suggest books that appeal to all children in third grade or fourth grade. The book that is too difficult for one may be just right for another. The child who clings to stories about a talking teddy bear may be slow to try a book that is advertised as "scary." Another who is just the same age may demand a book about the Loch Ness Monster and eat it up. However, certain trends show up which are worth considering.

"It's got to be funny" was the verdict of one nine-year-old when asked about the books he and his friends prefer. On any list or any bookshelf, the joke books and riddle books seem to be the most widely read. A three-or four-line joke or riddle delivers its punch so quickly that the newly independent reader feels rewarded and goes on for more.

Parents can only hope that joy in reading will someday encourage the child to reach beyond these four-line gags.

In third grade many children cling to the exaggerated

humor of the easy picture books they knew in second grade. *Lyle, Lyle Crocodile* and *You Look Ridiculous Said the Rhinoceros to the Hippopotamus*, both by Bernard Waber, continue to be favorites.

One step more advanced are the hilarious tall tales created by Sid Fleischman about McBroom, the one-acre farmer who planted and harvested an entire crop of beans in an hour. *McBroom Tells a Lie* and *McBroom and the Beanstalk* are typical.

Exaggeration is always good for a laugh with kids. McBroom does it the noisy way, with a tall-tale gag every few lines. Many longer stories pay out their humor slowly and build to a more credible and equally funny ending. One of these is an old favorite, *Mr. Popper's Penguins*, by Richard and Florence Atwater. Not until the third chapter do the Atwaters hint that this will be a funny story. Perhaps this is a good reason for you to read those first chapters aloud. Then the child will take over eagerly.

Pippi Longstocking, by a Swedish author, Astrid Lindgren, is the first of a series about a little girl who does with a flourish what every child longs to do: from rolling out cookies on the floor to walking a tightrope in a circus and lifting two policemen by their belts and dropping them over the fence. Pippi lives with her monkey and horse, does not go to school, and has a chest of gold coins to spend as she wishes. Children think Pippi is hilarious and pretty lucky too.

Pippi's humor grows out of exaggeration and her mastery of the impossible. However, some of the stories which third and fourth graders consider the funniest are completely realistic, recounting the adventures of real children like themselves.

Among these stories—and heading the list in popularity among both boys and girls—are the books by Beverly Cleary. These include *Henry Huggins, Henry and Beezus, Ramona the Pest*, and *Ramona and Her Father*. The situations are completely believable; the children are handled with the utmost sympathy; at every turn the humor bubbles over. Many third and fourth graders can read the Beverly Cleary books on their own, but they are great for reading aloud too.

Mysteries and whodunits are eagerly sought by the eight-to-tens. Third graders can read the Crosby Bonsall "mysteries"

—all so mild and humorous that they may not satisfy those wanting something that is hair-raising. Among the Bonsall books are *The Case of the Cat's Meow* and *The Case of the Double Cross*.

A notch higher on the difficulty gauge are two books by David A. Adler: *Cam Jansen and the Mystery of the Stolen Diamonds* and *Cam Jansen and the Mystery of the U.F.O.* Both are humorous, breezy, slightly baffling, and easy enough for the third grader to have fun with.

A search of library shelves or lists of recommended books will help you locate slightly more advanced books with greater suspense and excitement. Even the titles reach out to grab you. *The Fireball Mystery* by Mary Adrian, *Marco Moonlight* by Clyde Robert Bulla, and *Deadline for McGurk* and *The Great Rabbit Rip-off* by E. W. Hildick are among the possibilities.

For readers who are more interested in how a mystery is solved than in its threatening atmosphere, there are several stories about a young Sherlock Holmes at work. *Encyclopedia Brown, Boy Detective* is the first of a series by Donald J. Sobol. Each is a short mystery solved by a ten-year-old sleuth. Young readers with a flair for science will welcome the juvenile unraveler of puzzles, who is the hero of *Einstein Anderson, Science Sleuth* and *Einstein Anderson Shocks His Friends* by Seymour Simon. Those who want to do a little detective work on their own will latch onto *How to Write Codes and Send Secret Messages* by John Peterson.

Movie and TV tie-ins create immediate popularity for books of the same title or the same theme. Children rush to the library for these books. For several years, the prime example has been the television series based on *Little House on the Prairie* by Laura Ingalls Wilder. Librarians have been swamped with calls for this book and its sequels. When movie houses were showing that exquisite film, *The Black Stallion*, library shelves were swept bare of the Walter Farley horse stories.

In recent years dozens of children's books have been used as the basis for major movies and television programs. "Pippi Longstocking," "Charlotte's Web," and "Misty of Chincoteague" are among the TV programs which have spurred interest in the original books of the same titles.

Watch the newspapers and TV schedules for announcements of coming movies and television programs based on children's books. Then save time for them in your family. If the children have enjoyed the television program, hunt up the original book and plunge in.

You should be aware that tie-ins can cause problems too. When a book is adapted for a television program, it may be changed drastically. New characters may be added and scenes may be altered. Sometimes it seems that the title is the only thing that book and TV program have in common. After the first year of television programming, "Little House on the Prairie" showed only slight resemblance to the book or its sequels.

Children who turn from the television show to the book may be disappointed. One fourth grader living near Buffalo enjoyed the programs of "Little House" but did not like the book enough to finish. His explanation was: "The book's all wrong. I know because I watch the TV program."

Parents can help by explaining why book and television program are different and what to expect from each. Further, if you read the first few chapters aloud, you may be able to help the child bridge the media gap happily.

Sometimes the book on which a television program is based proves far beyond the reading level of an enthusiastic viewer. This happened with the TV cartoon version of *The Lion, the Witch and the Wardrobe* by C. S. Lewis. After that program, some children who turned to the library for the original book were disappointed because it is too difficult for many third graders although enjoyed by some fourth and fifth graders. The same disappointment occurred after the TV showing of "Little Women," "Black Beauty," and "National Velvet."

There are abridged and simplified versions of some of these titles, but they seem flat and colorless when compared to the original books. Probably the most effective way to convert the TV viewer's enthusiasm into greater appreciation of reading is to read the original story aloud, perhaps in a family group. As you read together and talk over the latest chapter, I think you will find children more appreciative of the rich significance of the story. Perhaps in another year or two, when reading skills are stronger, the same children will read the original book on their own.

Frequently an informational program on television provides

a good springboard to reading about the same subject. For example, when TV news programs showed the devastation caused by the eruption of Mount St. Helens in the state of Washington, books and magazine articles on the subject were in great demand. Perhaps you can help your children locate such newsworthy places on the map and then read news articles with them to supplement the short mention in a TV newscast.

Television sports programs are a leading attraction for countless children who then come to the library for related books. "I think some of them watch TV sports all Saturday and Sunday," one school librarian concluded. "They charge in here on Monday to get books about teams and stars they have seen on TV." Children seem to like all sports: football, baseball, soccer, basketball, skiing, ice skating, weight lifting, drag racing, boxing, wrestling, hockey, gymnastics.

When they ask for sports books, they are really asking for footnotes on the news: more about the running back they saw on TV yesterday or the bantamweight championship contenders in next week's bout. It is the kind of information adults get from newspapers and magazines.

There are easy-to-read factual books about sports, which children grab. Many are illustrated with action photographs, some in full color. But often they are dated by the time they are published, and the book about last year's champions is not what modern TV fans are looking for.

Furthermore, when they read the text, they may find it is more difficult than it looks. There are few anecdotes to make the sports heroes seem like living personalities. The text is factual, but nothing more.

Librarians tell me that even seven- and eight-year-olds ask for books of this kind. Are they following the lead of older youngsters so they will appear to be just as grown-up? Or, as someone suggested, are they using the TV sports book as a way to get Dad's attention at home? In any case, such a book is a one-shot—not a book to go back to or talk about, not food for thought or question.

Possibly you can help to satisfy a child's curiosity by reading newspaper accounts of the players and teams in the spotlight. And certainly you can help a child understand why no book can have a hot story about this season's winners, much less last night's champions.

If the child is choosing a book about drag racing or karting as a way to get Dad's attention, the message is clear: Make time for Dad to read with the child some of the unforgettable children's books that have suspense, humor, imagination, and beauty.

SHALL WE READ ALOUD TO THOSE WHO CAN READ INDEPENDENTLY?

Yes, by all means! They like the sound of language, and they revel in having your undivided attention.

But shouldn't children be reading for themselves as soon as they can? Won't it spoil them to read to them?

Of course they should, but they should have the fun of being read to as well. Furthermore, read-aloud time is ideal for introducing new books to the whole family.

Children like to sample before selecting a book. In the library they will dip into one book after another before making a choice. Sometimes those samples are all too brief, and the decision goes against the book for that reason. But if several chapters are read aloud at home, listeners get a real feeling for characters and setting and are ready to go ahead on their own.

Some books—like cherished friends—grow on you slowly. It would be too bad to miss these gems because they were introduced hurriedly.

The human voice does a great deal to endear a story to the listener. Characters come alive when their conversation is heard, particularly by children who are accustomed to the sounds of language from long hours of radio and television listening.

In choosing stories to read aloud, I like to begin with those the children suggest. If a child is able to read a story aloud, by all means lend encouragement. Or take turns— you read a page or chapter and then the child reads a part to you.

I find that children look forward, also, to having the adult bring a surprise selection to read aloud. The book you choose may be one that ties into the season or to some situation that has significance in the family. Maybe it is a cat story to honor a new pet or a ghost story for Halloween.

Or you may be one of those parents who long to extend your children's experience to include stories that are less blatant and sensational than the usual television fare. Perhaps you want to share some of the humor that is more subtle than the "laugh-track" variety, to stretch imagination to include the worlds of history and fantasy. As one mother put it: "I'd like to give them some quiet books, stories that make their imprint slowly, but will keep children thinking."

Let me tell you of some of the books that I have read aloud with children who seemed to share my satisfaction and came back with more comments and questions after each read-aloud session.

At the top of the list—the very top—I put *Charlotte's Web* by E. B. White with charming illustrations by Garth Williams. It is the story of the most lovable spider in all literature. The book opens with a startling note of realism: "Where's Papa going with that ax?" Eight-year-old Fern saves the runt in a litter of pigs and names him Wilbur. In the barn cellar, Wilbur's friend and mentor is Charlotte, the spider who writes messages in her web. Her wisdom and compassion have few equals.

For seven- and eight-year-olds this is a winning story of animals that talk. Those a bit older relish the innuendos of Charlotte's conversation. Even those children who have seemed indifferent to everything at school melt over the approach of Charlotte's death.

Another talking animal story which children relish tells of a musical cricket from Connecticut who finds friendship and beauty in a New York subway station. This is *The Cricket in Times Square* by George Selden, also illustrated by Garth Williams. A fast-talking Broadway mouse, Harry the Cat, and Mario the newsboy welcome Chester the Cricket and introduce him to the joys of subway life.

A well-written animal story has great appeal whether it is fantasy or reality. Among the realistic animal stories, few can equal those written by Marguerite Henry. Hers are usually horse stories—*Misty of Chincoteague* and *Sea Star*, for example—which children read eagerly. But my favorite on her list is *Brighty of the Grand Canyon*, the story of a little wild burro found by an old prospector on Bright Angel Creek in the Grand Canyon. It reveals a beautiful friendship between man and burro.

And as love of animals is taking over, I would surely want to read aloud some of the poems from *Prayers From*

Illustration by Tomie de Paola in *Can't You Make Them Behave, King George?*

the Ark written by Carmen Bernos de Gasztold and translated from the French by Rumer Godden. Each of the short poems is the prayer of one of the animals on Noah's Ark: the rooster who boasts "It is I who make the sun rise," the old horse who prays for "a gentle death," the little ducks who plead for "plenty of little slugs and other luscious things to eat," and so on. There is gentle humor as well as pathos in these tiny prayers, and I find that children take them to their hearts. (For more poetry suggestions, turn to Chapter 7, "Poetry Is for Everyone.")

Books that relate to history—both fiction and nonfiction—are welcomed also, but they sometimes need a personal introduction. Reading aloud makes a good beginning. Just right for this age are the minibiographies by Jean Fritz— *And Then What Happened, Paul Revere?, Can't You Make Them Behave, King George?,* and *What's the Big Idea, Ben Franklin?* Each is short (forty-seven pages), humorous, conversational, and historically accurate.

Also short, lively, and easy to read are several books by Ferdinand N. Monjo which are written from a child's viewpoint: *Me and Willie and Pa* (about Abraham Lincoln). *Grand Papa and Ellen Aroon* (about Thomas Jefferson and his granddaughter), and so on.

Children are interested in other children of course, and in these days of changing family structure and life style, they seem especially concerned about those children struggling to adjust to change.

In *"Hey, What's Wrong With This One?"* Maia Wojciechowska tells of three motherless boys who decide it's time for their father to get them a new mother, and they offer to help. Back of the boys' yelling and fighting, lies a deep sensitivity that helps bring a happy solution to the troubled household. This book is good for a lot of laughs and some sober thinking too.

The Great Gilly Hopkins by Katherine Paterson offers much to talk about and ponder over, for it is the story of a rebellious eleven-year-old who has been shunted from one foster home to another, always expecting her real mother to come to her rescue.

Another great favorite, perhaps because it was an After School Special on ABC, is Betsy Byars's *The Pinballs*, about three foster children who gradually learn to care for each other and to value themselves.

Warm family relations prevail in *Roosevelt Grady* by Louisa R. Shotwell. This is the story of black migrant workers who struggle under constant economic hardship as well as racial discrimination.

And finally somewhere along the way, I would want to introduce two books that children like "even though they hurt," as one boy put it. These are *Annie and the Old One* by Miska Miles and *A Taste of Blackberries* by Doris Buchanan Smith. In the first a little Navajo girl tries each day to postpone her grandmother's death. The second is a boy's report of his pal's death from a bee sting while they were picking blackberries. Both are beautifully written and very moving. Old age and death become more clearly a part of life.

These are only a few you can start with. As you read aloud and draw children into talking about such books and the ideas they bring forth, you will find more links to more books, more reading, and more talking. Gently does it!

6

More Grown-Up and More Demanding

Youngsters in fifth and sixth grade today seem to become more grown-up and more demanding with each day. Some expect the privileges once reserved for high school students although avoiding the responsibilities that go with maturity.

Many resent being called children. Even eleven-year-olds will call themselves "the preteens" and take on the ways and dress of the older set. They remind you that a thirteen-year-old is a teenager.

Among fifth and sixth graders, TV viewing is beginning to drop off slightly but still averaged more than three hours a day in 1980. At this age youngsters are seeking and meeting more projects outside of school than previously. Athletic activities, movies, clubs, and rather unorganized hanging around occupy much of their after-school time. Radio, cassettes, and some television programs give them the music they love. Often their heroes are the music-makers of the latest hit tune.

At this age, many girls seem to be preoccupied with clothes, nail polish, eye shadow, and hair styling. "It takes Lisa forty-five minutes every morning just to fix her hair," wailed the mother of a sixth grader. Frequently boys of the same age go through a similar ritual of styling and blow-drying their hair before the mirror each morning.

For every generalization, there are countless exceptions. Furthermore, the youngster who seems so blasé one day may be a naive child the next, with tastes and behavior swinging between the two extremes. Often the girls seem more grown-up than the boys; at least they work harder to appear sophisticated. But sitting beside that sixth grader with heavy cheek blush and raspberry red lips may be a quiet little girl who is as quaintly childlike as her grand-mother used to be.

Sometimes fifth and sixth graders seem almost a genera-tion apart. According to one suburban school librarian, fifth graders come in to learn and to be shown new things. After only a month in sixth grade, the girls, in particular, seem above all of that. "The girls fade away as readers," reports this librarian, "but the boys keep reading mystery stories and books about sports." What about the girls? "They want sex-oriented novels so they bring paperbacks from home," was the reply.

It is a truism to say that children differ. In fifth and sixth grades the differences seem far greater than in earlier grades. This may be one reason why many school systems have set up middle schools for grades 6, 7, and 8. (In those communities the elementary schools include kindergarten through grade 5; the high school grades 9 through 12.) As sixth graders associate more closely with seventh and eighth graders, they take on more advanced interests and ways.

Most fifth graders read less than they did the year be-fore. Sixth graders, by and large, read still less, presumably because of more activities outside of school. Often they choose the easiest books, which give quick, sure enter-tainment. Or they search for books which will answer questions stemming from their accelerated maturity. Abor-tion, illegitimacy, homosexuality, rape, divorce, desertion, drug abuse, alcoholism, mental retardation, and insanity are among the subjects brought out of the closet to play in full view on the television screen and now through chil-dren's books. Children who think of themselves as "the preteens" want to be all-knowing in the areas once re-served for adults. Television whets their appetites, and peer pressure does the rest.

Those who have seen the lurid detail of certain prime-time TV specials, lap up the peer approval that brings. In one school, where fourth, fifth, and sixth graders voted on their favorite book of the year, top place went to *The Amityville Horror*, which children had seen as a movie and on TV. Apparently only a few had read even a part of the book. Voting for it as "my favorite" may have been an effort to establish the status of a full-fledged teenager.

Informational books are read more eagerly at this age than fiction about the same subject. Thus factual books about sports heroes and teams are preferred to fiction about football, basketball, ice hockey, or soccer. Photographs in an informational book make it doubly attractive to fifth- and sixth-grade readers.

Librarians and paperback book clubs report that one of the most popular paperback books is the *Guinness Book of World Records*, which is jammed with facts and illustrated with photographs. Children dip in here and there to read about the tallest man or the fattest woman with zest.

The book made up of bits and pieces that can be read in any order, or with no order at all, is what one librarian calls "a non-book." Collections of riddles, jokes, and believe-it-or-nots fit her category of non-books. Kids go for them because they are easy to read, require no thinking, and demand no emotional commitment. They also furnish quotes that enable one child to reach out to others positively. Even the very shy youngster will use a riddle or *Guinness* world record as a conversation opener and lead to friendship. So "non-books" serve a purpose.

However, the segmented nature of the non-book invites sampling rather than continuity in reading. Because *Guinness* readers get no experience in carrying over situations or impressions from one segment to another, they do not develop the ability to follow a story line or the progression of facts that develop in reading a book of fiction or biography from beginning to end.

Fifth and sixth graders have a strong sense of independence and are often cool to adult suggestions. Yet they are easily influenced by group approval, group mores, and the leadership of an adult whose choices strike a vibrant note.

Teachers and school librarians are learning that they must be imaginative when introducing books to fifth and sixth graders. Reading aloud remains one of the best ways to lure young readers into reading on their own. A personal introduction from someone the child respects is often more effective than a general list from which each child must make a choice.

When the introduction comes from an acknowledged

leader among the children, it is very influential. To capitalize on this, the school librarian may recruit fifth and sixth graders to serve as library aides, book-talk specialists in classrooms, tutors for younger children, and book selection advisors to the librarian. Everybody benefits. If the school has a paperback bookstore, children who serve as salesmen soon become avid readers.

In fifth and sixth grade, youngsters do more research than previously, more critical writing, and more evaluation of what they read. Classroom use of a single literature anthology is giving way to an assortment of paperback books from which students can make a choice. Young people almost always prefer paperbacks. Thus they are more likely to read whole books instead of samples. Furthermore, the good school program encourages children to read widely in science and social studies, not simply in English or language arts.

There are relatively few books which all fifth graders or all sixth graders enjoy. While some cling to cartoon books, others reach for adult titles. City kids are likely to reject animal stories while small town and rural readers go for them. Beverly Cleary books are just as popular with both boys and girls in sixth grade as in the fourth and fifth. Judy Blume continues to be popular with sixth-grade girls who have been reading her books for several years. Given a choice, fifth and sixth graders pick up books which are dramatically varied in content and reading level.

The book with a strikingly different title captures immediate attention and often converts the indifferent reader. Note a few of the popular ones: *How to Eat Fried Worms, The Cat Ate My Gymsuit, Freaky Friday, My Dad Lives in a Downtown Hotel, Are You There, God? It's Me, Margaret,* and *Can You Sue Your Parents for Malpractice?* As one librarian put it, "A title can make or break a book with kids today."

Perhaps this love of startling titles is another indication that fifth and sixth graders want books that jolt the commonplace. Their yen for the exaggerated shows up, too, in the immediate popularity of the "supermags"—*Bananas, Dynamite,* and *Wow!*—published by the paperback book clubs and listed along with books on monthly order sheets. The "supermags" are heavily influenced by television and offer more to look at than to read. They seem to be equally popular with poor readers and good.

All of this complicates the job of guiding the fifth or sixth grader in choosing books. Coercion won't work. Heavy-handed advising won't work. Indeed, many a parent has learned that "A word to the wise is infuriating" when offered to the preteens.

BOOKS FOR THE PRETEENS

Parents and grandparents often expect fifth and sixth graders to like the same books they enjoyed as children. This can happen, but some of the books you remember may be slow going for today's children who are used to shorter books which are more simply written and which build to a higher level of suspense. Or you may have forgotten when you read a certain book and try to introduce it too early. Before you recommend one of your childhood favorites, read it again and see how it fits your child in the late twentieth century.

Movie and TV tie-ins win a large readership for almost any title today. If a book is adapted to a movie or a television program, thousands of copies are sold even though the mass-media version bears little resemblance to the original.

After watching a high-pitched TV drama, children often find the book is too slow, too tedious, to be appealing. Or they discover that the book on which the TV program was based is a long, complicated adult tome few children can comprehend. We hear of the sixth grader who saw the many TV installments of "Roots" and then read the book with pleasure; but for that rare one, there are hundreds who signed off after a few pages. The experience gave reading a low rating for them.

Parents might help to ward off this kind of disappointment by pointing out the length and complexity of such a book as *Roots* and suggesting another book on the same theme which would be easier to read.

The movie or TV tie-in makes a great introduction to a children's book, but it does not guarantee readership by any means. Parents who watch such a program with their children, talk about it together, and then read the book together will realize the most lasting results.

In recent years many children's books have been used by TV and film directors as the basis for major productions. Among those recently adapted to television or movie are *Roll of Thunder, Hear My Cry* by Mildred D. Taylor, *The Great Gilly Hopkins* by Katherine Paterson, *The Black Stallion* by Walter Farley, and *Island of the Blue Dolphins* by Scott O'Dell. All of them have what it takes for a good family show: suspense, strong emotional pull, good characterization, and originality. Children and adults enjoyed these shows with equal enthusiasm. Interestingly enough, many adults are unaware that these popular programs originated in children's literature.

Watch the newspapers and TV magazines for announcements of such novels and TV programs and make time for them in your family. Ask the school librarian and public librarian to keep you posted on good things to come. Then watch with your children and help to make the bridge from viewing to real reading.

Monsters, witchcraft, and astrology command a devoted following among fifth and sixth graders. It's not fiction they want, but stories about "real" monsters. Jeanne Bendick's *The Mystery in Lochness* fills the bill exactly.

Books in the Eerie Series, published by J. B. Lippincott, are very popular: *Meet the Werewolf* and *Meet the Vampire* by Georgess McHargue and *Space Monsters* and *Creatures From Lost Worlds* by Seymour Simon.

Larry Kettelkamp's *Haunted Houses*, which is illustrated with photos, adds to the broad bill of fare for those who want factual reports on the supernatural.

Well-sustained suspense assures the popularity of a book for young readers. Indeed, the word *mystery, secret,* or *ghost* in the title seems to have a magnetic effect. Children who have been digging into the informational books about witches and ghosts welcome stories with a background they recognize as authentic.

Young readers looking for suspense easily locate books which proclaim this quality in their titles: *The Ghost of Tillie Jean Cassaway*, for example, or *The Mystery of Lincoln Detweiler and the Dog Who Barked Spanish*. Such titles give assurance that the stories will follow the formula and deliver suspense.

Children may need help in finding the books in which great excitement, drama, and suspense unfold without specific announcement in the title.

John Bellairs gives just what they want in *The House With a Clock in Its Walls* and its sequels, *The Figure in the Shadows* and *The Letter, the Witch, and the Ring*. According to one librarian, "All are wildly popular." *The House of Dies Drear* by Virginia Hamilton combines ghosts of the Underground Railroad and a neighborhood hoax to create suspense.

Yet suspense does not depend upon ghosts, mysteries, sorcerers, and amulets. It can build up without any of these in a story that may have even greater originality and stronger emotional pull.

One such story is *Julie of the Wolves* by Jean Craighead George, which tells of a thirteen-year-old Eskimo girl, lost without food or compass on the Alaskan tundra, but accepted by a pack of wolves who enable her to survive.

Several stories with a historical setting have the suspense that the ten-to-twelves crave. Avi's *Night Journeys* is one of these—an exciting tale of two runaway indentured servants, age ten and eleven, in Pennsylvania of 1767. A number of World War II stories build up to a high pitch of suspense as well.

In *Flight of the Sparrow*, Julia Cunningham keeps her readers in a breathless state as a tiny French street waif recounts a series of harrowing struggles to save the lives of her "family" and survive herself. The intense loyalty of this little band of rejected youngsters makes the story a very satisfying one.

Strong emotional content is enough to make almost any book popular at this age level although fifth and sixth graders do everything possible to avoid showing any sentiment. The boy who wouldn't be caught dead giving his mother or sister a kiss will shower affection on his dog.

Some of the stories with strong emotional pull are about animals and the people to whom they give their allegiance. The classic example is *Lassie Come Home* by Eric Knight, the story of a dog who traveled hundreds of miles to get home again. Another is *Gentle Ben* by Walt Morey, the tale of a lonely boy and an Alaskan brown bear. *Old Yeller* by Fred Gipson tells of a stray dog who becomes the inseparable companion of a Texas farm boy in the 1860s until their bitter separation. Several horse stories have the same emotional appeal: *Misty of Chincoteague* by Marguerite Henry and *The Black Stallion* by Walter Farley, for example.

All have been converted to highly successful movies or television programs. "Lassie," of course, has been stretched over so many TV installments that it bears little resemblance to the book, but it is still a good bridge to reading, particularly if parents help to make the personal introduction to the book.

Deep person-to-person loyalty comes out in many popular books for children. Betsy Byars is an author who is particularly successful in drawing her readers into the emotional commitments of her characters. In her Newbery Award book, *The Summer of the Swans*, she tells of a shy, sensitive eighth grader who is trying to protect her retarded younger brother.

Katherine Paterson is another author who builds up a reader's emotional involvement in the fate of her characters. In *The Great Gilly Hopkins*, readers identify with the rebellious foster child, who hates everything and everybody until she gets herself and her world in better perspective. In *Bridge to Terabithia*, friendship flowers between a boy and girl who at first seem an extreme contrast. Tragedy strikes, leaving the boy to build on that extraordinary friendship and put his emotional self together again. After reading this book, one sixth grader said, "I'll never be the same."

Sometimes such books get off to a slow start and lose readers then and there. This is less likely to happen if the first chapters are read aloud. Often the very sound of the rhythmical language of a Katherine Paterson book will hold the young listener until the plot takes over. Then there is no stopping.

Deeply personal problems are basic to the plot in more and more of the books written for young readers today. Many of them depict heroes and heroines who must struggle with personal tragedy before they can go on with their lives. *The Night Swimmers* by Betsy Byars tells of the false bravado of a girl who must make a home for the two younger brothers who need her and at the same time resent her. Lois Lowry's

A Summer to Die is the poignant story of a girl who realizes her older sister is dying.

In *A Figure of Speech*, Norma Fox Mazer tells of a thirteen-year-old's struggle to break her family's heartless pressures on the eighty-three-year-old grandfather who lives in the basement. *Summer of My German Soldier* by Bette Greene pictures a twelve-year-old Jewish girl who is rejected by her parents because she befriends a German prisoner of war in Arkansas during World War II and is sent to reform school.

Parents don't show up well in stories like these. Family life is often marked with tension, if not total disintegration. Again and again, youngsters in these stories reach out for sympathy and understanding, but it is not their parents who help them make sense out of their lives.

Several of my young friends reject this kind of book entirely. "I don't like gray books," one of them explained.

The same girl and her friends devour the books by Judy Blume, which deal with the problems of growing up in suburbia. Her characters are not faced with agonizing hunger, child abuse, physical deformity, or sudden death. Parents, though fumbling and sometimes indifferent, are there to fall back on.

The personal concerns Judy Blume writes about are the ones that trouble suburban youngsters from a comfortable background: being overweight (*Blubber*), their own sexual development (*Are You There, God? It's Me, Margaret*), parents' divorce (*It's Not the End of the World*), the friend who is a shoplifter (*Then Again, Maybe I Won't*).

The topics Judy Blume speaks of were once taboo in books for children, but they are not new to children who often worry in silence. Teachers tell me that these books help children open up, talk to each other, and even talk with adults about deep personal concerns. "So Judy Blume serves an important purpose," they point out.

For Judy Blume fans there are similar novels that are even funnier: Constance C. Greene's trio about Alexandra: *A Girl Called Al, I Know You, Al,* and *Your Old Pal, Al*; and Lois Lowry's *Anastasia Krupnik*.

Imagination takes over in some of the most beautifully written and most intriguing books for young readers. In general, these are more appealing to good readers, but both teachers and librarians report that when read aloud they are very popular across the board.

A highly imaginative story may be laid in a familiar setting as real as the house next door, but at some point fantasy takes over. The reader suspends disbelief, and the impossible seems possible. This is what happens in *Charlotte's Web,* a story third and fourth graders melt over.

The love of animal fantasy continues as children become fifth and sixth graders and meet such books as *Rabbit Hill* by Robert Lawson and *Mrs. Frisby and the Rats of NIMH* by Robert O'Brien. The little animals of *Rabbit Hill* speak, think, read, and act like human beings, but they remain animals whose chief concern is survival in their rural setting. *Mrs. Frisby and the Rats of NIMH* is a more intricate story with a touch of science fiction. (The rats have escaped from a laboratory where they were given injections to sharpen their intellect.) Both books are good choices for reading aloud.

In a sixth grade I visited in Evanston, Illinois, *Watership Down* by Richard Adams was being read aloud, a chapter a day, and the kids were hanging on every word. First published in England as a children's book, *Watership Down* (444 pages long) was published in the United States for adults. In essence, it is the story of rabbits who are forced to establish a new warren and must cope with the threat of man's civilization. The rabbits have their own civilization and religion, even a language unique to rabbits. It is a remarkable book for reading aloud in the family.

Fantasies which involve human beings often begin with a realistic setting. The British are particularly successful in starting with the everyday here-and-now and branching off into imaginative happenings. Eileen Dunlop of Scotland has done this particularly well in *Elizabeth Elizabeth* and *The House on Mayferry Street.* In the first, twelve-year-old Elizabeth finds a mirror that takes her into the eighteenth century where she is the Elizabeth who occupied the mansion in that period. The scene of *A House on Mayferry Street* is a shabby old dwelling in Edinburgh where mysterious whispers, even the music of a flute, influence the lives of the Ramsay family.

A String in the Harp by Nancy Bond is a more intricate fantasy which takes place in Wales, where an American family is living for a year. Twelve-year-old Peter, who is hostile to the whole experience, finds a key which enables him to see the past. Peter's visions assume credibility as he strugggles to survive family tensions.

In the same general category is *The Dark Is Rising*, a five-volume sequence by Susan Cooper. The series is based on the myths, legends, and geography of Cornwall and links the times of King Arthur with three children of today. These books have strong appeal for many fifth and sixth graders.

A number of writers of fantasy locate their stories in an imaginary world. C. S. Lewis creates the country of Narnia for *The Lion, the Witch and the Wardrobe* and six others in a series. Lloyd Alexander dreams up the imaginary land of Prydain for a series of five books, including *The Book of Three, The Black Cauldron,* and *The Castle of Llyr.* All have devoted followers.

As youngsters read these books of fantasy—or hear them read aloud—they become aware of subtle commentary on the people, events, and values of the real world. Often the imaginative tale sets the reader thinking and questioning as the realistic tale does not. For many youngsters this brings real satisfaction.

In the same way, poetry takes over and becomes the great favorite of many youngsters. The kind of poetry they meet and the way it is introduced will probably determine their response. For suggestions, see Chapter 7, "Poetry Is for Everyone."

7

Poetry Is for Everyone

Children of all ages love poetry. They like to sing it and chant familiar lines or to create an interpretive dance suggested by a poem. They are fascinated by the voice of the poet recorded for them. They plunge into making films and sound filmstrips of the poems they have read and those they have written. For hours they will listen to recordings in order to find the right musical background for a poem.

Never have there been so many poetry books for children—many of them well-illustrated paperbacks containing some of the choicest poems by outstanding poets. Many of these poems were published for adults, but the children have taken them over. Some originated in the oral literature of primitive peoples and only recently have been translated and published for modern readers. Some are such exotic verse forms as haiku and tanka from ancient Japan or the ultramodern concrete poems, which position words and phrases to make a picture or create a special sound effect.

The variety is endless. And the enthusiasm of children is endless—provided they can become involved in the poem and provided the poem sings out to them.

If your experience has brought you to a different feeling about poetry, I am ready to guess that you never got involved in poetry through singing, chanting, dancing, painting, filming, or writing your own free verse. Further, you may have been introduced to poetry through the "vivisection method" whereby each line was analyzed and haggled over until you had only the bloody remains of a poem to be shoved into the discard pile, never to live again.

Eve Merriam, the poet, proposes a very different approach to poetry in "How to Eat a Poem":

> *Don't be polite.*
> *Bite in.*
> *Pick it up with your fingers and lick the juice that*
>   *may run down your chin.*
> *It is ready and ripe now, whenever you are.* *

This is what we have been doing in the Poetry Workshop at Lehigh University where teachers experiment with ways to bring children and poetry together. We bite right into the poem and soon are licking up the juice. We use no verbal preliminaries or motivation lest they get between us and the poem.

I find that involvement in a poem springs more easily when child and adult sit close together, perhaps on the floor or tucked into an oversize easy chair. When you sit shoulder to shoulder, the emotional involvement in a poem seems to come quickly and easily.

IMPROMPTU CHORAL READING

I like to begin with poems or songs which have a great deal of repetition so that a child can readily chime in on repeated lines and phrases. One favorite poem is so old that it is part of our oral folk literature. It begins:

> *If all the seas were one sea*
>   *What a great sea that would be!*

It continues the same pattern which is so quickly identified that even a five-year-old can figure out the alternate lines.

Parent:	*If all the trees were one tree*
Child:	*What a great tree that would be!*
Parent:	*If all the axes were one axe*
Child:	*What a great axe that would be!*
Parent:	*If all the men were one man*
Child:	*What a great man that would be!*

---

*From *It Doesn't Always Have to Rhyme* by Eve Merriam.

Then comes the narrator's section:

> *And if the great man took the great axe*
> *And cut down the great tree*
> *And let it fall in the great sea . . .*

Then you both sing out:

> *What a great SPLASH that would be!*

On the first try, you and the child may be feeling your way through words and lines that both of you are unsure of. But when you try it again, you will get more excitement—and more drama—into the words. And children will revel in it.

Another favorite for impromptu choral reading is Beatrice Schenk de Regniers's "If We Walked on Our Hands." Each stanza winds up with the refrain

> *What a mixed-up*
> *fixed-up*
> *topsy-turvy*
> *sit-u-a-tion.*[*]

Even a three-year-old will go for this one and chime in on that topsy-turvy chorus.

The Poetry Troupe, compiled by Isabel Wilner, is an anthology of poems selected because they encourage children to share in the reading. Several are question-and-answer poems ("Did You Feed My Cow?," "Roosters," and "Witch, Witch," for example). They immediately suggest two-part reading—one of you reading the question, the other the answer. A number of poems in this anthology have a repeated line that becomes a chorus which children pick up easily and love to chime in on. ("Old Snake Has Gone to Sleep" by Margaret Wise Brown, for example, and "Quack!" by Walter de la Mare.)

The nonsense poems of N. M. Bodecker often give an irresistible invitation to complete a rhyme. If you read the first line of a Bodecker couplet, your young poetry buff will

---

*From *Something Special* by Beatrice Schenk de Regniers.

easily and happily finish the second with a fitting rhyme. Try this one:

> *"Let's marry,"*
> *said the cherry.*

> *"Why me?"*
> *said the pea.**

And so it continues for forty couplets . . . and forty chances to come up with the right rhyme.

Another Bodecker poem, "Booteries and Fluteries and Flatteries and Things," becomes great fun with listeners chiming in.

You will find that many poems lend themselves to this kind of group reading, often with sound effects. For great fun try: "The Pickety Fence" by David McCord, "Weather Is Full of the Nicest Sounds" by Aileen Fisher, "The Mysterious Cat" by Vachel Lindsay, and "The Washing Machine" by Patricia Hubbell.

Not only do children enjoy what they call "doing a poem," but they quickly build a repertoire of poems they know by ear because they have become involved from the very beginning.

Favorite songs with lots of repetition give the opportunity for involvement too: "The Wheels of the Bus Go Round and Round," for example, or "The Bear Went Over the Mountain," and "Aiken Drum."

Improvisation follows easily, with you and the child suggesting new lines to fit the old pattern. "Aiken Drum" is a favorite vehicle for this:

> STANZA: *There was a man lived in the moon*
> *lived in the moon, lived in the moon*
> *There was a man lived in the moon*
> *and his name was Aiken Drum.*

> CHORUS: *And he played upon a ladle,*
> *a ladle, a ladle,*
> *And he played upon a ladle,*
> *and his name was Aiken Drum.*

---

*From the poem " 'Let's Marry!' Said the Cherry" which is found in the book of the same title by N. M. Bodecker.

Then each stanza tells what he is wearing:

His hat was made of good cream cheese,
of good cream cheese, of good
cream cheese

And then:

His coat was made of good roast beef,
of good roast beef, of good
*roast beef.**

Children love to think up new possibilities such as "His hat was made of bubble gum, of bubble gum, of bubble gum" or "His coat was made of pizza pie, of pizza pie, of pizza pie."

"She'll Be Comin' Round the Mountain" was completely changed by eleven-year-olds who dropped the six white horses and sang

She'll be comin' on a Honda
when she comes. . . .Yippee!

Often a child will concoct a new line or couplet while the song is underway and sing out his or her innovation as a solo which others pick up spontaneously. When children have participated in the creation of a song and have brought in others to sing their words, they get a very special feeling about the melody of language.

MUSIC AND POETRY

I am sure I have always known that poetry is meant to be heard and that poetry and music go hand in hand. But it is only through the Poetry Workshop that I have learned that music and poetry are inseparable. We use more and more music with the reading of poetry, and we find it has a magnetic effect on children and young people.

Sometimes we begin with the old spiritual, "Kum Ba Yah":

---

*Music for this Scottish folk song is found in several of the song books listed in Chapter 16.

Someone's singing, Lord, Kum ba yah . . .

Then: *Someone's praying, Lord, Kum ba yah . . .**

This is a song children like to extend with their own stanzas, such as

> *Someone's laughing, Lord . . .* and
> *Someone's dancing, Lord. . . .*

They soon learn that the rhythm must change with the meaning so they sing lightly and gaily, "Someone's laughing, Lord"—even "Someone's giggling, Lord"—and they become very wide-eyed and pensive as they sing, "Someone's lonely, Lord," or "Someone's suffering, Lord."

Often the children will hum the melody of "Kum Ba Yah" as background to the reading of such poems as "The Dream Keeper" or "April Rain Song" by Langston Hughes. Quickly they will change the tempo of their humming to fit the mood of the poem.

"One Wide River to Cross" is an obvious favorite to sing softly as background music for the poems in *Prayers From the Ark* by the French poet, Carmen Bernos de Gasztold. It is one of the most popular books I have ever introduced to children. The first poem is "Noah's Prayer" with Noah appealing to God for relief from the continuous downpour and the cries of animals on board. It is followed by the prayer of each of the animals—the little duck, the elephant, the old horse, the cat, the rooster, and so on. With each prayer, the tempo changes. You hear the butterfly dipping and fluttering in "The Prayer of the Butterfly."

"The Prayer of the Ox" plods slowly and evenly:

> *Dear God, give me time.*
> *Men are always so driven!*
> *Give me time to eat.*
> *Give me time to plod.*
> *Give me time to sleep.*
> *Give me time to think.†*

---

*Melody for "Kum Ba Yah" is given in *Sing Together Children* listed under "Song Books" in Chapter 16.

†From *Prayers From the Ark* by Carmen Bernos de Gasztold. English translation by Rumer Godden.

Frequently children write their own prayers from the Ark and read these with musical background, perhaps taping the combination. Each child likes to put himself or herself in the place of an animal and pour forth a prayer that, in reality, seems to be the child's. Usually it is the prayer of a lowly creature, frightened by the threats and violence of some larger creature, such as man. Note these poems from nine-year-olds:

The Prayer of the Skunk

Dear God,
Why did you make
me smell so bad?
Nobody likes me,
except you.
My aroma does protect me.
Help me to use it
*wisely and sparingly.**

ANDY FREEH

The Prayer of the Rabbit

Oh, Lord,
Why did you make me so tasty?
Hunters like to
shoot, skin,
and eat me.
But there's one thing
I'm thankful for—
little children
*always love me.**

BOBBY GLICK

If you play an autoharp or guitar, bring it out for your poetry hour. Just a little strumming—even an occasional chord—will add magic to the reading of poetry.

---

*From *Noah's Friends Pray* by Grade Four, Nockamixon School, Revere, Pa. Margaret Koch, teacher.

MOVEMENT AND POETRY

Those swept up in the rhythm and music of poetry soon want to express their reactions through movement. Not simply with foot tapping or finger strumming, but real body movement—swaying slowly with lines that move quietly and gently, arms reaching upward or folded close to the chest if that seems what the poem calls for.

A good way to begin is to sit on the floor in a totally relaxed position—legs outstretched, arms hanging limp, head dropping, and eyes closed. As a poem is read, each person moves as the poem suggests—rising to a kneeling position or crumpling closer to the floor, standing, swaying, snapping fingers—whatever the rhythm and the meaning of the poem demand.

With eyes closed, you get a strange sense of oneness with the poet who seems to be telling you what to do and the pace for every move. The poet speaks directly to you and seems to be thinking your thoughts—a very satisfying kind of involvement.

Try it with "The Prayer of the Ox." As the poem is read, move in the same slow rhythm. As you plod along, you will feel the heavy weariness of the ox and understand his complaint. Your body helps you understand and feel.

PAINTING AND SCULPTURE

Given a little encouragement, children move easily into the visual arts to express their reaction to a poem. At first their art work may be very literal: one "proud mysterious cat" with a slave kneeling before her to illustrate Vachel Lindsay's poem "The Mysterious Cat." But soon children see the fun of trying to visualize the mystery in the poem and the echo of repeated lines. Or it may be an impressionistic sort of collage for such a poem as Carl Sandburg's "Arithmetic," which includes the lines

> *Arithmetic is where numbers fly*
> *like pigeons in and out of your head.**

---

*From *The Complete Poems of Carl Sandburg*.

With collages, string paintings, wire coat-hanger sculpture, junk sculpture, papier-mâché and pipecleaner figures, and art work of all sorts, children can give their interpretation of a poem, either literally or imaginatively, and thus grow closer to the poet and the poem. We have found that children gain momentum when they see their teacher working on a similar art project independently while they work on theirs. It is not unusual for the children's creations to show more individuality and sensitivity than the teacher's, but a good teacher is used to that. Try it at home and see what happens.

WHEN CHILDREN WRITE POETRY

One of the great ways to sharpen children's awareness of poetry as an art is to show them how to express themselves in poetic language. Once they are able to use words with imagination and rhythm, they become sensitive to the language and melody of experienced poets.

If you are over thirty and have never written any poetry, you may panic at the thought of writing a poem yourself. Even if you have made a few tries, you probably remember little more than searching for a word to rhyme with *gathered* and finding nothing but *lathered,* which made no sense at all. Or you may recall tapping out the rhythm with your fingers and realizing you needed another beat in the last line—but you'd said all you had to say.

Eve Merriam solves these problems in the titles of two of her books of poetry for children: *There Is No Rhyme for Silver* and *It Doesn't Always Have to Rhyme.*

Poetry does not have to rhyme. Only experienced writers with an extensive vocabulary and a very inventive way with language can use rhyme effectively and naturally. Rarely does a beginner have this skill.

Not all lines of a poem have to be the same length or have the same number of accented syllables. Free verse may have one or two words in one line and ten in the next, provided the ideas expressed are imaginative and the language rhythmical.

Once children accept the fact of free verse (no rhyme and no limiting pattern of accented syllables per line), they are free to roll into poetry, writing with their own fresh phrases and imaginative word pictures. Free verse is used by some of the best-known poets in the United States and Europe today. Its only requirements are imagination and a sense of rhythm appropriate to the theme.

Children have both. Once they are free to use these natural talents, they can produce very lovely and sensitive poetry. In recent years, several books of poetry by children have been published. Some have grown out of the poets-in-residence program which has brought experienced poets into the schools to lead children in the reading and writing of poetry.

As a beginning, encourage your child to speak freely and imaginatively about sounds, colors, and feelings. Perhaps you will be able to record some of his or her choice phrases. "It's as quiet as the cotton in the aspirin bottle," said one nine-year-old. "Quiet as your cheeks get red in the snow," said another.

"Gray is a feeling like forgetting your lunch," said an eight-year-old, and "Love is warm/Like the spring seashore sand," spoke a kindergarten child.

With this kind of creative thinking as a start, children can go on to more careful observation and more extended images. Here is the poem of Fay Longshaw, a ten-year-old in Warwickshire, England:

Old People

Old people,
Neglected people,
Like an unwanted toy put down
And then forgotten.

Sitting back in a chair asleep
Their mouths open,
Their eyes shut tightly
Cutting themselves off from the
outside world.

Unhappy people,
Sad people
Living in the past,
Remembering the happy days,
And dreading the future.

Children who learn to observe carefully and then dictate or write their poetic ideas are appreciative of the poet's imagery when they hear a poem read or meet it in print.

POETRY WITH CHILD APPEAL

In selecting poetry for several anthologies, I have always had the help of children. I like to meet them in small groups of no more than ten or twelve over a period of several months to read poetry and learn which poems they would like to have in a book to read again. Few have ever had an adult ask their advice about poetry before, and they assume the responsibility with pride and seriousness.

Frequently these children have voted down a poem I had assumed would be among their first choices. When I asked why this poem or that failed to get top rating, the answer was frequently, "It's too sweet." I have come to think this is a child's most serious indictment.

By this time, I am well aware that in the past we have given children poetry that cloys with its pretty little birds, sweet-smelling flowers, and sparkling dew drops.

Asked why they like a particular poem, children will frequently say, "I like it because it's real." "Real" means something that speaks to them directly, unhampered by poetic diction and extended images. A poem about city traffic and the litter on city streets may seem "real" to them if it is written simply, without poetic flourishes. One about skiing or mountain climbing may be called "real" even by those who have never taken part in such rugged activities, but only if the language of the poet convinces them that he was there, and that they, too, might be there. The poet must establish direct communication with the child.

"THE POET IS JUST LIKE ME. HE FEELS."

One time I met with fourth graders who had become deeply involved in poetry and were discussing why they found poetry so appealing. From a welter of suggestions came this from a ten-year-old boy: "I like poetry because the poet is just like me. He feels." The other children nodded agreement as though satisfied that he had put into words what they had been trying to say.

I had never before realized how deeply children appreciate the *feeling* side of literature. Again and again, I have found convincing evidence of children's longing for literature that touches them as people who feel, who laugh and cry, who are sometimes lonely and emotionally hurt, who may quiver with anxiety or sing for joy.

Laughter makes a good beginning for the poetry hour for children of all ages. Mother Goose includes short humorous verses which are sure winners with the very young: "Hickory, dickory, dock," "Tweedledum and Tweedledee," "Dickery, dickery, dare," "Mother, may I go out to swim?" and hundreds more.

Father Fox's Pennyrhymes by Clyde Watson has the musical lilt and zany charm of Mother Goose in the real New England of Father Fox, who wears stout work overalls and drinks hot cider by the open fire. There are funny jingles here, and some that are sheer nonsense—all made more intriguing by the detailed watercolor illustrations by the author's sister, Wendy Watson.

Some of the most comical poems for children tell a story, often with wonderful rhythm, rhyme, and alliteration. "The Owl and the Pussy-Cat" by Edward Lear is an old-timer with timeless humor.

"When Daddy Fell Into the Pond" by Alfred Noyes is a sure hit with youngsters of eight and up—indeed for any age wanting to see Daddy dripping with duckweed. The same youngsters welcome "Adventures of Isabel" by Ogden Nash who tells of a young lady who was about to be devoured by an enormous bear. But:

> She washed her hands and she straightened
> her hair up,
> Then Isabel quietly ate the bear up.*

Unforgettable comic characters appear in many children's poems: "Godfrey Gordon Gustavus Gore" by William Brighty Rands is about "the boy who would never shut a door"; "Jonathan Bing" by Beatrice Curtis Brown tells of the forgetful young man who wore only his pajamas when he "went out to visit the King"; and John Ciardi's Arvin Marvin Lillisbee Fitch who "rode a broomstick like a witch."

---

*From *Many Long Years* by Ogden Nash.

Sometimes a gentle kind of humor appeals to the very young, as in the poems of A. A. Milne, whose two collections of poetry written for his own son are also in paperback: *When We Were Very Young* and *Now We Are Six*.

Bolder humor shows up in poetry written more recently, such as that of Karla Kuskin in "Hughbert and the Glue" (Hughbert glues up his whole world) and "Catherine" (who makes a birthday cake of mud, sticks, and stones). Or of Shel Silverstein in "Mr. Spats" (who had twenty-six hats), Jack Prelutsky in "Adelaide" ("the more she ate, the less she weighed"), and Spike Milligan in "Malice at Buckingham Palace."

Children appreciate the humor of mixed-up word concoctions. Laura E. Richards was a master of these. (Remember the "elephant who tried to use the telephant" and "Little Tom Tickleby/Answer me quickleby"?)

Eve Merriam has her own distinctive way of mixing up words to make sense. Try this from her poem, "Weather":

> *A juddle a pump aluddle a dump a*
> *Puddmuddle jump in and slide!**

No one who has repeated those lines a few times has trouble reading them.

Always popular are the quick short poems with a surprise ending such as "The Purple Cow" and "I Wish That My Room Had a Floor" by Gelett Burgess and the limericks of Edward Lear ("There was an old man with a beard," "There was an old man from Peru," and many more in his *Complete Nonsense Book*).

Surely the most popular of the modern humorous poets is Shel Silverstein whose books *Where the Sidewalk Ends* and *A Light in the Attic* are adored by children and their parents. His illustrations are as wacky as his verses.

William Cole has brought together some of the best humorous poems in his anthologies, *Oh, What Nonsense!* and *Oh, How Silly!*—each with hilarious illustrations.

Scary poems, like spooky stories, have a big following among the young, who like the eerie feeling when ghosts cry and witches ride. For a Halloween sampling, be sure to include

---

*From *Catch a Little Rhyme* by Eve Merriam.

Illustration by Shel Silverstein in *Where the Sidewalk Ends*

Myra Cohn Livingston's "October Magic," John Ciardi's "What Night Would It Be?" and Walter de la Mare's "Some One." Several very popular poems combine the humorous and the scary: "Beware, My Child" by Shel Silverstein (about the threat of a snaggle-toothed beast) and "Please, Johnny!" by John Ciardi (about "The Shreek" who is "a shiverous beast.") No one would ever call them too sweet.

Two collections of poetry by Jack Prelutsky are also very popular: *Nightmares: Poems to Trouble Your Sleep* and *The Headless Horseman Rides Tonight: More Poems to Trouble Your Sleep*. Both are illustrated by Arnold Lobel.

Tenderness and sympathy are moods that draw many children to poetry. Yet many adults have failed to recognize the underlying seriousness in children and their feeling of compassion. Free to choose a topic to write about, youngsters often select injustice, poverty, death, or physical suffering.

You expect them to like "The Story of the Baby Squirrel" in which Dorothy Aldis tells the sad and universal tale of a missing pet, or *Listen, Rabbit* by Aileen Fisher, a little boy's first-person account of his friendship with a wild rabbit. But it may surprise you to know that they respond warmly to the poem, "Mother to Son" by Langston Hughes. This is a mother who holds her head high, undaunted, although as she says, "Life for me ain't been no crystal stair."*

Perhaps it is a sign of the earlier maturity of children that they are concerned about the tragedies of life.

WHO AM I?

Given assurance that they may write freely, many children struggle with the question, "Who am I?" Others push on to ask, "Where am I heading?" Such introspection may seem unchildlike to adults who have not sat down again and again for poetry sessions with children willing to share their thoughts. Yet, in many ways, today's children show themselves to be unchildlike in the old sense of the term.

I think it is this introspective side of children that leads them to David McCord's poem, "This Is My Rock," one of the most popular we have introduced to middle graders. Each child seems to hear himself or herself saying with the poet:

> *And here I run*
> *To steal the secret of the sun.†*

Perhaps this is why many children welcome poems written in the first person, such as those of Lilian Moore in her little book, *I Feel the Same Way*. Myra Cohn Livingston has several "I poems," as one boy called them, and they invariably win friends among children: "The Trouble Is—" explains "*no one* appreciates me"‡ and "One for Novella Nelson" winds up with "Me, I'm not alone/I've got myself."§

POETRY WITH A MESSAGE

The earliest poetry for children had a religious message which was often rather threatening as "In Adam's fall/we sinned all." That was three hundred years ago and is thought of only as a relic today. Then came poetry that hammered home a lesson about being kind and polite and obedient little children. The didactic poem is seldom seen today. Both would be rejected if modern children met them in their reading.

But these children often write and read poetry with a message and seem to feel real satisfaction in so doing. Instead of a lesson about the conduct of the individual child, as in the older poetry, the modern message may be about social problems of which the child is an inseparable part. There are poems about pollution, about the suffering of minority groups, about the filth and brutality of city streets, about man's inhumanity to man.

Children respond positively to the poetry of black writers such as Lucille Clifton, Eloise Greenfield, Gwendolyn Brooks, Langston Hughes, Nikki Giovanni, and June Jordan. Several excellent anthologies of black poetry win the sympathetic involvement of young people. Two of these—*I Am the Darker Brother* and *Black Out Loud*—were edited by Arnold Adoff.

Many of the pop/rock lyrics which come to grips with social problems are very popular with youngsters in elementary school. To grandparents and some parents, these lyrics may seem a long way from the traditional poetry of childhood. The repetition grows monotonous, perhaps, and the rhythm borders on the weird if you grew up with "The Village Blacksmith" and "Come, little leaves, said the wind one day." But this is the rhythm that our youngsters know and to which they are attuned. This is the repetition of our oral language culture as heard continuously on television and radio. The poetry of protest is part of our culture, and children—even the little ones—are ready for it.

FIND THE TIME—CHOOSE THE PLACE

The time for poetry will vary. You may want to add several poems to your daily read-aloud hour, selecting those that will tie into stories or events of the day. If your children have learned to love poetry by chiming in on familiar lines, you may find almost any family outing can include poetry.

In many families with young children, bedtime is a good time for poetry because listeners are relaxed and interruptions are minimal. But don't overlook the possibilities of the lull on a rainy day or a hot summer afternoon.

It helps to set the stage for poetry. If you plan to read several poems, be sure your listeners are comfortable. One of my friends always takes a book of poetry on family picnics and opens it on the bank of a peaceful stream—or reads by the dying glow of a campfire.

When poems become friends, certain ones turn up to suit special occasions. Countless mothers have quoted the poems of their childhood when walking with their four-year-olds: poems such as "My Shadow" by Robert Louis Stevenson or "Mrs. Peck-Pigeon" by Eleanor Farjeon. A dog down the street may suggest Marchette Chute's little poem, "My Dog," which begins

> *His nose is short and scrubby;*
> *His ears hang rather low.*[*]

It is no exaggeration to say there is a poem for every occasion. (Remember Christina Rossetti's "Mix a Pancake/ Stir a Pancake"?) Both the poem and the occasion will become more significant when taken together.

If you have been on a picnic, Dorothy Aldis's "The Picnic" will be welcomed. A trip to the seashore will be a natural introduction for Myra Cohn Livingston's "Low Tide" and "German Shepherd" or the lovely sea poems of May Swenson. The first try on roller skates should be accompanied by Myra Cohn Livingston's "74th Street" and the end of vacation will have much more significance with Eve Merriam's "Leavetaking."

And if you need some support in the proposal to cut back on time for television and stereo, you can have no better back-up than Eve Merriam's poem, "Umbilical," and John Ciardi's "Jimmy Jet and the TV Set."

Holidays invite poetry, too. We have choice poems for

---

*From *Around and About* by Marchette Chute.

.

almost any day you can name: Christmas, Hanukkah, Valentine's Day, Fourth of July, Easter . . . even Groundhog Day . . . and of course, birthdays. (Consult *Poetry for Holidays* and *More Poetry for Holidays* edited by Nancy Larrick.)

BOOKS OF POETRY FOR CHILDREN

You should have several good books of poetry for children at hand, preferably those that both you and the children will enjoy. An annotated list of poetry books is given on pages 226–228. Perhaps the place to begin is with one of the excellent anthologies of poems for all ages by many poets.

When children get to know a particular poet, they should have the opportunity to own a whole book of his poems. Books by individual poets are included in the annotated list on pages 223–226.

8

Build on Their Interests

Fifty years ago teachers, librarians, and parents set up lists of books every child should know, and children were expected to read those that adults had decided were appropriate. As adults introduced these preselected books, they found themselves trying to build a base of interest in the child. They provided what was called motivation to read—a reason, a drive, to read.

This was a slow way to go at it, indeed a backhanded way. For every child has certain topics, certain activities he or she is excited about. If we can introduce books that fit some driving fascination in each child, we are more likely to develop a persistent reader.

Children's interests are widely varied and may change frequently. For one child it may be magic, monsters, or motor bikes; for another, it may be jokes, jet planes, or gerbils.

When children play, they sometimes become so engrossed that they actually forget about eating. The same vigorous absorption can be directed to reading provided the child finds the right books. The second grader who is fascinated by dinosaurs may read half a dozen books about them. This enthusiasm may push him or her to read third- and fourth-grade books which might otherwise seem too hard.

One eight-year-old who collected snakes spurned reading until his third-grade teacher suggested two or three books about snakes. A new world opened up. David read and read. By the end of the year his reading level had jumped three grades.

DISCOVERING WHAT TURNS THEM ON

Some children are very outspoken about their interests. Others are reserved. A child may develop a deep concern at school and not mention it at home. Or there may be a slight curiosity that can be strengthened.

If you know what attracts your child, you can find books that will supplement this interest. Discovering a child's concerns is not always easy, for they may change from week to week—and the range is almost unlimited. But if children are sure you are a sympathetic listener, they are likely to talk. You might compare notes with the teacher, who may know of involvement and ambitions you have not heard about.

Often you can get a line on a child's interests by a few casual questions: If you could do the one thing you most want to do, what would it be? If we could take a one-day trip, where would you go? If we could live in another country or another age, what would be your choice? If you had a museum, what would you put in it?

Or turn the conversation to "one thing I wonder about." If you toss in some wonderings of your own, you may encourage the child to speak more freely than otherwise.

Often a child's wondering is in the form of a very exact question: "I wonder what's at the bottom of the ocean?" Or, "I wonder what kind of bird that is?" Such questions lead naturally to a search for the answer in encyclopedia, dictionary, or children's book. A thoughtful parent will try to help find the right book. (See Chapter 15, "Tools for Book Selection.")

One word of caution: Once you discover your child's special interest, don't make too big a thing of it. If you present book after book and ask question after question, the child may begin to feel that you have taken over. So make your role as casual as you can, and let the child ask for further collaboration.

DEVELOPING NEW INTERESTS

Childhood is the time for sampling and exploring. Even the youngest have questions. By encouraging the questions, we encourage more exploring and the building of new interests. There is no better route to reading.

Wherever you live, you are surrounded with the stuff that questions are made of. The weather is a good example. Where does rain come from? How did it get into the clouds? What is snow? What is fog? How can you make a cloud in the kitchen? Why is the grass wet this morning? Why are days longer in summer? Why is it colder in winter?

These simple questions are intriguing to children. They lead to other questions—questions about the wind and air currents and gravity, for example. Easy science experiments can be set up to explain simple facts about the weather. All these questions and activities can lead to reading, and a number of books fit this interest beautifully.

The natural curiosity of the young child may produce a string of questions that fray the patience of parents, but it should never be discouraged. Through the desire to find out, the child, like a small rabbit sampling the leaves of various plants, gets the background that will give meaning to reading in later years. Unknowingly a youngster is preparing for reading by asking question after question. When school starts, there will be more ideas to talk about and write about. When that child reads, he or she will have much more to bring to the printed page and will have developed the habit of looking for new ideas and new experiences.

Your response to the curiosity of your child will have influence for years to come. If you fall back on any of the time-worn dodges ("Can't you see I'm busy," "Go ask your father," "Wait a minute," "You are interrupting me," etc.), the child may conclude that questions are annoying, if not downright bad, and exploration should be discontinued. Yet curiosity and outreach are the very traits to foster if you wish your child to be successful in school, in a career, and in personal living. Wise teachers cherish the student who asks questions. Wise parents do the same.

There are many areas in which you can provide new experiences and thus stimulate questions. A few examples:

Acquiring a pet. That decision will bring pleasure, plus a considerable amount of education. The animal gives much to talk about and read about. The child will welcome a book about the species or breed. Often, however, the kind of pet in the story is of less consequence than the deep loyalty between the pet and its human pal.

Planting seeds. Even a few nasturtium seeds in a pot or a row of lettuce or radishes in the yard will provide excitement. (Lettuce is a prudent choice because it should be pulled up early.) With a garden of their own, children become more interested in all plant life—and have more questions to ask.

Local visits. The visit can be to the supermarket, the post office, the dairy, the fire station, or a factory. Take the child behind the scenes where it is possible to linger and explore. At the post office buy a stamp for a letter addressed to the child, and ask the clerk to cancel it as the young addressee watches. That letter will be treasured when it is delivered the next day—and it may even make the child anxious to write a letter to Granddad. The airport is always exciting, of course. If there is a fish hatchery within range, you are lucky.

Short trips. Zoos and museums are ideal for the young provided you don't try to take in everything. Fifteen minutes at the monkey house is better than a wearying tour of the whole zoo. City dwellers may find a wonderful barnyard only a short drive from town—or a woods carpeted with spring beauties and dogtooth violets. Suburban children will be thrilled by a city subway or a ferryboat ride.

Longer trips. You don't need to make a long and expensive trip to interest a child. What the child wants is to see new things and get new ideas. Your role is to look once again with the eyes of a child and to find excitement in his or her discoveries. A small child will find it enough to walk by a stream, while an older brother may choose the swamp beside an abandoned railroad or a study in depth of a junkyard.

To some people a swamp is simply muck, but to others it is an exciting world of plants, insects, and animals. To the child with a mechanical turn, a junkyard is fascinating. Big rusty cogwheels will excite one explorer as much as the other is moved by marsh marigolds. And in both areas—machinery and nature—there are endless questions to be pursued.

Nine- to twelve-year-old children prefer an all-day trip and are ready to help with preparations. Is there a state park in your area? An historic shrine? A great bridge? A mountain? Invite the youngsters to work out a good route on the road map. They might write for literature about the place to be visited.

One mother told me that her nine-year-old sends for road maps in advance of a trip. He and his father choose the route. Along the way, the boy jots down interesting facts and questions to be looked up when he gets home. "They are the questions we all want answered but usually forget," the mother added. "Besides, they get us all reading."

ROCODILE,

Monkey,   Buffalo,   Hare,

Illustration by Alice and Martin Provensen in *A Peaceable Kingdom*

Any trip opens new approaches to nature and science, provided the driver is willing to pull off the road and stop from time to time, or to explore back roads. If you carry in the glove compartment several field guides to birds, wild flowers, and trees you can make on-the-spot identifications.

Not many drivers slow down to read historical markers along the highway. Yet those markers usually give just enough information to raise further questions. Why was this battle important? Did it accomplish anything beyond killing? What was this area like two hundred years ago? You will find many children's books about historical events and personalities. Your questions about cause and effect, right and wrong, will give your child an example of critical thinking.

There are appealing books about various regions of the United States. In the Pennsylvania German area where I lived for a number of years, curiosity is quickened by countless things. What is the meaning of the geometrical symbols painted on old barns? Why do some Amish people still travel in horse-drawn buggies? What are the strange words used on certain restaurant menus? Questions like these are answered in three good stories by Marguerite de Angeli: *Henner's Lydia, Skippack School,* and *Yonie Wondernose.* All tell of the customs and folklore of the Pennsylvania Germans. Many of the author's illustrations repeat the painted decorations which early settlers of Pennsylvania put on their houses, furniture, books, and even their birth certificates.

Colonial Williamsburg, the Mississippi Valley, New England, the Southwest, the Northwest, the Far West, and many other regions are well presented in books for children. If you plan a long trip to another region, or a move to another state, buy and read before you go. The gasoline won't seem so expensive if you fill the family's minds as well as your tank.

It is still possible in many parts of the United States to ride that glorious and vanishing conveyance, the passenger train. Steam power for sizable mileage is found in Colorado and New Mexico on two narrow-gauge lines. Local diesel-powered or electric trains are available in most metropolitan areas. A young father of my acquaintance devoted one Sunday morning to a train ride for his children, who were thrilled by the long tunnel north of Perkasie, Pennsylvania. There is, of course, a wealth of children's books about trains and the history of railroading.

Holidays, which adults often take for granted, are very important to children. Christmas, Easter, and Halloween are major events in the child's year, and all of them have been well covered in children's literature.

Christmas in your family will have greater significance if you read aloud such books as *Baboushka and the Three Kings* by Ruth Robbins, *A Certain Small Shepherd* by Rebecca Caudill, and *How Brown Mouse Kept Christmas* by Clyde Watson. And at Easter introduce Aileen Fisher's *Listen, Rabbit* for the younger children to revel in.

On holidays that celebrate the birthdays of famous men

(unfortunately none celebrates a famous woman as yet), you have the perfect opportunity to introduce such biographical books as *Where Do You Think You're Going, Christopher Columbus?* and *What's the Big Idea, Ben Franklin?* by Jean Fritz.

Hobbies may lead to further interests and further reading, too. Many children from six to twelve have at least one hobby, which may last for only a few days or may continue a lifetime. I think it is safe to say there is a good children's book about each of the major hobbies pursued by youngsters of twelve and under.

Would-be gymnasts will find valuable information and encouragement in *A Very Young Gymnast* by Jill Krementz. Dance students will thrill over her book entitled *A Very Young Dancer,* which tells of a girl's preparation for and performance in the New York City Ballet's "Nutcracker Suite."

For budding magicians there are such splendid how-to books as *Magic Secrets* and *Funny Magic* by Rose Wyler and Gerald Ames. Those eager to put on a magic show should read *Give a Magic Show* by Burton and Rita Marks.

Not all hobbies lead to reading, of course. Collecting bottle tops, for example, may lead to a dead end. But the love of collecting and the skill of gathering, sorting, trading, and storing could be switched to a more worthwhile hobby if the possibilities are made clear.

One of the most significant hobbies is stamp collecting, which is a natural lead to geography and history. However, a child may need some help in seeing the possibilities and in getting underway. This is a hobby that may last for many years, and books will make it more enjoyable along the way.

People can lead to reading, too. Children are always meeting people who interest them: a new child in school, a new family down the street, a new hero on TV.

New neighbors make children wonder about the place they came from. If it was a foreign country, count yourself as blessed. Foreign languages, songs, customs, and interests can be the pathway to absorbing books and stories.

An uncle or older brother working in a distant country provides a good reason for finding out more than his letters tell.

Indeed, every waking hour is full of people, events, and things that can draw a child to a book. Your grand opportunity lies in encouraging your child's curiosity.

Yet, more and more, I hear of children who have no hobbies, no special interests beyond television. In the sixth grade of one rural elementary school, more than half of the students cited television as their one hobby. Their teacher reports that the weekly period for "hobbies and crafts" finds children sitting idle because they are not interested in the kinds of activities that once made this the most popular period. "All they want is television," she said in despair. "It's their whole life!"

Perhaps these TV addicts need more stimulating activities than hobbies and crafts that can be brought out of the closet on call for a free period. A visit to an abandoned quarry to collect ferns and rock specimens might stimulate more questions and, hence, lead to more reading. The tour of an old churchyard and inspection of ancient tombstones could be stimulating in a very different way. In our town fifth graders converged on the local church where a new pipe organ was being installed, asked questions of the workers, and came away with much to talk about and look up in books. Expeditions such as these can stir children's curiosity and spark them into reaching out for more information.

Don't be afraid of launching into areas which are new to you. Children like the feeling of learning along with those who are older than they. That very experience may encourage them to keep questioning and learning when they become adults.

Don't hesitate to raise questions you cannot answer. Most adults are hazy on the details of science, geography, and history. This very lack of information is a good reason to say, "Let's look it up!" Your children will then become accustomed to using the almanac, dictionary, atlas, and encyclopedia—a habit that will help them all of their lives. (See Chapter 9, "Let's Look It Up!")

To find books related to your child's questions and

interests, consult the book lists described in Chapter 15, "Tools for Book Selection." Most librarians can also advise you about appropriate titles for your child's age and interests.

9

Let's Look It Up!

The key to learning is questioning. For many young children, asking a question comes as naturally as breathing. Sometimes it seems there is a question with almost every breath. Why? How big? How do you know?

Children's questions are cause for rejoicing, for that means they are thinking. Adults, as well as older children in the family, can encourage this questioning attitude by taking the questions seriously and helping to find the answers. Or they can embarrass the younger one and stifle his pursuit of knowledge by ridiculing a naive query. ("Hey, Mom, did you hear Jimmie ask how come an island keeps on floating?") Furthermore, unless answers are forthcoming—genuine answers, not those tossed off in ignorance or exasperation—a child soon begins to stifle the urge to inquire.

Many questions are not easy to answer unless you have the sort of encyclopedic mind which permits instant retrieval of authoritative information. Often a child's question is about a familiar subject ("What's a comet?"). But when you try to formulate an answer, you find yourself short of facts. Children's questions increasingly point to areas and topics that are new to adults. Hence the need for a reference book.

When you say, "Let's look it up," and reach for a dictionary or other reference book, you are making it clear that you take the child's question seriously, that you, too, want to extend your information, and that there is a way to do it quickly and easily at home.

Although very young children can only "read" the pictures in a reference book, they are becoming involved in the search for information and feel a part of the reading process. Those who can read a few lines or paragraphs with your help are starting a habit that will benefit them the rest of their lives: the habit of going to books for information and satisfaction.

The time to search for an answer is right when it is asked, not next week when you plan a visit to the public library. Strike while the question is hot. To do that you need some basic reference books in your home. There are many kinds of reference books which will help you find answers for preschool children and which elementary school children can learn to use on their own.

The reference books to be considered for the average home are a dictionary, an almanac and book of facts, an atlas, and an encyclopedia.

MANY KINDS OF DICTIONARIES

A dictionary is a multipurpose reference book. It comes in many sizes, styles, and prices.

A picture dictionary is the simplest book to carry the name dictionary. Although it lists words in alphabetical order with illustrations and sometimes sentences to show the meaning of each word, a picture dictionary is not a reference book in any sense. It is better described as a picture book which gives information about words and often a great deal of entertainment to young children. (For information about specific books of this kind, see annotations under the heading "Picture Dictionaries," p. 177 in Chapter 16, "Books They Like.")

A school dictionary (also called a junior dictionary) is much larger and more detailed than a picture dictionary. It shows how each word is divided into syllables, how it is pronounced, what it means (often several meanings), and what part of speech it is. Pictures are included, sometimes maps .

Several good school dictionaries for elementary school children are described below in alphabetical order:

The American Heritage School Dictionary. Houghton Mifflin Co., 1977. For grades 3–9.

The Random House School Dictionary. Random House, 1978. For grades 5–8.

Webster's New Elementary Dictionary. G & C. Merriam Co., 1970. For grades 3–8. Paperback edition, Pocket Books.

Webster's Intermediate Dictionary. G. & C. Merriam Co., 1977. For grades 7–9.

These dictionaries vary greatly in size—from 18,000 entries in one to over 57,000 in another. Even more important, the content varies greatly.

One of the greatest jobs in compiling a dictionary for young readers is choosing the words to be listed and defined. New words are coming into common usage all of the time, and new meanings are being given to old familiar words. Which should be included?

For example, the word *astronaut* was not in any of the children's dictionaries just a few short years ago. Now, even four- and five-year-olds know the word so it is included in all of the children's dictionaries.

There is an interesting story about *The American Heritage School Dictionary*, first published in 1972. To determine which words should be included in this dictionary for grades 3–9, a computer analysis was made of the printed language which children of those grades meet at school in textbooks, library books, atlases, encyclopedias, and magazines. The definitions and sample sentences in this dictionary come directly from the computer report of the way words are actually used in sentences these youngsters are reading.

Although the recently revised dictionaries include new words and new meanings for old words, many young readers want even more. Most homes, therefore, will find use for a college dictionary.

A college dictionary, written for college students and other adults, includes around 150,000 entries. For each word, it gives syllabication, pronunciation, and more definitions and more advanced ones than those in a junior dictionary. Three college dictionaries you will find useful:

The American Heritage Dictionary. Dell paperback, 1977.

The Random House College Dictionary. Random House, 1975.

Webster's New Collegiate Dictionary. G. & C. Merriam Co., 1980.

These dictionaries are authoritative, well illustrated, and constantly being revised to include new material. In addition to definitions, all college dictionaries give the derivation of a word. Thus, the reader learns that the word *comet* (described as having "a misty envelope that may form a tail that streams away from the sun") comes from the Greek word meaning "long-haired." This kind of information is interesting and important to the curious child.

A college dictionary may be difficult for a child to use independently because the type is small and the vocabulary is rather advanced. When several definitions are given for a word, a child may have trouble finding the one which applies. He or she may be confused by the abbreviations for the origin of the word (*MF, ML, OE,* and *Gk,* for example) and the fields where it has special meaning (*Bot., Zool., Naut.,* among many).

Yet the college dictionary will interest children in the upper elementary grades. Suppose the curious fourth grader hears the word *détente* used by a TV news commentator and wonders what it means. It does not appear in all school dictionaries. One college dictionary has the definition—"a relaxation of international tension"—and the young TV viewer is satisfied. However, some college dictionary definitions are too involved or use words too difficult for a child to handle. The happy solution is to have a school dictionary for the child to use independently and a college dictionary for you to use together. Certainly the more advanced dictionary offers a great deal that is stimulating to a child and to parents as well.

Many dictionaries not listed in this chapter are sold in drugstores, supermarkets, and chain stores, as well as book stores. Some are good, some not so good. Before you buy, look up several words you know well and see what you think of the definitions. Are they clear and accurate? Does the dictionary have good illustrations and maps? Is the type legible? Then consult the public librarian or school librarian who can give you suggestions and show you the dictionaries used in the library.

LEARNING TO USE THE DICTIONARY

If children are to get the most out of a dictionary, they should understand how to use it. You can help by introducing the distinctive features. First explore the dictionary yourself and then, with your young reader, find answers to such questions as these:

1. *How is pronunciation indicated?* Sometimes the key is given at the bottom of the right-hand page. Or, it may be noted in a box in the upper right corner. Be sure to read the explanation in the front of the book. Then, with your child try to apply the pronunciation key to words you are both interested in. Remember that your dictionary at home may have a different pronunciation key from the one the child uses at school.

2. *How is syllable division shown? Which syllable is accented?*

3. *How is the origin of the word shown?* Help the child interpret abbreviations.

4. *What additional information is included in back-of-the-book appendices?* Note that some dictionaries incorporate all material in the A-to-Z listing of entries and thus have no appendix.

As soon as children learn to use a dictionary, they have broad resources at their command—resources that will help them with their reading and in dozens of other ways. A parent can easily help a child develop the dictionary habit because there are many occasions for looking up words at home.

After a family visit to a nearby cave someone asks, "What is the difference between a *stalactite* and a *stalagmite?*" The dictionary will define each and show pictures. (The *stalactite* hangs tight from the ceiling; the *stalagmite* builds up from the floor of the cave.)

"How many pints in a gallon?" Under *gallon,* the dictionary gives the answer: eight.

"Why is Ferris wheel written with a capital *F?*" Under *Ferris wheel, The Random House School Dictionary* explains it was named after the inventor, G. W. G. Ferris.

"What is the capital of Massachusetts?" Under *Massachusetts*, the RHSD notes Boston is the capital.

"Someone pronounces *helicopter* as though it were *heelicopter*; which is right?" (Either is correct.)

At first children are unlikely to question the pronunciation of an adult. But they can be shown that skepticism is fun. They can learn to translate the dictionary's letters and diacritical marks into sounds. They will be pleased when they master this skill. And they will be more alert to pronunciation, including their own.

The best thing about the dictionary habit is that the more ingrained it becomes the more the reader benefits.

ATLASES

An atlas is another reference book which children find interesting as well as helpful. Several good ones which children can use comfortably:

Goode's World Atlas. Rand McNally Co., 15th edition, 1978. For grade 5 and up.

Rand McNally Picture Atlas of the World. 1979. For grades 4–7.

World Atlas for Students. Hammond and Co., 1980. For grades 8–12.

Here again you should take time to show a child how to use the atlas and how to read maps. Pupils in the upper grades learn these things at school, but repetition at home will help. With your guidance, even children from six to eight can become interested in using maps.

For this kind of family use, road maps are especially effective. Before your next automobile trip, get out the road map and show the children where you are and where you are going: "Here is Quakertown. And here is US 309 going south to Philadelphia. Here we cross the Pennsylvania Turnpike."

Or you can raise the question of the best route to take to your weekend camping spot: "This route is shorter, but it is on the throughway, which is monotonous. How can we find a road that will be more interesting, or more scenic? How can we tell whether this back road is hard surfaced?"

Several of the oil companies have prepared excellent

road atlases which are for sale at local filling stations. One of the best books of this kind is *Rand McNally Road Atlas* (Rand McNally, 1981). It is excellent for home planning as well as highway traveling.

ALMANACS AND BOOKS OF FACTS

An almanac is an inexpensive book with hundreds of pages of facts and figures updated annually. By using the detailed index, you can quickly find population figures; names of congressmen and many other officials; biographies of U. S. presidents; World Series winners for more than fifty years; descriptions of foreign countries; data on the highest mountains, the longest rivers, the highest dams, the fastest trains, the worst shipwrecks—and many thousands of other facts.

Two almanacs that are widely used in homes and libraries are:

The Information Please Almanac. Simon and Schuster.
The World Almanac and Book of Facts. Newspaper Enterprises Inc. Paperback edition, Doubleday.

These almanacs are ideal for getting facts quickly. Both books contain far more than you would expect to find in a single volume. Because they are designed for adults, they have very small type. But today's child of nine to twelve often wants adult information and is perfectly willing to cope with small type and crowded pages.

A quite different annually revised book of facts intriguing to young readers is the *Guinness Book of World Records,* Bantam Books paperback. Appealing to grade five and up, it contains factual records—the highest, longest, fastest, lightest, etc.—about science, natural phenomena, geography, outer space, mechanics, business, law, sports, freaks—almost any subject you can think of.

ENCYCLOPEDIAS FOR FAMILY USE

When a quick, brief answer is needed, the dictionary or almanac may suffice. But when you want more comprehensive information, you need a good encyclopedia. It can also serve as a springboard to further reading.

Junior encyclopedias, often referred to as "family encyclopedias," consist of twenty volumes or more. The recommended junior encyclopedias are suitable for readers in the elementary grades and junior and senior high school. However, many families go on using their junior encyclopedias long after the children are grown and off to college.

Three which are widely recommended by teachers and librarians are listed below:

Compton's Encyclopedia. For grades 4–10. Encyclopaedia Britannica Educational Corporation, 425 N. Michigan Avenue, Chicago, IL 60611.

The New Book of Knowledge. For grades 3–6. Grolier Educational Corp., Sherman Turnpike, Danbury, CT 06816.

World Book Encyclopedia. For grades 4–12. World Book— Childcraft International, Inc., Rm. 510, Merchandise Mart Plaza, Chicago, IL 60654.

All contain factual articles arranged alphabetically as in an adult encyclopedia. The material is accurate, well written, and generously illustrated with photographs, maps, charts, and drawings. These sets can be bought only through a salesman, not in department stores or bookstores.

WHY HAVE AN ENCYCLOPEDIA AT HOME?

With encyclopedias costing a lot of money, why buy one for children to use at home? Can't they use the encyclopedias at school?

They can use a school encyclopedia, of course, but children are five years old before entering kindergarten, so at least four years of their curiosity will have to wait for the school encyclopedia. Furthermore, children spend far more time at home than at school, so they can use the home encyclopedia more readily and more frequently. And don't forget that, as an adult trying to encourage a child's search for information, you will be using the home encyclopedia too.

Should you buy an encyclopedia before children learn to read? Even before they learn to use it at school?

I would say YES to both questions because it is at the very earliest age that children begin to reach out to learn about the world around them. Even the three-year-old will ask about rain and snow, about how the apartment elevator works, about wheels and sliding doors, about a bleary television image or the transistor radio. He or she will come to you with questions and look to you for answers which can be understood and depended upon. And you will be raising questions with the children—about the balloon caught in the treetop and the one that drifted to the floor or the frost on your windowpane.

Today's children may ask more advanced and more perplexing questions than previous generations because they are learning about so many faraway places and complex situations on television. Along with stimulating information via TV, they may be getting a good deal of misinformation which you and the encyclopedia can set straight.

Every now and then I hear a parent speak of an encyclopedia as an aid to homework with the implication that that is its chief purpose. It can help with schoolwork, of course. But if a child goes to the encyclopedia only to get help with homework, it is like going to the piano only to practice the scales and missing the joy of real music.

At school children are usually introduced to an encyclopedia in the third or fourth grade. When they reach senior high school, they may be ready for an adult encyclopedia.

If you buy an encyclopedia when a child is only three or four, will it be out of date when he begins to use it six or seven years later? Some entries will be obsolete, of course; and if there has been a census, population figures for cities and states will be different. The latest inventions and names of current public officials will not be included. But the great bulk of the material in an encyclopedia is little changed from one year to the next.

One edition can serve a whole series of children in the family, especially if it is supplemented with current yearbooks, almanacs, and other informational books.

POINTERS ON BUYING AN ENCYCLOPEDIA

An encyclopedia is an expensive tool and a long-term family investment, so it is prudent to investigate carefully before you buy. Don't give in to the fast-talking salesman who says, "You have been selected to receive a free set . . ." or "I can offer you a reduced rate if you sign today."

The facts are that quality encyclopedias are not given away and their prices are not cut.

Before you buy an encyclopedia, consider the two kinds: junior or family encyclopedias which can be read by children in grades four through six, and often of interest to high school students and adults; and adult encyclopedias which are much more difficult to read, with fewer illustrations, and of interest chiefly to advanced readers.

You can be sure that any encyclopedia will be used by several different age levels in the family, not just the ages for which it was planned. I know of six-year-olds who enjoy a junior encyclopedia even though they can read very little. And I know many parents who continue to use the junior encyclopedia as their chief reference source after children have left for college.

You can learn a great deal about encyclopedias for young readers from your school librarian and public librarian. Explain your needs: the ages of your children, the other reference books you have, and what you want from an encyclopedia in your home. Then ask to see the encyclopedias in the library and to learn how they rate with the children and with librarians who have made comparisons. If you bring your child into such a conference, he or she may feel involved immediately and hence more inclined to use the books when they are installed at home.

Failure to check carefully on the recommended encyclopedias may leave you in the plight of one of our neighbors: "We bought an expensive encyclopedia, but the children never can find what they need. Nobody uses it." I looked up a librarians' chart of information on encyclopedias and found my neighbor's set marked "Not recommended." Others in the same price range were classified by librarians as "Excellent" and "Recommended."

When you have investigated various sets, write to the publisher to ask a salesman to call. He will bring a set of books for you to examine and will tell you about them.

Insist upon time to look at the books. If the salesman will not leave a sample volume for you to study overnight and try out with your children, do not sign his purchase order. Take time to study the encyclopedia in your school library or public library.

As you browse through the pages, consider such questions as these: Are the pages inviting? Are the pictures sharp and clear? Are they pictures which stir interest and questions? Is the type a good size? (Remember the young reader is used to larger type than adults meet daily.) Sample the articles to see how information is handled. Is the language simple enough to be read by children or understood by them? Do you think this material will hold your child's attention and encourage further reading—perhaps in other volumes of this encyclopedia?

One good way to sample a set of books is to look up a topic on which you are well informed. Is it easy to locate? Is it accurate and up to date? Does it tell you where to find more about the same subject or related topics?

What will happen when your children are grown? Will these books still be of use to you? Sample some of the articles with your own interests in mind.

Frequently a salesman will quote a higher price for a "package," which may include better binding, an annual yearbook, and such extras as a dictionary or atlas. If you pay in installments—as many people do—the total is higher than if you pay cash on the line. Special bindings cost more.

Before you buy an encyclopedia, give a thought to how you and your children will use this expensive set of books. No encyclopedia will reach off the shelf to grab the child, you know. The first move will be up to you. Will you take time to show the child how to use these books? And will you continue to set an example by looking up topics under discussion and then reading with the child who needs encouragement? Books left untouched on the shelf are a poor investment indeed.

GETTING THE MOST FROM YOUR ENCYCLOPEDIA

When your new encyclopedia arrives, put it where every member of the family can use it easily. There should be a good light and comfortable chair nearby. If children have a part in these decisions, so much the better.

Next, acquaint yourself with the way your encyclopedia is organized. Each one is a little different and needs some study and practice.

In the three recommended junior encyclopedias, articles are arranged alphabetically, with the key letter of each volume printed clearly on the spine. Yet each set also has an index which will assure your finding related articles, not just the one in the most obvious volume.

Both *Compton's Encyclopedia* and *The New Book of Knowledge* have an index in each volume with references to articles in that volume and to related articles in other volumes. Throughout each index, there are brief biographies and summaries of subjects not included among the main entries.

The final volume of the *World Book Encyclopedia* is a Research Guide and Index of over 1,000 pages. It includes more than 150,000 entries plus 200 Reading and Study Guides. These guides give extensive reference to other sources: books to read, related audio-visual materials, and places to go for further information.

Once you have learned how your encyclopedia is organized, pick a sample topic and look it up in the index or in the alphabetical arrangement of articles. Then look up the related articles to get a more complete story. The more you use the books, the better you can guide your child.

In most cases, the encyclopedia will have to be introduced and explained to children. Help them select the volume in which the article on their subject is likely to appear. Then help them use the index and the cross references to related articles.

You will find that each entry starts with a dictionary-type definition that tells you exactly what the subject is about. It begins with simple sentences and explanations and proceeds in stages to more advanced material appearing later in the article. The very young reader may need only the first few paragraphs; more mature youngsters—looking for more advanced material—will read to the end.

Each encyclopedia is somewhat different from all the others. You and your children will have to become the masters of yours. The odds are you will have a wonderful time.

10

Who Am I? What Do I Value?

As children grow up, they begin a search for their identity as individuals. "Who am I?" each one asks. "What do I value?" Children may not verbalize these questions; indeed, they may never face themselves so frankly. But as they approach adolescence and adulthood, they give signs of uncertainty and concern about themselves and their relations with others.

While children are still in elementary school, parents are looking ahead to the time when their boy or girl will be in high school or college. They wonder what will happen when their children are away from the family nest, choosing their own friends, and making decisions that will affect their entire lives.

Invariably these thoughts lead back to the present. Parents ask themselves: "How can we prepare our children for the future? How can we help while they are growing up?"

Usually the questions relate to children as individuals. Will each one be a happy person? Or will he or she be dogged through life by the hate syndrome gnawing on the eight-year-old who said, "I hate school. I hate to write letters. I hate vegetables. I hate piano lessons."

Will that little girl learn to live happily with other people? Even those who may be quite different from herself? Will she get satisfaction from daily living and radiate her positive feelings? Will she learn to cherish every living thing and thus grow in compassion as she grows in knowledge? Will she work out a scale of values for herself and be willing to stand up for what is right?

Intangible goals are hard to measure and hard to achieve. But we know that almost everything in a child's life can influence personal growth. Books can be an important influence too—those you read to children and those they read independently.

Writers in the 1800s were convinced that through reading a child would grow up to be good or bad. To make sure that each story had the proper effect, they added a moral at the end. Probably no lesson of this kind ever transformed a bad boy into a good one. It seems more likely that young readers skipped these warnings altogether.

Modern children's stories do not preach sermons, but many of them tell of someone who has a problem. Quite naturally young readers ponder the decision made by the fictional hero or heroine. They put themselves in the same situation and wonder what they would do in the same spot. Thus they may begin to develop a personal sense of values.

Or children may read of people who are different from themselves—of different race, nationality, or religion. They may grow up to appreciate individuals who are different because they have learned to know them through books.

Although the author's first purpose is to tell a good story, children may get more than excitement and suspense from the narrative. They may begin to establish empathy for different kinds of people they meet.

If so, children's reading is helping them grow up as persons who are qualified to live and work with others. Quite literally they are finding themselves and establishing their values through books.

CHILDREN HAVE THEIR PROBLEMS

By adult standards the problems of children may seem slight. A ten-year-old girl worries about being taller than anyone in her class. To her father who is over six feet, this is something to be proud of so he does a little teasing. To his daughter this may be the most critical issue of the moment.

Children often hide their deep-seated worries. If encouraged to talk, they may hint of tragedy.

"I wonder why other children do be so mean all the time," wrote one fourth grader. "I have no one to play with."

"My brother was hit by a truck. I wonder if he will ever walk again," wrote another.

"I wonder about my father," wrote another child. "I mean, how come he left us."

A third grader on Lincoln's birthday asked what had become of Lincoln. When she learned he had been assassinated more than a hundred years ago, she burst into tears and asked, "Why does everybody have to die?" Her father had had no idea that she had long been troubled over the inevitability of death.

Many children in these circumstances let their worries and resentments smolder. As a cover-up, they will sometimes strike out in a totally different direction with harsh words and even violence.

Grownups need to watch for signs of hurt and anxiety, such as shyness, irritation, and belligerence. These attitudes may be a bid for attention when the child feels bypassed by busy parents.

I have come to realize that to a child one of the great marks of parental neglect is the failure to listen. In several thousand poems, letters, and short prose pieces from children which I have read in recent years, a repeated cry of the children is that parents don't take time to listen.

Reading aloud to a child may help to build the warm personal relationship which the child needs. Talking about the story or poem may lead to discussion of situations that are frustrating and people whose actions are puzzling, if not downright threatening.

At this stage it may help to introduce a poem or story of someone who also has an anxiety. This should be done carefully lest the sensitive child be hurt further. It certainly won't help to say, "This is a story about a boy who is shy too." In no case can we expect a book to cure, but it may encourage the child to talk about his or her worry and to start thinking constructively.

LONELINESS, RESENTMENT, AND FAMILY TENSIONS

Although children may not speak of it, many have a deep sense of loneliness. The little girl who feels she has no one to play with may be comforted by the picture book *Play With Me* by Marie Hall Ets. She may take courage from the success story of the little girl pictured in *Fiona's Bee* by Beverly Keller.

Sibling rivalry disturbs many children too. The youngest may gain courage from the events of *Keep Running, Allen!* by Clyde Robert Bulla. It is an easy-to-read story of the youngest of three children who struggles to keep up with the others, then turns the tables on them.

Indeed, any story that tells of the triumph of the youngest or the smallest seems to bring satisfaction to children. I think many of the old folk tales are enjoyed for just this reason.

The middle child of the family—who longs for the privileges accorded the oldest and the special dispensations given the baby—may see things in a new light after hearing *The Middle Moffat* by Eleanor Estes or ... *And Now Miguel* by Joseph Krumgold. Both are true to life and at the same time very reassuring.

In *Brother Mouky and the Falling Sun,* a small black boy faces up to his resentment of his brother and finds a way to calm his feelings and arrive at forgiveness. Far from being preachy, this poetic little story is deeply moving for any age.

The youngsters who feel they are being forced by the adult world into an uncongenial role will welcome *Shadow of a Bull* by Maia Wojciechowska, in which the son of a famous Spanish toreador resists the pressure to follow his father's profession. Manolo knows he doesn't want to kill—not even to uphold his father's name and meet community expectations, but it takes time for him to build up the courage of his conviction.

In a number of books, family anxiety and stress stem from the physical or mental disability of one of the children. *Mine for Keeps* by Jean Little tells of a little girl crippled by cerebral palsy. Both *Me Too* by Vera and Bill Cleaver and *The Summer of the Swans* by Betsy Byars chronicle the sorrow and conflict over a mentally retarded child in the family.

In *My Brother Steven Is Retarded* by Harriet Langsam Sobol, an eleven-year-old tells of her older brother with rare understanding and compassion. Black-and-white photographs add to the authenticity of her report.

Parents are a problem to many children too, and this is difficult to talk about at home. But when these children

Illustration by Alan Tiegreen in *Ramona and Her Father*

write letters and poems, the tensions are revealed. "I don't understand them. They are impossible," wrote a twelve-year-old girl in Michigan. "We talked and talked. Yet we are as distant as always," said a fourteen-year-old of her parents.

In *Freaky Friday,* by Mary Rodgers, thirteen-year-old Annabel Andrews has a chance to see life through her mother's eyes when she wakes up one Friday and finds she is her own mother and must cope with the freaky problems that are her mother's daily diet. *Freaky Friday* is exaggerated, hilarious, and very revealing—for both generations.

Separation, divorce, and remarriage are situations many children face, and some have trouble adjusting to. For the very young, Joan M. Lexau introduces the subject of divorce in *Me Day.* It is the story of a little boy waiting for a letter from his father whom he misses bitterly. Judy Blume's *It's Not the End of the World* handles the inevitability of a breakup in a family with three children. Even more distressing is the story told by Peggy Mann in *My Dad Lives in a Downtown Hotel.* Family tensions mount in *The Grizzly* by Annabel and Edgar Johnson. In this story eleven-year-old David, whose parents are separated, faces up to wilderness dangers with an autocratic father he barely knows.

How could these children have handled their worries more effectively? What would have helped each child grow more sympathetic and stronger through these trying times? Questions of this sort might set a child thinking more constructively and creatively, but they must be handled with care.

One librarian has told me of the concern some children feel for the family problems faced by their friends. Frequently a child from a stable, tension-free family locates a book that he or she thinks might help a friend with troubles at home. Then both will bring the book in to discuss with the librarian. "So we all feel better," she added.

For children involved in such family problems, there is excellent guidance in a number of simply written books published by Lerner. *A Look at Divorce* by Margaret S. Pursell notes some of the causes of divorce, the possible outcomes, and the child's adjustment. (Other Lerner Awareness Books deal with adoption, alcoholism, birth, death, physical handicaps, and aging.)

There are also very heartwarming books which reflect beautiful family relationships. For the youngest none can surpass *Catch Me & Kiss Me & Say It Again* by Clyde Watson, a collection of happy rhymes which radiate the warmth of loving parents.

Beautiful father-son relationships are revealed in two moving stories for children of six to eight: *Willie Blows a Mean Horn* by Ianthe Thomas and *The Wentletrap Trap* by Jean Craighead George.

And in *Ramona and Her Father* and *Ramona and Her Mother,* Beverly Cleary tells of a spunky little girl and the strong ties she has with understanding parents.

In *Roll of Thunder, Hear My Cry,* Mildred D. Taylor pictures the deep loyalty of a black family battling to survive persecution by white neighbors.

Family solidarity is important, too. *The Real Me* by Betty Miles is the story of a girl's effort to combat sexism at school and on the newspaper route. Family backing makes her struggle easier. Through the joys and tragedy of *Bridge to Terabithia* by Katherine Paterson, two sets of parents prove wonderfully supportive.

Reading such books and talking about them together may be a way of bringing your whole family into the kind of harmony you have only dreamed of.

LIFE AND DEATH

Questions of life and death concern children deeply. On television documentaries as well as the soaps, they meet vivid glimpses of life and death, sometimes very informative, sometimes frightening.

Human reproduction and childbirth are subjects of both curiosity and anxiety even to very young children. A number of books with excellent illustrations give straightforward information. They make a good opener for the child's questions and informal conversation which can relieve the anxiety that may be building up. *Inside Mom: An Illustrated Account of Conception, Pregnancy, and Childbirth* by Sylvia Caveney and Simon Stern gives detailed information in a reassuring tone. *A Look at Birth*, a Lerner Awareness Book by Joan Samson, tells of fetal development and infant behavior. While too difficult for the youngest to read independently, these books are good read-aloud material as well as discussion starters for all ages.

New Baby Comes by Julian May is simple enough for children in the primary grades to read on their own. *A Baby Is Born* by Milton Levine and Jean H. Seligman is a bit more difficult to read, but all ages will find the pictures unusually informative.

A number of picture books deal with the young child's anxiety over the new baby in the family. In *Everett Anderson's Nine Month Long* by Lucille Clifton, a small black boy worries and wonders. In *Nobody Asked Me If I Wanted a Baby Sister* by Martha Alexander, Oliver protests and then learns to cope. In *Go and Hush the Baby*, Betsy Byars gives a very positive story of the boy who uses all his ingenuity to entertain his baby brother.

Old age and death, once avoided in books for young children, are now being considered in an appealing array of titles. *A Treasure Hunt* by Christopher Wilson is a charming story about the active daily lives of the elderly and dispels some of the prejudice surrounding them.

Nana Upstairs & Nana Downstairs, written and illustrated by Tomie de Paola, tells of small Tommy's love for his grandmother and great-grandmother and the adjustment he must make to death.

For more advanced readers, there are excellent books of fiction in which death is pivotal to the story: *Bridge to Terabithia* by Katherine Paterson, *There Are Two Kinds of Terrible* by Peggy Mann, *A Gathering of Days: A New England Girl's Journal, 1830–32* by Joan W. Blos, and many more.

The curiosity is there—even among preschool children. With appealing books which are sensitively written, you may be able to direct a child's questions and concern into something deeper and wiser.

LEARNING TO APPRECIATE OTHER PEOPLE

Part of growing up is learning to appreciate other people despite their differences. But, until recent years, most children's books showed only a sunny, fair-skinned world. Blacks were seldom included, and life of the inner city slums was bypassed. With this segregated kind of reading fare, middle-class white children got a distorted picture of their world, and the black and Hispanic city children felt left out.

Fortunately we are now getting beautiful books which acknowledge the fact of our multicolored society, and all can benefit. *The Snowy Day,* written and illustrated by Ezra Jack Keats, shows an engaging little black boy playing happily in city snow. Inner-city life of a black family in Harlem has been brilliantly pictured by a young black artist and author, John Steptoe, in *Stevie* and *Train Ride.* With parents working all day, Steptoe's children are on their own to explore the city and meet its people, including junkies, cops, karate experts, and killers. Their language is the black idiom of the street.

I Am the Darker Brother and *Black Out Loud* are beautiful books of black poetry compiled by Arnold Adoff. These are poems with winning rhythm and much to think about.

For middle-grade children, there are innumerable black family stories which are very stirring. *The Hundred Penny*

He walked with his toes
pointing in, like that:

Illustration by Ezra Jack Keats in *The Snowy Day*

Box by Sharon Bell Mathis is the tale of a boy's love for
the 100-year-old great-great-aunt who comes to live in
his family. *The Jazz Man* by Mary Hays Weik tells of a
lame black boy marooned in an upstairs apartment who
seems to live by the sound of music from the neighbor he
calls the Jazz Man.

Tensions, privation, even brutal cruelty, emerge in some
of these stories of black families. One that is unforgettable
is *Sounder* by William Armstrong, which reveals the bitter
injustices heaped on a nameless black sharecropper and
his family.

Now there are excellent books about American Indians,
about Hispanics living in the United States, indeed, about
many minority groups who are struggling to survive in the
face of social and economic injustice.

These books—and many more—show appreciation for
people of all ages, all races. They are well written and

appealing to children. The problems are introduced naturally and in situations that are convincing. When you read such books as these, you may discover that they absorb even your adult interest.

ESTABLISHING VALUES

Many of the most popular books for young readers tell of people who are asking questions, making decisions, and taking a stand for what they believe. That often means making a sacrifice or a whole series of sacrifices. It may even require perseverance in the face of torment, suffering, and extreme danger.

In *Night Journeys* by Avi, a young boy of 1767 is determined to help two runaway children who, young as they are, have been branded as indentured servants. Pursued by an armed vigilante, the three youngsters take frightening risks. Will they make it to safety? Should they have risked their lives so that the two can be free? Children enjoy probing questions of this sort and arriving at a decision.

For older readers, Jean Fritz has created a convincing character in *Brady,* the story of a boy during the Civil War who faces up to the issue of slavery and develops the courage and initiative to work for the Underground Railroad. What would others think of his commitment? What recrimination might he suffer? Is the act worth the risks?

Some fictional characters grapple with social problems in their community and take a position on an issue of consequence. In *Plain Lane Christmas,* C. Walter Hodges tells how people living and working on Plain Lane organize to fight the urban renewal which threatens to destroy their neighborhood.

And in *How the Children Stopped the Wars,* Jan Wahl gives a vivid story about the children's stand against the horrors and pointlessness of war.

There are three titles I would like to mention as exemplifying books that can build values. All are sensitively written, with the message subtly interwoven throughout.

The simplest perhaps is *The Seeing Stick* written by Jane Yolen and illustrated by Remy Charlip and Demetra Marsalis. It is the tale of a little blind princess and the mysterious old man who teaches her to see with her fingers and, becoming aware of the beauties of the world around her, to flower as one who cares.

The second is a tiny book that is disarmingly simple: *Neighbors* written and illustrated by M. B. Goffstein. For a whole year two neighbors shyly reach out to each other and finally become friends. What kept them apart so long? How did friendship triumph?

The third is a longer book of fiction about a mystery girl who seems to come from nowhere. She improves the lives of all she meets and then vanishes leaving only a memory behind. This book is *Tuppenny* by Julia Cunningham. Was Tuppenny real? Why will she always be remembered with gratitude? What does she symbolize in the lives of all of us?

Do young readers see a parallel in their lives—a little blind princess who learns to "see," neighbors who must overcome deep shyness in order to become friends, a Tuppenny at work to nurture the lives of those in trouble? Are they developing a sense of values which will include equality and justice even for the downtrodden? We don't know, of course, and perhaps never will.

Certainly some children will think more critically and act more thoughtfully after reading such books. But no book can do it alone, not even a shelf full of books. The example of sensitive parents and teachers counts tremendously. We can hope that reading a good book and talking it over may bring things into better focus while the child is growing up.

11

Don't Be Afraid

Ask any parent, "Do you wish your child to be prepared to deal with the real world or with a make-believe world?" The almost certain answer will be, "The real world—of course." Yet many parents contradict themselves when they guide their children's reading.

Consciously or unconsciously, they want to protect their children from the harsh, the brutal, and the controversial. So they look for books which they call "suitable," forgetting that the television world, of which children are a part, is all the while drawing them away from what their grandparents would have labeled "suitable" for innocent children.

Children today are not innocent in the sense our grandmothers used the term. They are far more knowledgeable about the harsh facts of life than their parents imagine.

Yet many adults—parents, teachers, and librarians among them—continue to seek the "suitable" book and bypass or even outlaw the book which reflects today's world. Usually a "suitable" book reflects the mores prevailing in the socioeconomic community of their own childhood. Violence wasn't acceptable in nice neighborhoods, and violence should not be part of the book world. There weren't any drug problems or sex problems (at least they weren't discussed), so these topics are not deemed suitable for literature. Blacks and Puerto Ricans were not in every community, so why read about them? And who wants a sad book about the miseries of poverty?

The same kind of thinking results in "the happy ending complex," which motivates many adults who choose books for children. They want every book to end with the chief characters living happily ever after. The typical Lois Lenski protagonist invariably escapes her migrant worker's shack and settles into a little white house with ruffled curtains and climbing roses. Louisa R. Shotwell's *Roosevelt Grady* is far more realistic, even though the boy's three-part dream is realized: his father gets a job which will keep him in one place for a while, the family finds a decent place to live (although it is only a converted bus), and the younger brother has a chance to have his crippled foot corrected.

Lois Lenski and *Roosevelt Grady* qualify as "suitable" because they wind up on a hopeful note. In such books the migrant workers, black and white, are going up on the American-dream escalator, operated by benign whites who deal out hope to those beneath them. Millions of children know from their own experience that this is a false picture of life.

Inner-city teachers tell me their kids debunk the happy-ending formula and prefer the unresolved problem stories that appear in *Scope Magazine*. "They're real," the young readers say. Yet many parents and teachers discourage young people from reading books which deal realistically with racial conflict, inner-city violence, and minority-group frustration.

If you listen to children, you know that their experiences and concerns are drastically different from those of a generation ago. They are likely to reject a sweet poem about the modest violet and accept one about littered streets. A sixth grader parodied Robert Louis Stevenson's poem, "The Swing," to read, "How would you like to go up in the air/Up in the air so stinking?"

One teacher read *Happiness Is a Warm Puppy* to her seventh graders and then suggested they divide into three sections, each to write a joint commentary about any topic they wished. The kids went to work and produced three group poems. The topics were loneliness, pain, and war. None would be found on the traditional lists of appropriate themes for children.

Many reasons are given for playing down or bypassing the book which deals honestly with our pluralistic society. Basically, there is an overwhelming fear of controversy, particularly in the schools. Academic students in one community were exasperated when their high school English teacher directed them not to order *Nigger, House of Tomorrow,* and *Goodbye, Columbus,* which appeared at various times on their paperback book club selection lists. The books were considered "too controversial."

If reading and children's books are to reach their full potential in our pluralistic society, we must conquer the prevailing prejudice and fear of controversy among adults who work with children.

As a beginning, it is important for parents and teachers to consult frequently with children to find out what they are interested in and how they respond to certain poems, stories, and biographies. In my children's literature classes for teachers, I ask students to recruit two or three children as their helpers and guides—not to teach the children, but to hear and heed what the children have to say. Often these junior reading partners provide a new concept of suitability. One sixth grader advised his teacher, "A book has got to have a lot of guts, not a lot of blah."

Poetry can be a valuable test of a child's interests and concerns. You may learn some new things about your child if you offer a few short poems on various themes and ask which he or she would recommend to others. One fourteen-year-old girl who had shunned poetry became enthusiastic over a group of poems about the city. "The trouble with poetry at school," she said, "is that it's all covered over with the beautiful. This is real."

Such books as *The Hundred Penny Box, Sounder,* and *Roll of Thunder, Hear My Cry* are a new experience to most of the teachers I meet. I suspect that few parents have read them—or even looked at them. Although young people are turning more and more to books written for adults, it is a rare adult who reads a contemporary juvenile novel. Perhaps that is one reason why the generation gap has become an unnecessary chasm.

Teachers don't go for these books until they have tried some of the shorter stories, such as *Stevie* or *The Jazz Man,* which can be read aloud in a single class session. Even after hearing the story, some teachers in my classes remain detached, resisting involvement in "unsuitable" situations.

The detachment breaks down when classmates present the book and lead discussion. The younger teachers do a great job raising questions which bring the story into the context of today's social and economic issues.

"What about the grammatical errors in *Stevie?*" someone will ask. Another will reply: "What's important—a double negative or a child's frustration?"

"Do we want kids reading about a father who doesn't work?" was one question about *The Jazz Man.*

"But jobs are hard to get, especially for the guy who is black," another teacher replied.

The book that has the most shattering effect on the teachers in my classes is *Sounder.* Some of these teachers say the physical suffering is too cruel to present to children. Too bad the father had to steal, but of course a thief must go to jail. At the beginning of a discussion of *Sounder* I have not heard anyone ask why some people are trapped in hideous poverty to become the chattels of others. That's the way things are, many adults are saying, but let's hide it from the children as long as we can.

And there the story would drop if we had not had repeated experiences with open questions in class. These are questions which lead the discussion to personal reaction and critical thinking as distinguished from mere fact retrieval. In talking about *Sounder,* questions like these brought immediate involvement:

How did you feel when Sounder was shot? How do you think the boy felt? Why do so many tragedies beset this family? Why was it hard for these people to overcome their problems? Why do you suppose the author gave no names to the people in the story?

The nature and sequence of the questions depend upon the responses of the children and the questions they raise along the way. The discussion becomes a spontaneous network of conjecture and personal reaction, rather than the common game of fact retrieval.

When this approach is used in the study of children's literature, teachers seldom remain detached or indifferent. Their basic compassion breaks through as they learn to shake off their habitual restraint and risk personal commitment.

Teachers need the encouragement and support of parents who want their children to know the world they live in and to take part in making it a better society. Children's books which deal vividly and realistically with current issues can become a positive educational force for individuals and for the community.

You can begin to introduce such books at home and to initiate the kind of open-question discussion which will bring out children's experiences and possibly their anxieties. Fiction and nonfiction about sex, divorce, desertion, drugs, street gangs, poverty, pollution, and war may seem bitter fare for the youngster you still think of as your baby. However, these are subjects children get on television, the people and scenes they meet as they walk down the street. Suitable or not, this is life today in the United States. Don't be afraid to discuss the books that can help to make life more significant for your children.

II

GETTING THE MATERIALS THEY NEED

12

Using the Public Library and the School Library

If children are to learn to read and to enjoy reading, they need appealing reading materials. Those who have books in the home are most likely to become good readers.

One of your big jobs as a parent, then, is to find books that appeal to your youngster—books to look at and talk about, books for you to read aloud, books for older children to read on their own.

Many excellent books can be borrowed from the public library and the school library.

THE PUBLIC LIBRARY

Almost every public library has a children's department or children's room. There you will find books for pleasure and for information, book lists, reference books, and anything else related to children's reading. Some have puppets, puzzles, and toys for children as well as a collection of books especially for parents. All can be borrowed by those who have library cards.

Many libraries are large enough to have a children's librarian—an excellent person for you to consult. Frequently he or she has free book lists and bookmarks as well as information about library programs for children and their parents.

Story hours are popular occasions in most public libraries. These are set up for various age levels, sometimes with a program for parents going on simultaneously.

Some libraries put their story hour programs on radio

and television. Thus your child can look and listen at home and go to the library afterward to get the books referred to.

During the summer many public libraries have a special vacation reading program for children. This provides an opportunity to encounter new books, take part in a variety

Illustration by Lorinda Bryan Cauley in *The Goose and the Golden Coins*

of activities, and make new friends. Children who keep reading throughout the summer avoid the vacation slump in reading scores that sometimes shows up in September.

Many public libraries now stock paperbacks for children to borrow. Some also maintain a sales rack of paperbacks to buy. These are proving tremendously popular. Librarians say the paperbacks tend to increase readership of hardcover books as well.

Children will feel closer to the library when they begin their visits early and have plenty of time to linger and look. When old enough for the story hour, the youngster should be introduced to the librarian and get a library card in his or her name. Children will soon find their way to the picture books and, later, to adventure stories, biographies, and informational books. Hasten the day when they will visit the library under their own steam to browse among the books and borrow for home reading.

THE SCHOOL LIBRARY OR MEDIA CENTER

The American Association of School Librarians recommends that all teaching aids be centered in one place in the school: books, magazines, newspapers, films, filmstrips, slides, cassettes, recordings, maps, photographs, posters, anything that will enrich the educational program. Hence, the name Instructional Materials Center or Media Center is often used in lieu of School Library. The new name recognizes the tremendous variety of educational materials currently being used in both elementary and secondary schools.

Students who earn the best grades in college are usually the ones who were library users in high school. And the high school youngsters who use the library the most are those who got the habit in elementary school. No wonder, then, that educators agree, "You need a good library to teach reading today."

Today's children need books more than ever. They are interested in more things. They are encouraged to probe deeply and think critically. There is more to learn today, and there are more good books for children to read. Also, there are more films, filmstrips, and recordings to make reading appealing and learning intriguing.

Students are encouraged to reach out in all directions

through all sorts of materials and experiences. Textbooks are no longer the all-pervasive learning aid. Some schools encourage teachers to use a rich array of library books— paperback as well as hardcover—to supplement the textbooks or to provide a more stimulating replacement. It is argued that thirty children reading thirty different books are better off—through swapping of books and ideas—than the same children with thirty identical books.

Social studies classes are reading historical fiction and biography, tall tales, and legends. Science teachers introduce informational books, books of experiments, and biographies of great scientists. Poems are being read and folk songs are being sung as part of daily class study.

Reading lessons may center exclusively on library books, which some children find more exciting and more challenging than the traditional readers. In most classrooms, there are library books which children can turn to whenever they have a free moment. Sometimes neighboring classes exchange books or children bring books—especially paperbacks—for the "swap shelf" where the rule is "Leave one; take one."

Almost every state requires each elementary school to have a school library, or instructional materials center, with a librarian in charge. Children may borrow individually, and the teacher may get an assortment for the entire class. The librarian becomes the school's central source of information about books and children's interests.

Often the librarian has a story hour in the library or gives book talks in various classes to introduce appealing books.

Many instructional materials centers maintain a paperback bookstore or rack where children may buy their own books. Records show that book borrowing increases with book purchases.

Sometimes fifth and sixth graders are enlisted as part-time assistants to the librarian. They arrange and shelve books, charge them out to students or to their classrooms, set up displays about a special occasion or topic, and give book talks. Often these library aides assume full responsibility for presenting a book program for younger children.

Sometimes parents and others in the community are invited to give the same kind of assistance. Thus while helping the children, they are learning more about children's literature and what children think about certain books.

While the school librarian's first job is to advise children and teachers, he or she is prepared to help parents too. Furthermore, librarians are well aware that interest and encouragement from home are needed to increase a child's reading skills and joy in reading. Some school libraries are open one or two evenings a week so that children can bring their parents to see the library and borrow books.

As a further service to parents and as a stimulus to the children, a school book fair is often arranged by the school librarian or the parent-teacher organization. Hundreds of books are displayed with all the color and drama of a country fair. During the day children visit the fair in classroom groups to see and handle the books and sometimes to place purchase orders. They are invited to bring their parents after school and in the evening. This gives a splendid opportunity for you to hear about books from your children and learn what they find intriguing. Usually books may be ordered at the book fair to be delivered in a few weeks.

Printed book lists are often distributed by the school librarian. Additional lists of recommended books are likely to be on file in the school library. For further suggestions, see Chapter 15, "Tools for Book Selection."

Be sure that you get acquainted with the librarian in your child's school. He or she can give you practical suggestions about children and the books they enjoy.

13

Building a Home Library

In the New York Public Library I came across a Mother Goose book that I had owned as a child. It was a large and beautiful edition illustrated by Jessie Willcox Smith. As I sat at one of the children's tables, I felt that I was with an old and cherished friend.

I suddenly realized that my images of Mistress Mary and Peter, Peter, Pumpkin Eater were the ones I had absorbed from these illustrations many years ago. Here were Jack and Jill, too, just as I had been picturing them. It had been so long since I had looked at these drawings that I had forgotten the source of my own visualization. In a very literal sense this book—and particularly these illustrations—had become a part of me.

My copy of this edition of Mother Goose had been a present from my godmother, whose Christmas gifts were always exciting. She had given me *The Water Babies* by Charles Kingsley, and Hawthorne's *Wonder Book*. These, too, were exquisitely illustrated.

Those three books I recall in almost uncanny detail.

What had she given me on other Christmases? Always something very choice, I am sure, though I cannot remember what. Only the books survive.

AT HOME WITH BOOKS

Perhaps you have had a similar experience with books of your childhood. If so, I think you will agree there is nothing like having some books that are your own.

144

The child who owns even a few choice books is sure to think of books as friends. They become part of that youngster.

Today books are often crowded out of the home. Space is limited. Families move frequently, and books are heavy to move. Besides, some people argue, there are books in the school library and the public library. Why buy when you can borrow?

Borrowing has many advantages, of course. The most important is that the library can offer a much wider choice than any home. But borrowing is no substitute for owning.

I can't recall any borrowed book that has influenced me as have the books I have owned and lived with. Borrowing is for short-term reading. That is just right for some books, but there are others we need to go back to. My Mother Goose book meant more to me because I could turn to it day after day, year after year.

This kind of living with books puts reading on a very personal level. A child who can turn to a book again and again sees it as a part of life. Even a small home library can build lifelong friendships.

BOOKS FOR YOUR HOME LIBRARY

Certain books are basic to every home library. Other candidates vary according to the tastes and interests of the family.

Probably the first book in every child's collection should be a Mother Goose book. There are Mother Goose books of all kinds and prices. (See the list in Chapter 2, "Listening, Singing, and Talking Prepare for Reading.") Although there are many inexpensive books of Mother Goose rhymes, I hope you will get at least one that is a thing of beauty. It may seem expensive, but actually it will cost a good deal less than some of the toys and gadgets for younger children. Remember: this handsome book is probably the child's first introduction to the printed word. Its pictures may be the ones remembered longest.

Equally important is a song book which includes lullabies and the folk songs of childhood. (Several are listed in Chapter 2 along with the Mother Goose books.)

Be sure to include several books of poetry. Chapter 7, "Poetry Is for Everyone," tells about many popular books

Illustration by Eric Carle in *Twelve Tales From Aesop*

of poetry in both hardcover and paperback with suggestions for using them with children.

By all means add one or more collections of stories too—
fairy tales and legends, myths, tall tales, and well-known
animal stories. These stories, like the poems, are wonderful
for reading aloud.

In addition, there should be picture books, storybooks, and informational books selected for each child's particular interests. Christmas and birthday gifts can add to the collection. The availability of beautiful and inexpensive paperbacks for children makes a good home library within the reach of almost every family.

For suggestions about how and where to make book purchases, see Chapter 14, "Buying Books for Children." For recommendations about what books for what age levels, consult Chapter 15, "Tools for Book Selection," and Chapter 16, "Books They Like."

Reference books—dictionaries, encyclopedias, almanacs, and atlases—are tremendously important to children, even those under five. For information about recommended reference books for the home, how and where to buy them, consult Chapter 9, "Let's Look It Up!"

ENLISTING CHILDREN'S HELP

In developing a home library, it is important to have the children's help so they will have a greater sense of ownership.

As soon as children are walking and able to carry things around, show them where their own books are to be kept. Then encourage them to return them to that place as a way of establishing pride of ownership.

As a child grows older, ask his or her help in choosing books. A trip to the bookstore to select a birthday present may introduce the child to many books and increase satisfaction in the final choice.

Some families set aside money to buy at least one book each month. The choice of the book may be the subject of much discussion. In one family of my acquaintance the children frequently decide to buy a book they have all read several times on library loan. Thus, they make sure of having an old friend they can turn to again and again.

14

Buying Books for Children

When you buy books for children, they see them as important in your eyes. Consequently books assume greater significance to children. Pride in ownership contributes to their interest in reading.

"But books are expensive," you say. "Can we afford them?"

Books are more expensive than they were when you were a child, of course, but so is everything else.

Many of the best books for children cost as much as $8.95 or $9.95 in the hardcover edition. Those with full-color illustrations throughout may cost more. Where there is a paperback edition, the same book may cost five or six dollars less than the hardcover book.

Let me cite 1982 prices for several full-color children's books in the two editions:

	Hardcover	Paperback
London Bridge Is Falling Down by Peter Spier	$ 6.95	$1.95
Marguerite de Angeli's Book of Nursery and Mother Goose Rhymes	$12.95	$5.95
Little Tóot by Hardie Gramatky	$ 8.95	$4.95

Usually the paperback has the same text and illustrations as the hardcover edition. In some paperbacks, printing of the artwork is equal to that in the hardcover. The difference in price is usually due to the difference in the quality of binding and paper. Obviously the binding on a hardcover book will outlast the less sturdy cover of the paperback, but in both editions the pages are equally susceptible to wear and tear.

If a child reads a book only once, the hardcover price may seem high. Even a paperback picture book at $1.49 may seem a poor investment if it is read just once, then cast aside.

But "just once" isn't the way children read the books they like. They go back to read them again and again.

A little child looks at the pictures and talks about them. He or she will ask to have the book read again and again. The youngest may even take the book to bed as though the book were a soft teddy bear to cuddle up to. An older child may read a favorite book four or five times and then lend it to friends or add it to the "swap shelf" at school. If you add an inscription in the front of the book to commemorate a special occasion such as Christmas or a birthday or the name of the donor, the book becomes a special treasure.

Recently several mothers of college students have reported the number of children's books those young people still treasure. "Be sure not to throw away my kids' books," they say as they shove off for college. Owning children's books has been a source of continuing pleasure for those young people for years, and they don't want it to end.

If $8.95 or $9.95 seems like a lot of money for a child's hardcover book, take a look at the price tags on children's toys nowadays. Even at Woolworth's, where we expect low prices, children's toys may cost fifteen dollars and more. At an exclusive toy shop, the prices may be five times as high.

These toys represent a sizable investment in dollars, yet many give only passing pleasure. Seldom are they a positive influence on a child's thinking or way of life. They are unlikely to strengthen a youngster's chances of becoming a more sensitive individual.

One month after Christmas or a birthday, take an inventory of the toys and games at your house. Wheels are off trucks. Ladders from the fire engine are scattered under the bed with plastic spacemen. Strategic pieces are missing from every boxed game.

Children need toys and games, of course, but they also need good books. If you are a budget watcher, remember that the influence of a good book may last long after the plastic space capsule has fallen apart.

PAPERBACKS FOR CHILDREN

Forty years ago there were almost no paperback books for children. By 1981 there were close to 20,000 different children's titles in paperback with more coming off press every month.

Until recently most paperback books were reprints of hardcover books that had been published a year or two before. By the 1980s, the major paperback publishers were bringing out paperback originals as well as reprints of hardcover books.

The paperbacks for children include beautiful picture books printed in full color for the very young, books of poetry, folk tales and folk songs, science experiments, informational books, junior novels of adventure, mystery, romance, and fantasy, as well as books of riddles, gags, and facts. Many tie in with current movies and television programs. There are paperback reference books too: dictionaries, almanacs, and books of facts.

Paperbacks seem to have an almost mystical appeal for young readers. Ask children to choose between the hardcover and paperback editions of the same book, and they almost invariably pick the paperback. They seem to prefer the bright covers, the soft feel of the paperback, and the fact that it fits easily into a blue jeans pocket.

At first adults may worry about the durability of paperbacks. Are they sturdy enough for kids to handle? Will they last? By now there is ample evidence that the new glues used on paperbacks may be just as durable as the side-sewing once considered necessary in children's books. Many school librarians report that paperbacks survive as many as twenty-five circulations to elementary school children. That means twenty-five different children have checked the book out, carried it around in a back pocket or bicycle rack, read it in three or four sittings, packed it up to return to school, and checked it in again. If a book can survive all of that twenty-five times and still live for more borrowing and reading, it will surely hold up with honor for family reading.

Remember, too, that children reach for books that are

timely. They want to read a book with movie or TV tie-in. They want the life story of this season's pro-football heroes and their teams. For children the demands stirred by television are urgent. They want the books while the subject is hot.

Because paperback book publishing is speedier than hardcover book publishing, it can produce books children want before their enthusiasm cools or vanishes entirely. Hardcover publishing does not move that fast. For children, relevance is often more important than lifetime bindings.

WHERE TO BUY BOOKS FOR CHILDREN

Children's books are not so readily available as soft drinks and bubble gum, but they can be purchased through many sources:

1. *Paperback book clubs* which operate through the schools. (See page 152.)
2. *Hardcover book clubs* which mail books direct to the home of each subscriber. (See page 153.)
3. *Local bookstores* or the book section of a department store.
4. *A growing number of chain drugstores, supermarkets, and toy stores.*
5. *Mail-order services* of out-of-town bookstores and department stores.

BUYING THROUGH THE BOOK CLUBS

It is estimated that close to 22.5 million children in the United States purchase books regularly through children's book clubs at school or at home.

Book club membership has obvious advantages: the child receives new books at regular intervals, the books are of fair to good quality, and prices are lower than bookstore prices.

Talk to your child about book club membership. If he or she has a share in making the decision, interest will be greater. Children's book clubs are of two kinds: those distributing paperbacks and those distributing hardcover books.

PAPERBACK BOOK CLUBS

These are the largest distributors of paperback books for children in the country. It is estimated that close to eighteen million children buy an average of seven books a year through the paperback book clubs.

These clubs distribute paperback editions of books from many publishers and, increasingly, those published by the book club itself. Prices in 1981 ranged from 60¢ to $1.25.

Because book clubs sell large quantities, they can list lower prices. Note the following comparison of 1982 prices for two popular children's books:

	Hardcover Price	Trade Paperback Price*	Paperback Club Price
Mouse Tales (64 pp. full color)	$6.95	$2.95	60¢
Little House on the Prairie (352 pp. black & white)	$8.95	$2.95	95¢

A classroom book club is operated by the teacher who receives an annotated book list for each child at regular intervals. Each child checks the books he or she wishes to order from the list. Books are delivered in bulk to the teacher, who distributes the books, collects the money, and forwards it to book club headquarters. In many classrooms, children assist in the bookkeeping, collection of money, and book distribution. Excitement mounts when the carton of books arrives and children get their orders. As one boy put it, "It's just like Christmas every month."

Books listed by the paperback book clubs vary in quality of content, artwork, paper, and printing. Almost every offering lists one or more of the prize-winning books which meet every standard of excellence, even in the cheaper paperback binding. These include good stories,

*The trade paperback is sold in bookstores, department stores, and specialty shops.

biographies, books of poetry, and beautifully illustrated picture books.

At the other end of the spectrum are the joke books, magic trick books and "supermags," which make no claim to literary excellence but often lure a nonreader into reading.

Information about elementary school paperback book clubs follows (prices are subject to change):

Scholastic Book Clubs, 904 Sylvan Avenue, Englewood Cliffs, NJ 07632

> *Grade levels:* Three clubs: See-Saw Book Program, kindergarten and grade 1; Lucky Book Club, grades 2 and 3; Arrow Book Club, grades 4 to 6.
>
> *Kinds of books:* Fiction, nonfiction, poetry, stories, riddles, posters, records, book-and-record sets.
>
> *When books are sent:* See-Saw Books and Lucky Book Club, seven times during the school year; Arrow Book Club, eight.
>
> *Price:* 60¢ to $1.95.
>
> *How to join:* Through school or classroom club.

Xerox Paperback Book Clubs, Box 1195, Education Center, Columbus, OH 43216

> *Levels:* Three clubs: Buddy Books, kindergarten and grade 1; Goodtime Books, grades 2 and 3; Discovering Books, grades 4 to 6.
>
> *Kinds of books:* Fiction, nonfiction, science, riddles, puzzles, how-to-do-its, posters.
>
> *When books are sent:* Eight times during school year.
>
> *Price:* 75c to $1.95.
>
> *How to join:* Through school or classroom book club.

HARDCOVER BOOK CLUBS

These clubs distribute the hardcover books of many publishers. Prices are considerably lower than those of the same books in the bookstore. To become a club member, each child fills out an application form which must be signed by parent or other adult. At regular intervals a book is mailed to the child at home with a bill to the parent or other adult donor. Every member within a specified age range receives the same book. Thus, in a hardcover book club the child does not have the opportunity to choose a book, but in the paperback club he has to make a selection from many.

Parents seem willing to leave the choice of titles to book club editors, who are careful to keep this trust by avoiding what might be considered controversial themes (urban squalor, racial strife, sex, and drugs in particular). Consequently the books may appear to be somewhat bland for the older readers in this age of TV violence.

I am told that most members of the hardcover book clubs are preschoolers, kindergarteners, and first graders. Perhaps as children get older, they prefer to make their own selections, which they are able to do through the paperback clubs.

Information about the hardcover book clubs follows (prices are subject to change):

Children's Choice Book Club (a Scholastic Club), Box 984, Hicksville, NY 11801
Age level: 3 to 7.
Kinds of books: Fiction and nonfiction picture books, classics, and contemporary favorites.
When books are sent: Every six weeks two books are sent, with minimagazine for children, and parents' letter.
Price: $7.56 which covers two books, minimagazine, parents' letter, and shipping costs.
How to join: By mail to club headquarters.

I Can Read Book Club, 1250 Fairwood Avenue, Columbus, OH 43216
Age level: 4 to 8.
Kinds of books: Fiction and nonfiction published originally by Harper & Row under the title "I Can Read Books."
When books are sent: 6 week intervals.
Price: $2.99 to $3.49 per book plus postage and handling.
How to join: By mail to club headquarters.

Junior Literary Guild, Customer Service Center, 245 Park Avenue, New York, NY 10167
Age levels: K, ages 3 and 4; P, ages 5 and 6; E, ages 7 and 8; A, ages 9 and 10; B, ages 11 and 12; C, ages 12 and up (Advanced Readers).
Kinds of books: Fiction and nonfiction of general interest and variety.

When books are sent: Monthly.
Price: $3.25 per book plus shipping.
How to join: By mail to club headquarters.

Illustration by Mercer Mayer in *Everyone Knows What a Dragon Looks Like*

Parents Magazine's Read Aloud and Easy Reading Program, Box 161, Bergenfield, NJ 07621
Age level: 2 to 7.
Kinds of books: Illustrated books for "little listeners and beginning readers."
When books are sent: Monthly.
Price: $4.33 per book ($7.74 if two books are ordered) plus postage and handling.
How to join: By mail to club headquarters.

Sweet Pickles Book Club, 1250 Fairwood Avenue, Columbus, OH 43216
Age level: 3 to 7.

Kinds of books: Easy-to-read fiction published originally by Holt, Rinehart & Winston.
When books are sent: 6 week intervals.
Price: $2.99 per book plus postage and handling.
How to join: By mail to club headquarters.

Weekly Reader Children's Book Club, 1250 Fairwood Avenue, Columbus, OH 43216
Age level: Three age groups—3 to 7; 8 and 9; 10 and 11.
Kinds of books: Primarily fiction, some nonfiction.
When books are sent: 6 week intervals.
Price: $2.99 to $3.49 per book plus postage and handling.
How to join: By mail to club headquarters.

YOUR LOCAL BOOKSTORE

If you have a good bookstore in your community or a department store with a well-stocked book section, you are fortunate indeed. You have not only a marketplace but a splendid source of information.

Visit a bookstore when you have time to browse among the attractive display racks with their book jackets in full view. Books are grouped by subject or by age level—science, sports, picture books for the very young, etc. Usually the bookseller can recommend an appropriate book for a particular child. Or he or she can turn to reference lists to find one. Sometimes there are free or inexpensive book lists on sale.

All too often parents visit a bookstore without bringing the child for whom a book is being sought. Yet the book displays are very appealing to children, even to four- and five-year-olds. Clean hands and due respect for property are required, of course.

If a child can help buy a book, the trip to the bookstore will have even greater interest. With birthday money to spend for a book of his or her own choice, interest in reading and pride in owning books will increase.

The better bookstores and department stores carry selected books from many publishers. If they don't have the book you want, they will order it for you. Be sure to allow six to eight weeks for an order to be filled.

The supermarket, the drugstore, the newsstand, and department stores may carry children's books too, especially at Christmas. Usually these have arrived as a package from only two or three publishers, so the assortment is limited. The self-service stores offer no guidance and do not order books on request.

To find a bookseller who stocks a good assortment of children's books, watch the ads in major newspapers. You should also check the listings under "Book Dealers—Retail" in the yellow pages of your telephone directory. Or write to the American Booksellers Association, 122 E. 42 St., New York, NY 10017, and ask for the name and address of a nearby place to buy children's books. A children's librarian in the public library or a school librarian can probably advise on good sources.

When you find a satisfactory bookstore or book department, ask to be put on its mailing list for information about children's books.

BUYING BOOKS BY MAIL

Suppose you have no bookstore in your town, what can you do? Order by mail. You will get efficient service from many metropolitan bookstores that have big mail-order departments. Also, some mail-order houses list children's books in their catalogues, particularly at Christmas.

In addition, there are jobbers and mail-order houses which specialize in paperbacks for children. Their catalogues describe the books of many publishers, sometimes offer a special price on packets of books (grouped by age level or theme), and include an order form. To locate a jobber in your area, consult the librarian as well as the yellow pages of your telephone directory.

15

Tools for Book Selection

"A book is an unlimited investment in the human mind and spirit," says the Children's Book Council.* "Its selection deserves at least as much time as we devote to choosing clothes for our children."

You need more than time—you need some tools that will help you find the books your child will enjoy. One excellent tool is a four-page folder, "Choosing a Child's Book," published by the Children's Book Council, 67 Irving Place, New York, NY 10003. For a free copy, send a stamped, self-addressed No. 10 envelope. The folder gives sound advice plus descriptions of book lists, their sources, and their prices. It also includes information about periodicals and books about children's reading.

Fortunately there are many annotated lists of recommended books for children. Most have been compiled by teachers and librarians who know what books children enjoy. (See also Chapter 16, "Books They Like.")

You will find good annotated lists in your school library and in the public library. The larger bookstores also have them. If you have two or three of these lists, you will find them valuable in locating new titles. As children begin to read independently, they also will turn to the lists.

---

*The Children's Book Council is a nonprofit organization of publishers of children's books which sponsors Children's Book Week and an extensive program to promote children's books and children's reading.

HOW TO USE A BOOK LIST

Most lists of recommended children's books are set up to answer two big questions: (1) How can I find a book about a particular subject? and (2) What book is recommended for a particular age level?

Suppose your nine-year-old has seen a TV film about dolphins and wants to read about them. What books can you recommend? The index of the book list may have an entry under "Dolphins." Or it may have a general section on animals where you will find brief descriptions of several recommended books about dolphins. From the annotations, you should be able to tell which one seems most appropriate for your child.

Make a note of the title, author, and publisher of each book that sounds promising. If it is an anthology of poetry or stories, record the name of the editor or compiler who made the selections. If no author or editor is given—as with Mother Goose books—be sure to record the name of the illustrator. This may be the important clue to finding the book you want.

Later you can look for these books in the library or order through a bookstore.

Suppose you have no special subject or kind of book in mind, but simply want a book for a child of a particular age or grade. Some lists group books by age or grade level. This enables you to turn to the right group and scan the annotations for promising titles. Lists which do not group books by age level usually give estimated age level beside each title.

Whatever the list, take the age-level designation with a grain of salt. One five-year-old may be very advanced and reading independently while another is interested only in looking and listening. The book you read to your beginning reader may be much more advanced than the one he or she can read independently. At best, the age-level designation is only a crude guess.

RECOMMENDED BOOK LISTS

Schools and libraries have detailed reference books that tell about thousands of children's books. For home use a smaller list is more practical.

In many communities, lists of recommended children's books are prepared and distributed locally. Sometimes a school will send out a list to every family.

Some newspapers and magazines carry reviews of children's books. Note the titles that sound interesting for your youngster. When you talk to the teacher and the librarian or listen to a television program about children's books, jot down information about promising titles. If you encourage your child to do this too, you may soon have a joint list to use when you visit the library.

Some of the best-known lists of children's books are described below. All of them give a brief annotation for each book, the name of the publisher, the author or editor, the price (at the time the list was published), and the age level for which the book is recommended. Usually books are grouped by subject.

Study this list of lists and then order one or more for regular use at home. (Prices subject to change.)

About 100 Books: A Gateway to Better Intergroup Understanding by Ann G. Wolfe. Children's books reflecting events, trends, and unsolved problems in intergroup relations during recent years. 8th ed. 1977. (The American Jewish Committee, 165 East 56 Street, New York, NY 10022. $1.00.)

Adventuring With Books edited by Mary Lou White and the committee of the National Council of Teachers of English. More than 2,500 books for prekindergarten to grade 8 with annotations. Books are divided in thirteen categories for easy reference. 500 pages. 1981. (National Council of Teachers of English, 1111 Kenyon Rd., Urbana, IL 61801. $8.95.)

The Best of Children's Books, 1964–1978 edited by Virginia Haviland, et al. Lists 1,000 of the top children's books published in this fourteen-year period. Entries, for preschool-

ers to young adults, are divided into ten categories. (Supt.
of Documents, U. S. Government Printing Office, Washington, DC 20402. Use stock number S/N 030-001-00093-1.
$4.25.)

Bibliography of Books for Children. Annotated listing of
fiction, nonfiction, and reference books for children. 112
pages, updated triennially. 1980 edition. (Association for
Childhood Education International, 3615 Wisconsin Ave.
N.W., Washington, DC 20016. $5.95 plus 60¢ postage and
handling.)

Caldecott Medal Books and *Newbery Medal Books.* Two
pamphlets, each listing award-winning books. Published
annually in May. (Association for Library Service to Children, 50 East Huron Street, Chicago, IL 60611. Single
copy free with stamped self-addressed envelope. 3–50 copies, 20¢ each. Discount on quantities.)

Children's Books compiled by Virginia Haviland and
Committee. Annual list annotating about 200 outstanding
books of the year for preschool through junior high school,
grouped by theme. 16 pages. (Superintendent of Documents, U. S. Government Printing Office, Washington, DC
20402. Use stock number SN 030-001-00094-0. $1.75.)

Children's Books Too Good to Miss compiled by May Hill
Arbuthnot and others. Annotations for several hundred
choice books for children, with illustrations. 7th edition.
1980. (The Press of Case Western Reserve University,
11000 Cedar Road, Cleveland, OH 44106. $8.95.)

Children's Choices. Annotated list of children's books
selected by children across the country. Issued annually.
Single copy free with self-addressed envelope with postage
for two ounces. ("Children's Choices," Children's Book
Council, 67 Irving Place, New York, NY 10003.)

Excellent Paperbacks for Children. Annotated, selective
bibliography of quality paperbacks for children of two to
fourteen. 56 pages. 1979 edition. (Association for Childhood
Education International, 3615 Wisconsin Ave. N.W., Washington, DC 20016. $3.50 plus 60¢ for postage and handling.)

Let's Read Together: Books for Family Enjoyment, edited by a committee of the National Congress of Parents

and Teachers and the Association for Library Service to Children. Annotated list of about 750 titles for ages two to fifteen, grouped by reader interest and age level. 4th edition, 1981. (Association for Library Service to Children, 50 East Huron Street, Chicago, IL 60611. $5.00.)

Notable Children's Books compiled annually by the Book Evaluation Committee of the Association for Library Service to Children. Brief annotations for the 50 books selected as notable publications of the year. 6 pages. (Association for Library Service to Children, 50 East Huron Street, Chicago, IL 60611. Single copy free when accompanied by self-addressed stamped envelope, 3–50 copies, 20¢ each.)

Picture Books for Children edited by Patricia Jean Cianciolo and the Picture Book Committee of the National Council of Teachers of English. Annotated bibliography of picture books for children, selected for both artistic and literary excellence. Includes discussion of varied styles of illustrating and writing and 35 large black-and-white halftone illustrations from significant picture books. 254 pages. 1981. (Association for Library Service to Children, 50 East Huron Street, Chicago, IL 60611. $12.50.)

III

CHILDREN'S BOOKS AND MAGAZINES

16
Books They Like

Each year about 2,500 new children's books are published in the United States alone. They range from very easy picture books without words to advanced books which adults enjoy almost as much as their children.

The following list is a sampling of the 40,000 children's books now in print, which are well written, attractively illustrated, and appealing to children.

Books available in paperback are starred (*).

To indicate the general age range of children to whom each book is appealing, the following symbols are used:

N   Nursery School and Kindergarten (Age 5 and under)
P   Primary Grades (Ages 6, 7, and 8)
I   Intermediate Grades (Ages 9, 10, and 11)
A   Advanced Readers (Ages 10, 11, and 12)

NURSERY RHYMES AND PICTURE BOOKS

Mother Goose, Nursery Rhymes, and Good-Night Books

*Bedtime for Frances by Russell Hoban; illustrated by Garth Williams. Harper, 1960. Frances, an engaging little badger, resorts to all sorts of maneuvers in order to postpone bedtime. Continued in *Bread and Jam for Frances, Harper, 1964; Scholastic paperback and *A Bargain for Frances, Harper, 1970. N–P

Benny Rabbit and the Owl written and illustrated by Joseph Low. Greenwillow, 1978. A reassuring goodnight story. N–P

Book of Nursery and Mother Goose Rhymes illustrated by Marguerite de Angeli. Doubleday, 1954. Delicate illustrations and a wealth of familiar rhymes. N–P

Brian Wildsmith's Mother Goose. Watts, 1965. Eighty-six familiar rhymes and bold brilliant illustrations. N–P

Catch Me & Kiss Me & Say It Again by Clyde Watson; illustrated by Wendy Watson. Philomel, 1978. Happy rhymes for every occasion in the child's day—all radiating the warmth of a loving family. N

A Child's Good Night Book by Margaret Wise Brown, illustrated by Jean Chalot. Addison-Wesley, 1943. A charming bedtime picture story of animals getting ready for bed and finally of children saying their evening prayer for "small things that have no words." N

Goodnight, Goodnight written and illustrated by Eve Rice. Greenwillow, 1980. A dramatic good-night picture book about the city. N–P

Goodnight Moon by Margaret Wise Brown; illustrated by Clement Hurd. Harper, 1947. A lovely bedtime story of the bunny who says good night to everything in his room as it grows darker and darker. N

Granfa' Grig Had a Pig and Other Rhymes Without Reason From Mother Goose compiled and illustrated by Wallace Tripp. Little, Brown, 1976. Hundreds of rib-ticklers—old favorites and those less familiar—which will appeal to all ages. Brilliantly wacky illustrations in full color. N–P–I

Gray Goose & Gander & Other Mother Goose Rhymes collected and illustrated by Anne Rockwell. Crowell, 1980. Fifty-six short, humorous rhymes are shown, one to a page, with a cheerful color illustration for each. N–P

Gregory Griggs and Other Nursery Rhyme People selected and illustrated by Arnold Lobel. Greenwillow, 1978. A collection of Mother Goose rhymes about people, with charming full-color illustrations. N–P

Illustration by Eve Rice in *Goodnight, Goodnight*

Hi Diddle Diddle illustrated by Nola Langner. Scholastic, 1970. Forty-two of the simplest Mother Goose rhymes. N–P

Mother Goose illustrated by Gyo Fujikawa. Grosset, 1981. Ten familiar rhymes with full-color illustrations on 5″ × 6½″ board pages. Also *Come Out and Play*. N

Mother Goose illustrated by James Marshall. Farrar, 1979. Thirty-five of the funniest rhymes with comical illustrations in full color. N–P

*The Mother Goose Treasury compiled and illustrated by Raymond Briggs. Coward, 1966; Dell paperback. Over 400 rhymes and twice as many drawings and full-color paintings—vivid, dramatic, and boldly humorous. N–P

Oh What a Noise! illustrated by Uri Shulevitz; text adapted by Elizabeth Shub from *A Big Noise* by William Brighty Rands. Macmillan, 1971. A little boy resisting bedtime thinks of marvelous noises: the yowl of a cat, the roar of lions, etc., with drawings as wild as the noises. N–P

*Old Mother Hubbard and Her Dog illustrated by Evaline Ness. Holt, 1972. A Mother Goose favorite with stunning tongue-in-cheek illustrations in full color. N

Switch On the Night by Ray Bradbury; illustrated by Madeleine Gekiere. Pantheon, 1955. A little boy discovers that the dark is friendly and comforting, often funny. N

The Tall Book of Mother Goose illustrated by Feodor Rojankovsky. Harper, 1942. One hundred of the most popular rhymes with gay modern pictures. N–P

WORDLESS PICTURE BOOKS

*Ah-Choo by Mercer Mayer. Dial, 1976. A sneezing elephant creates chaos and wins a lady hippo's affection. The "AH-CHOO"s are the only words in print. N–P

*Bobo's Dream by Martha Alexander. Dial, 1970. Pictures tell the story of a small black boy and his dachshund, Bobo. Both build up courage when Bobo is threatened by a fierce mongrel. N–P

Changes, Changes by Pat Hutchins. Macmillan, 1971. A picture story about blocks that are changed to make a house, then a fire engine, then a boat, and so on. N–P

Deep in the Forest by Brinton Turkle. Dutton, 1976. A bear cub wanders into the home of a modern Goldilocks and creates havoc until frightened away. A charming wordless book. N–P

Dig, Drill, Dump, Fill by Tana Hoban. Greenwillow, 1975. Dramatic black-and-white photos show heavy-duty machines on the job. Wordless except for a glossary. Also **Push, Pull, Empty, Full,* Macmillan, 1972. N–P

Do You Want to Be My Friend? by Eric Carle. Crowell, 1971. The seven words of the title lead through an intriguing series of brilliant full-color pictures which tell a dramatic, even touching, story. N–P

Frog, Where Are You? by Mercer Mayer. Dial, 1969. A cheerful picture story about a boy and dog in search of their lost frog. N–P

Illustration by Fernando Krahn in *Here Comes Alex Pumpernickel!*

Here Comes Alex Pumpernickel! by Fernando Krahn. Atlantic-Little, Brown, 1981. This picture book tells of the disasters caused by Alex's curiosity and good intentions. *N–P*

The Midnight Adventures of Kelly, Dot, and Esmeralda by John S. Goodall. Atheneum, 1973. A sturdy koala bear (Kelly), a charming doll (Dot), and a demure mouse (Esmeralda) climb into the rural scene in a picture on the wall and row down the river. Also *Shrewbettina's Birthday*, Harcourt, 1970; and *The Adventures of Paddy Pork*, Harcourt, 1968. *N–P*

Noah's Ark by Peter Spier. Doubleday, 1977. The age-old story told in brilliant pictures with fascinating details that provide endless opportunity for looking and commenting. *P–I*

The Snowman by Raymond Briggs. Random, 1978. A small boy builds a snowman and dreams of their adventures together. A story told in 167 gentle pictures arranged in filmstrip sequence. *N–P*

*There's a Nightmare in My Closet by Mercer Mayer. Dial, 1968. A picture story for those who love a little scare. *P*

PICTURE BOOK STORIES

And It Rained written and illustrated by Ellen Raskin. Atheneum, 1969. Hilarious story and illustrations of a tea party in a tropical rain forest where the pig, the parrot, and the potto cope with weak tea and soggy biscuits. *P–I*

And to Think That I Saw It on Mulberry Street written and illustrated by Dr. Seuss. Vanguard, 1937. A horse-drawn wagon on Mulberry Street grows bigger and bigger as a small boy plans how he will tell about it when he gets home. *N–P*

*Blueberries for Sal written and illustrated by Robert McCloskey. Viking, 1948; Penguin paperback. How little Sal and her mother go blueberrying in Maine and meet Little Bear and his mother over the hill. Also, *One Morning in Maine* (when Sally loses her first tooth). Viking 1952. *N–P*

Catch a Little Fox by Beatrice Schenk de Regniers; illustrated by Brinton Turkle. Houghton, 1970. Variations on the old rhyme "Oh a-hunting we will go." N–P

The Cow Who Fell in the Canal by Phyllis Krasilovsky; illustrated by Peter Spier. Doubleday, 1972. Bored with her life, a Dutch cow named Hendrika goes on a great adventure. N–P

Crictor written and illustrated by Tomi Ungerer. Harper, 1958; Scholastic paperback. Hilarious picture story of a boa constrictor which is the pet of an elderly French schoolmistress. P

Crow Boy written and illustrated by Taro Yashima. Viking, 1955; Penguin paperback. Japanese children learn to appreciate the shy one. P

The 500 Hats of Bartholomew Cubbins written and illustrated by Dr. Seuss. Vanguard, 1938. Humorous story of a boy who takes off his hat before the king and finds another in its place, then another and another. N–P

George and Martha written and illustrated by James Marshall. Houghton, 1972. Five amusing little picture stories of two friendly hippos whose behavior confirms the value of true friendship. N–P

Georgie written and illustrated by Robert Bright. Doubleday, 1959. Georgie, a friendly little ghost, feels unwanted. P

Gilberto and the Wind written and illustrated by Marie Hall Ets. Viking, 1963; Penguin paperback. Exquisite picture story of a Mexican boy and his unpredictable friend, the wind. P

The Happy Lion by Louise Fatio; illustrated by Roger Duvoisin. McGraw, 1954. When the happy lion escapes from the zoo in a French town, he is dismayed to find people running away from him. Also *The Happy Lion Roars,* 1957, and *The Happy Lion in Africa,* 1955. N–P

Harry the Dirty Dog by Gene Zion; illustrated by Margaret B. Graham. Harper, 1956. Getting dirty is fun until Harry finds himself rejected by his family. N–P

How Brown Mouse Kept Christmas by Clyde Watson; illustrated by Wendy Watson. Farrar, 1980. Exquisite Christmas Eve tale to read aloud and savor. *N–P*

*If I Ran the Circus written and illustrated by Dr. Seuss. Random, 1956. A rhyming tale of tongue-twisting words, tall-tale exaggeration, and zany pictures. *N–P*

Inside, Outside, Upside Down by Stan and Jan Berenstain. Random, 1968. Nonsense verses and illustrations about a bearlike creature. *N–P*

*Ira Sleeps Over written and illustrated by Bernard Waber. Houghton, 1972. A little boy who is invited to sleep overnight with a friend next door struggles with the big question: Shall I take my teddy bear? *N–P*

Jumanji written and illustrated by Chris Van Allsburg. Houghton, 1981. Judy and Peter have exciting and bizarre adventures when they begin to play Jumanji, a board game that looks like many others. *P–I*

Illustration by Chris Van Allsburg in *Jumanji*

Little Toot written and illustrated by Hardie Gramatky. Putnam, 1939. A mischievous little tugboat finally earns the right to be called a hero. *N–P*

London Bridge Is Falling Down illustrated by Peter Spier. Doubleday, 1967. Beautifully detailed illustrations of the old song. *N–P–I*

Lyle, Lyle Crocodile written and illustrated by Bernard Waber. Houghton, 1965. The adventures of a pet crocodile and the human family he adopts. A continuation of *The House on East 88th Street*, 1962. Also *Lovable Lyle*, 1969, and *Lyle and the Birthday Party*, 1973. *P*

Madeline written and illustrated by Ludwig Bemelmans. Viking, 1939; Penguin paperback. Charming story of little girls in a French school and their intrepid leader, Madeline. Continued in *Madeline's Rescue*. *P–I*

Make Way for Ducklings written and illustrated by Robert McCloskey. Viking, 1941; Penguin paperback. The delightful story of a family of mallard ducks that lived in the Public Garden of Boston. *N–P*

Max written and illustrated by Rachel Isadora. Macmillan, 1976. On his way to baseball practice, Max visits his sister's dancing class and has a ball. *P–I*

May I Bring a Friend? by Beatrice Schenk de Regniers; illustrated by Beni Montresor. Atheneum, 1964. A small boy brings a giraffe, then a hippo, then monkeys on his daily visits to the king and queen. *N–P*

Millions of Cats written and illustrated by Wanda Gág. Coward, 1928. A very old man and woman wanted a cat and got "millions and billions and trillions of cats." *N–P*

Mother Rabbit's Son Tom written and illustrated by Dick Gackenbach. Harper, 1977. Two ministories about the young rabbit who will only eat hamburgers. *N–P*

Mr. Gumpy's Outing written and illustrated by John Burningham. Holt, 1971. When Mr. Gumpy decides to go for a boat ride, children and farm animals beg to go too and clamber aboard. All are warned, "Don't flap about," but they forget. *N–P*

Neighbors written and illustrated by M. B. Goffstein. Harper, 1979. For a whole year two neighbors shyly reach out to each other and finally become friends. *P–I*

*Play With Me written and illustrated by Marie Hall Ets. Viking, 1955; Penguin paperback. A little girl learns to win friends. A book of real beauty. *N–P*

*Sam, Bangs and Moonshine written and illustrated by Evaline Ness. Holt, 1966. The lonely daughter of a fisherman brings on near tragedy by tales of her mermaid mother. *P*

The Shopping Basket written and illustrated by John Burningham. Crowell, 1980. Steven goes shopping but on the way home is accosted by a bear, a monkey, a kangaroo, a goat, a pig, and an elephant who demand a share of the purchases. *P*

*The Snowy Day written and illustrated by Ezra Jack Keats. Viking, 1962; Penguin paperback. A small black boy's adventures in the snow are told with simple text and brilliant pictures. Continued in **Whistle for Willie, 1964. N–P*

Stevie written and illustrated by John Steptoe. Harper, 1969. A little boy in Harlem tells of his difficulties when cry-baby Stevie is added to the household. Also *Train Ride, 1971. P*

*The Story About Ping by Marjorie Flack; illustrated by Kurt Wiese. Viking, 1933; Penguin paperback. The adventures of a mischievous Chinese duck that is separated from the other ducks on a river houseboat. *N–P*

*Sylvester and the Magic Pebble written and illustrated by William Steig. Simon and Schuster, 1969; Windmill Books paperback. A brilliant picture story of a young donkey who finds a magic pebble which assures fulfillment of any wish. Also **Amos and Boris, Farrar, 1971; Penguin paperback. P*

Thy Friend, Obadiah written and illustrated by Brinton Turkle. Viking, 1969. Beautiful picture story of a little Quaker boy on Nantucket and his missing sea gull. *P*

The Two Reds by William Lipkind and Nicolas Mordvinoff. Harcourt, 1950. The adventures of a boy and a cat in a big city are shown with brilliant pictures. Also *Finders Keepers*, 1951. N–P

Where the Wild Things Are written and illustrated by Maurice Sendak. Harper, 1963. Max imagines a visit to the land where the wild things are and finds them friendly and beguiling. Favorite of children. N–P

Whose Mouse Are You? by Robert Kraus; illustrated by José Aruego. Macmillan, 1970. Through direct questions and answers, suggesting an old nursery rhyme, Mouse reveals his plight and his solution. N–P

William's Doll by Charlotte Zolotow; illustrated by William Pène du Bois. Harper, 1972. Though expert with his basketball and electric train, William wanted a doll above all. An endearing and persuasive little book. N–P

*Will I Have a Friend? by Miriam Cohen; illustrated by Lillian Hoban. Macmillan, 1967. Jim's great anxiety on entering school is "Will I have a friend?" A good picture of first experiences in nursery school. Also *Best Friends,* 1971, and *When Will I Read?* Greenwillow, 1977. N–P

*A Woggle of Witches written and illustrated by Adrienne Adams. Scribner's, 1971. Exquisitely illustrated account of witches on Halloween and what happens when they face a trick-or-treat contingent. N–P

ABC AND COUNTING BOOKS

ABC of Monsters written and illustrated by Deborah Niland. McGraw, 1978. Lovable, roly-poly monsters perform various antics to represent the letters. N–P

All in the Woodland Early: An ABC Book; lyrics and music by Jane Yolen; illustrated by Jane Breskin Zalben. Philomel, 1979. An enchanting animal alphabet book that sings its way from A to Z (Ant to Zemmi) with happy illustrations. N–P

Anno's Alphabet: An Adventure in Imagination illustrated by Mitsumasa Anno. Crowell, 1975. Each letter is shown as a solid piece of wood and on the facing page objects beginning with that letter, but no words. A wonderful book to talk about. Also *Anno's Journey*, Philomel, 1979. *N–P*

*Ape in a Cape written and illustrated by Fritz Eichenberg. Harcourt, 1952. This alphabet book of odd animals has just one illustration and single rhyming line on each page. *N–P*

Bruno Munari's ABC designed and illustrated by Bruno Munari. Philomel, 1960. Imagination, humor, bold color, and stunning design make this an intriguing book to read and look at again and again. Also *Bruno Munari's Zoo*. *N–P*

Celestino Piatti's Animal ABC illustrated by Celestino Piatti; English text by Jon Reid. Atheneum, 1966. A parade of animals with a humorous four-line verse that describes each. *N–P*

*Count and See with black-and-white photos by Tana Hoban. Macmillan, 1972. A dramatically modern counting book showing familiar objects to illustrate each number from 1 to 10, then by tens to 50, then 100. *N–P*

*Dancing in the Moon: Counting Rhymes written and illustrated by Fritz Eichenberg. Harcourt, 1956. Delightful to look at and to hear read aloud. *N–P*

Numbers illustrated by John J. Reiss. Bradbury, 1971. How many arms on the starfish, hours on the clock, flowers in a bunch? The pictures dramatically depict the giant numbers. *N–P*

One Dancing Drum by Gail Kredenser; illustrated by Stanley Mack. Phillips, 1971. Musicians with their instruments arrive in increasing numbers with each turn of the page to make a joyous and imaginative counting book. *N–P*

A Peaceable Kingdom: The Shaker Abecedarius illustrated by Alice and Martin Provensen. Viking, 1978. Twenty-six rhyming lines from a nineteenth century Shaker Manifesto, each introducing a letter of the alphabet with enchanting pictures of animals, quaint people, and Shaker artifacts. *N–P*

Picture Dictionaries

The Cat in the Hat Beginner Book Dictionary by the Cat Himself and P. D. Eastman. Random, 1964. Ludicrous drawings and text explain 766 words for the beginner— a dictionary to enjoy. *P*

Richard Scarry's ABC Word Book written and illustrated by Richard Scarry. Random, 1971. Lots of little pictures and plenty of humor. Also *Richard Scarry's Best Word Book Ever.* *P*

Richard Scarry's Storybook Dictionary written and illustrated by Richard Scarry. Western, 1966. Seven hundred words and 1,600 variant forms are introduced through wacky pictures and situations: an airplane lands on a barn, a mouse sits on a birthday cake, a badger pulls a frog from soft cement, etc. *N–P*

EASY-TO-READ BOOKS

Albert the Albatross written and illustrated by Syd Hoff. Harper, 1961. A strange bird finds the ocean by traveling on a lady's hat. Very easy reading. Also *Julius*, 1959. *P*

Andy and the Lion written and illustrated by James Daugherty. Viking, 1938. An amusing variation of "Androcles and the Lion," the old story of the Roman slave who pulled a thorn out of the lion's paw and thereby made a friend. *P*

Are You My Mother? written and illustrated by P. D. Eastman. Random, 1960. With only 100 different words, the author tells an amusing story about a baby bird in search of its mother. *P*

Caps for Sale written and illustrated by Esphyr Slobodkina. Addison-Wesley, 1947; Scholastic paperback. After a nap under a tree, a cap peddler discovers his caps are gone but sees the tree full of chattering monkeys, each wearing a cap. *P*

The Cat in the Hat written and illustrated by Dr. Seuss. Random, 1957. Hilarious story in verse of the wacky performance of a cat that comes to visit on a rainy day. Can be read by many first graders. Also *The Cat in the Hat Comes Back*, 1958. P

A Certain Small Shepherd by Rebecca Caudill; illustrated by William Pène du Bois. Holt, 1965; paperback. Exquisite story of a small mute boy in Appalachia and his Christmas miracle. P

Clifford the Big Red Dog written and illustrated by Norman Bridwell. Scholastic paperback, 1969. About a pet dog bigger than a two-story house. Very easy. Also *Clifford Gets a Job*, 1972, *Clifford Takes a Trip*, 1969, *Clifford the Small Red Puppy*, 1973, and *Clifford's Halloween*, 1970. P

Could Be Worse! written and illustrated by James Stevenson. Greenwillow, 1977; Penguin paperback. Grandpa's tall tale of his adventures gives the children a big surprise. P

Did You Carry the Flag Today, Charley? by Rebecca Caudill; illustrated by Nancy Grossman. Holt, 1971. A first

Illustration by Donald Crews in *Freight Train*

grader with incorrigible curiosity and zest finally wins the greatest honor in his Appalachian school. *P*

Freight Train written and illustrated by Donald Crews. Greenwillow, 1978. A few powerful words, a few brilliant pictures, and the freight train moves across the country, over the trestle, through the tunnel, and into the city. Also *Trucks,* 1980. *N–P*

*Frog and Toad Are Friends written and illustrated by Arnold Lobel. Harper, 1970. Tender affection between Frog and Toad pervades these five simple stories and gently amusing art. Continued in **Frog and Toad Together,* 1979. *N–P*

Garth Pig and the Ice Cream Lady written and illustrated by Mary Rayner. Atheneum, 1977. When Garth, the youngest of ten piglets, is kidnapped by a wolf disguised as an ice cream lady, the other nine go into action. *P*

Go, Dog, Go! written and illustrated by P. D. Eastman. Random, 1961. A Beginner Book about all kinds of dogs and their comical behavior. Also *Sam and the Firefly,* 1958. *P*

Little Bear by Else Holmelund Minarik; illustrated by Maurice Sendak. Harper, 1957. Four delightful stories about Little Bear's trip to the moon, his birthday party, his wishes, and his adventures, which can be read by many first and second graders. Also *Little Bear's Friend*, 1960, *Little Bear's Visit*, 1961, and *Father Bear Comes Home*, 1959. P

Mice on Ice by Jane Yolen; illustrated by Lawrence Di Fiori. Dutton, 1980. Ten easy-to-read ministories about the leader and cast of the Mice Capades, marked with humor, excitement, and tenderness. P

Mouse Tales written and illustrated by Arnold Lobel. Harper, 1972. Seven tiny stories told by Papa Mouse to the seven Mouse boys at bedtime—very simple, amusing, gentle, compassionate with quietly funny drawings. N–P

Nobody Listens to Andrew by Elizabeth Guilfoile, illustrated by Mary Stevens. Follett, 1957; Scholastic paperback. The simple story of a boy with big news which is ignored by all until the final big surprise. N–P

One Fish, Two Fish, Red Fish, Blue Fish written and illustrated by Dr. Seuss. Random, 1960. Rhyming nonsense for beginning readers. Also, *Hop on Pop*, 1963, and *Green Eggs and Ham*, 1960. N–P

Plain Lane Christmas written and illustrated by C. Walter Hodges. Coward, 1978. Residents and shopkeepers of a quaint old street organize to fight the urban renewal plans that threaten their neighborhood. N–P

This Little Pig by Miska Miles; illustrated by Leslie Morrill. Dutton, 1980. Easy-to-read story of the triumph of the runt in a litter of seven piglets. N–P

FOLK TALES, FAIRY TALES, FABLES, AND LEGENDS

Aesop's Fables retold by Anne Terry White; illustrated by Helen Siegl. Random, 1964. Fresh and vigorous retelling of the old fables. P

Alphonse, That Bearded One by Natalie Savage Carlson; illustrated by Nicolas Mordvinoff. Harcourt, 1954. Canadian folk tale of a bear cub, trained to be a soldier, who takes his master's place in the army. *P–I*

Amahl and the Night Visitors by Gian Carlo Menotti, adapted by Frances Frost. McGraw, 1962. Beautifully illustrated story based on the television opera of the crippled boy who sees the Three Wise Men at Christmas. *I–A*

American Tall Tales retold by Adrien Stoutenburg; illustrated by Richard M. Powers. Viking, 1966; Penguin paperback. Fresh stories of American work heroes—Paul Bunyan, John Henry, Mike Fink, etc. *I–A*

Baboushka and the Three Kings by Ruth Robbins; illustrated by Nicolas Sidjakov. Parnassus, 1960. An old Russian tale of the woman who was too busy to join the three kings in search of the Child but has tried to follow them ever since. *I*

Beat the Story-Drum, Pum-Pum: African Tales retold and illustrated by Ashley Bryan. Atheneum, 1980. Five Nigerian folk tales told in rhythmic language and bold woodcuts printed in ocher, red, and black. *P–I*

Call It Courage by Armstrong Sperry. Macmillan, 1940. A Polynesian legend of a chieftain's son who conquers his fears in harrowing adventures. *I–A*

Everyone Knows What a Dragon Looks Like by Jay Williams; illustrated by Mercer Mayer. Four Winds, 1976. A charming tale of a trusting small boy who helps save the city by believing in the dragon. *P*

Fables written and illustrated by Arnold Lobel. Harper, 1980. Short, original fables that laugh at people through the antics of animals. Glowing illustrations are fables in themselves. *P–I–A*

The Fairy Tale Treasury selected by Virginia Haviland; illustrated by Raymond Briggs. Coward, 1972; Dell paperback. Thirty-two of the best-loved fairy tales from all over the world with over 300 illustrations full of humor and originality. *P–I*

Favorite Fairy Tales Told in Scotland retold by Virginia Haviland; illustrated by Adrienne Adams. Little, Brown,

1963. Six stories for children to read on their own. Also *Favorite Fairy Tales Told in Denmark,* 1971, *Norway,* 1961, *Italy,* 1965, etc. *I*

The Goose and the Golden Coins retold and illustrated by Lorinda Bryan Cauley. Harcourt, 1981. The tale of the goose that dropped golden coins for the maidens who befriended her. Also **The Story of the Three Little Pigs.* Putnam, 1980. *N–P*

*Half a Kingdom: An Icelandic Folk Tale retold by Ann McGovern; illustrated by Nola Langner. Warne, 1977; Scholastic paperback. How a peasant girl conquers two ugly trolls, liberates the prince, and thereby wins half a kingdom plus a charming husband. *P–I*

Henny-Penny illustrated by Paul Galdone. Houghton, 1968. The English folk tale of the little hen that set out to tell the king that "the sky's a-going to fall." *N–P*

*How the Rooster Saved the Day by Arnold Lobel; illustrated by Anita Lobel. Greenwillow, 1977; Penguin paperback. Like a folk drama, the contest between rooster and robber unfolds with witty text and enchanting art. *N–P*

John Henry: An American Legend written and illustrated by Ezra Jack Keats. Pantheon, 1965. Greatly simplified story of the famous black pile driver, with large dramatic pictures in color. *I*

Kickle Snifters and Other Fearsome Critters Collected From American Folklore compiled by Alvin Schwartz; illustrated by Glen Rounds. Lippincott, 1976. Imaginary beasts of the tall tales with illustrated definitions in nonsensical terms. *I*

The Man Who Didn't Wash His Dishes by Phyllis Krasilovsky; illustrated by Barbara Cooney. Doubleday, 1950. An old tale of exaggerated humor. *P–I*

My Mother Is the Most Beautiful Woman in the World by Becky Reyher; illustrated by Ruth Gannett. Lothrop, 1945. In this old Russian folk tale a little girl who is lost describes her mother as the most beautiful woman in the world. *P–I*

The Night It Rained Pancakes adapted from a Russian folk tale by Mirra Ginsburg; illustrated by Douglas Florian. Greenwillow, 1980. How the crafty older brother uses the stupid younger brother and saves a pot of gold. *P*

The Old Woman and Her Pig illustrated by Paul Galdone. McGraw, 1961. The old nursery tale beautifully designed and illustrated. Also *Old Mother Hubbard and Her Dog*, McGraw, 1960; and **The Three Bears*, Houghton, 1972; Scholastic paperback. *N–P*

*Ol' Paul, the Mighty Logger by Glen Rounds. Holiday, 1976; Avon paperback. Roaring humor and frank horseplay prevail in this collection of tall tales about Paul Bunyan, the legendary lumberjack. *I–A*

The Old Woman and Her Pig and 10 Other Stories retold and illustrated by Anne Rockwell. Crowell, 1979. Very simple stories with charming illustrations. *N–P*

Rum Pum Pum, A Folk Tale From India retold by Maggie Duff; illustrated by José Aruego and Ariane Dewey. Macmillan, 1978. When Blackbird's wife is kidnapped by the king, he plots revenge and triumphs. Good for storytelling. *P–I*

The Seeing Stick by Jane Yolen; illustrated by Remy Charlip and Demetra Marsalis. Crowell, 1977. A mysterious old man teaches the little blind princess to see with her fingers and to blossom. *P–I*

The Stars in the Sky: A Scottish Tale retold by Joseph Jacobs; illustrated by Airdrie Amtmann. Farrar, 1979. Imaginative drawings make this old tale a delight. *P–I*

*Stone Soup retold and illustrated by Marcia Brown. Scribner's, 1947. Humorous tale of soup made from stones—plus carrots, cabbage, meat, and all the rest. *P–I*

The Tall Book of Nursery Tales illustrated by Feodor Rojankovsky. Harper, 1944. Twenty-four well-known nursery tales told simply with delightfully lifelike illustrations. *P*

*The Teeny Tiny Woman retold and illustrated by Barbara Seuling. Viking, 1976; Penguin paperback. A charm-

ing little ghost tale with a surprise ending that children love. *N–P*

*The Three Billy Goats Gruff edited and illustrated by Marcia Brown. Harcourt, 1957. An old folk tale with new illustrations that make the ogre as dreadful and the goats as gay, impertinent, and bold as ever. Also *Dick Whittington and His Cat*, Scribner's, 1950. *P–I*

The Three Little Pigs illustrated by Eric Blegvad. Atheneum, 1980. The English folk tale with intriguing pictures. *N–P*

The Three Wishes retold and illustrated by Paul Galdone. McGraw, 1961. Folk tale about the woodsman who used

Illustration by Leo and Diane Dillon in *Why Mosquitoes Buzz in People's Ears*

up his wishes before he knew it. Also *The Three Wishes* retold by M. Jean Craig. Scholastic paperback. *P–I*

The Time-Ago Tales of Jahdu by Virginia Hamilton; illustrated by Nonny Hogrogian. Macmillan, 1969. Four haunting stories, told by Mama Luka to a small black boy who comes to her Harlem apartment while his mother works—stories that tell of giants, banyan trees, and the creatures of Africa. Also *Time-Ago Lost: More Tales of Jahdu*, 1973. *I–A*

The Treasure retold and illustrated by Uri Shulevitz. Farrar, 1979. The tale of the man whose dreams send him forth to search for treasure. *P–I*

Twelve Tales From Aesop retold and illustrated by Eric Carle. Philomel, 1980. The fables retold in delightful style with brilliant illustrations. *N–P*

Why Mosquitoes Buzz in People's Ears: A West African Tale retold by Verna Aardema; illustrated by Leo and Diane Dillon. Dial, 1975. Mosquito tells a tall tale that sets off a chain reaction leading to disaster in the jungle. Also *Who's in Rabbit's House?* 1977. *P*

Wiley and the Hairy Man adapted from an American folk tale and illustrated by Molly Garrett Bang. Macmillan, 1976. How Wiley fooled the Hairy Man who lived in the swamp by the Tombigbee River. *P–I*

Zlateh the Goat and Other Stories by Isaac Bashevis Singer; illustrated by Maurice Sendak. Harper, 1966. Seven tales of visions and villages, of patient animals and everyday people—all springing from middle-European Jewish folklore. A book too good to miss. *I*

MODERN STORIES—REAL AND FANTASTIC

FUNNY STORIES

Alexander and the Terrible, Horrible, No Good, Very Bad Day by Judith Viorst; illustrated by Ray Cruz. Atheneum, 1972. A comical recital of the succession of tragedies which beset a small boy on just one day. Also *Alexander, Who Used to Be Rich, Last Sunday*, 1978. *P*

All the Way Home by Lore Segal; illustrated by James Marshall. Farrar, 1973. Picture story of a city mother bringing two howling kids home from the park and the creatures who join the procession. *P*

*The Day the Circus Came to Lone Tree written and illustrated by Glen Rounds. Holiday, 1973; Dell paperback. When cowboys in the crowd think the Lady Lion Tamer is about to be devoured, they rush to the rescue and chaos results—a hilarious story for any age. *P–I*

Ida Early Comes Over the Mountain by Robert Burch. Viking, 1980. Like an awkward scarecrow, Ida Early takes over as a housekeeper in a motherless family and charms the lot. *I*

*Lentil written and illustrated by Robert McCloskey. Viking, 1940; Penguin paperback. Practice in the bathtub improves Lentil's harmonica playing to the point where he wins real distinction. *P–I*

McBroom Tells a Lie by Sid Fleischman; illustrated by Walter H. Lorraine. Little, Brown, 1976. Easy-to-read story about a tall-tale hero who always comes out ahead. Also *McBroom and the Beanstalk,* 1978, and *McBroom Tells the Truth,* 1977. *P–I*

*No Kiss for Mother written and illustrated by Tomi Ungerer. Harper, 1973; Dell paperback. A rambunctious young cat rebels against his mother's persistent baby talk and kisses. *N–P*

*Nobody Asked Me If I Wanted a Baby Sister written and illustrated by Martha Alexander. Dial, 1971. How Oliver learns to cope with the new baby sister, told with humor and understanding. *N–P*

*Nothing Ever Happens on My Block written and illustrated by Ellen Raskin. Atheneum, 1966; Scholastic paperback. Comical picture-book story of a boy who complains that nothing happens on his block although the intriguing pictures tell a very different story. *N–P*

Pinkerton, Behave! written and illustrated by Steven Kellogg; Dial, 1979. Pinkerton, a dog as big as a pony, flunks out of obedience school but uses his bad habits to conquer

Illustration by Steven Kellogg in *Pinkerton, Behave!*

a burglar. A droll story of few words with hilarious illustrations. *P*

*Pippi Longstocking by Astrid Lindgren; illustrated by Louis S. Glanzman. Viking, 1950; Penguin paperback. Nine-year-old Pippi, who lives with her monkey, her horse, and her fortune in gold pieces, manages to create a sensation wherever she goes. Her adventures continue in several other books. *P–I*

Strega Nona retold and illustrated by Tomie de Paola. Prentice-Hall, 1975. Big Anthony uses the magic words to start spaghetti making, but doesn't know how to turn the magic off. A hilarious tale full of exaggeration. *P*

*Tell Me a Mitzi by Lore Segal; illustrated by Harriet Pincus. Farrar, 1970; Scholastic paperback. Three family stories of city children with individuality and charm, illustrated with boldly realistic and humorous drawings. *P–I*

*Who, Said Sue, Said Whoo? written and illustrated by Ellen Raskin. Atheneum, 1973. Like the cumulative rhyme of an old nonsense song, this amusing adventure story "chitter-chitter chatters" to a beautiful surprise with stunning pictures in brilliant colors. *N–P*

*You Look Ridiculous Said the Rhinoceros to the Hippopotamus written and illustrated by Bernard Waber. Houghton, 1966. A hippopotamus dreams she has acquired the best feature of each of her very critical friends. Also **An Anteater Named Arthur*, 1967. *P–I*

ANIMAL STORIES

*Abel's Island written and illustrated by William Steig. Farrar, 1976; Bantam paperback. Marooned on an uninhabited island for a year, a lovable and inventive gentleman mouse survives a series of disasters and comes through a hero. Ideal for family reading aloud. *P–I*

*The Biggest Bear written and illustrated by Lynd Ward. Houghton, 1952. A small boy brings home a bear cub that grows into a great problem. *N–P*

*The Black Stallion by Walter Farley. Random, 1941. There's breathtaking excitement in this story of a boy, a wild black stallion, a shipwreck, and a horse race. Also **Son of the Black Stallion*, 1947, **The Black Stallion and Satan*, 1949, and **The Island Stallion*, 1948. *I–A*

*Brighty of the Grand Canyon by Marguerite Henry; illustrated by Wesley Dennis. Rand, 1953. An old prospector finds a little wild burro on Bright Angel Creek in the Grand Canyon, and a lasting friendship develops. *I–A*

Charlotte's Web by E. B. White; illustrated by Garth Williams. Harper, 1952. A gentle spider saves the life of Wilbur the pig by spinning messages in her web. *P–I–A*

Cranes in My Corral by Dayton O. Hyde; illustrated by Lorence Bjorklund. Dial, 1971. An Oregon cattle rancher tells of raising four sandhill cranes—gay and affectionate, but true to the facts. *A*

The Cricket in Times Square by George Selden; illustrated by Garth Williams. Farrar, 1960; Dell paperback. The wonderful story of a cricket from Connecticut who spends the summer in a New York subway station, aided and abetted by three friends—a boy, a cat, and a fast-talking Broadway mouse. Continued in *Tucker's Countryside,* 1969; Avon paperback. *I–A*

The Cry of the Crow by Jean Craighead George. Harper, 1980. A poetic story of Mandy and her pet crow, who mimics the voice of the hunter. *I–A*

Curious George written and illustrated by H. A. Rey. Houghton, 1941. After wild adventures in a big city, George, a monkey with great curiosity, finds himself in a nice, safe zoo. Continued in *Curious George Takes a Job,* 1947, *Curious George Rides a Bike,* 1952, *Curious George Gets a Medal,* 1957, and *Curious George Learns the Alphabet,* 1963. *N–P*

Gentle Ben by Walt Morey; illustrated by John Schoenherr. Dutton, 1965; Avon paperback. The lonely son of a salmon fisherman befriends an Alaskan brown bear which has been mistreated, and then struggles to save him. *A*

The Incredible Journey, A Tale of Three Animals by Sheila Burnford; illustrated by Carl Burger. Little, Brown, 1961; Bantam paperback. A Siamese cat, an English bull terrier, and a Labrador retriever make their way painfully over hundreds of miles to get home again. *A*

Kävik the Wolf Dog by Walt Morey; illustrated by Peter Parnall. Dutton, 1968. When Andy rescures Kävik, a hardened sled dog, from plane wreckage and nurses him back to health, a beautiful friendship is formed. Kävik's long trek from Seattle back to Alaska and Andy is beautifully told. *A*

Lassie Come Home by Eric Knight; illustrated by Don Bolognese. Holt, rev. ed., 1971; Dell paperback. A collie dog, taken hundreds of miles from home, makes her way back to meet her master at the schoolhouse gate. *A*

The Midnight Fox by Betsy Byars; illustrated by Ann Grifalconi. Viking, 1968; Avon paperback. A city boy who is indifferent to nature and wildlife spends the summer in the country where he learns to know a black fox which he protects from his uncle's gun. *I–A*

Mississippi Possum by Miska Miles; illustrated by John Schoenherr. Little, Brown, 1965. Beautifully illustrated story of a baby possum that follows a black family to escape a Mississippi River flood. *P–I*

Misty of Chincoteague by Marguerite Henry; illustrated by Wesley Dennis. Rand, 1947. At the spring roundup of wild ponies from Chincoteague Island, two children adopt a wild pony. Continued in *Sea Star*, 1949. *I–A*

Mr. Popper's Penguins by Richard and Florence Atwater; illustrated by Robert Lawson. Little, Brown, 1938; Dell paperback. Mr. Popper turns over his house to Captain Cook, a penguin presented by an Antarctic explorer. Before long twelve penguins are ruling the Popper household. *P–I*

Mrs. Frisby and the Rats of NIMH by Robert C. O'Brien; illustrated by Zena Bernstein. Atheneum, 1971. Super-rats, trained in laboratory experiments, come to the aid of a sickly mouse child and his anxious mother. This is science fiction that tells much about the ways of our society. *A*

Owls in the Family by Farley Mowat; illustrated by Robert Frankenberg. Little, Brown, 1961; Bantam paperback. The true, first-person story of a Canadian boy and his two pet owls. *P–I*

Rabbit Hill written and illustrated by Robert Lawson. Viking, 1944; Penguin paperback. When new folks come to the big house, the animals on Rabbit Hill have many interesting adventures. Continued in *The Tough Winter*, 1954; Penguin paperback. *I–A*

Socks by Beverly Cleary; illustrated by Beatrice Darwin. Morrow, 1973; Dell paperback. Socks, a young tabby cat, rules the Bricker household happily until their infant son is born. His triumph over rejection and competition makes an amusing and touching story. *I*

The Story of Ferdinand by Munro Leaf; illustrated by Robert Lawson. Viking, 1936; Penguin paperback. Comical story of the young Spanish bull who would rather sit and smell the flowers than be in a bullfight. *P–I*

The Tale of Peter Rabbit written and illustrated by Beatrix Potter. Warne, 1902; Dover paperback. Also French and Spanish editions. A favorite of all generations. *N–P*

The Trumpet of the Swan by E. B. White; illustrated by Edward Frascino. Harper, 1970. Louis, the one mute cygnet born to a family of trumpeter swans, is given a trumpet and begins a distinguished musical career and fine relationship with human beings. *A*

Watership Down by Richard Adams. Macmillan, 1974; Avon paperback. A long, detailed, but vital fantasy about the breakup of a rabbit warren and the frantic search for a new community where the rabbits can maintain their unique language, folklore, and cultural patterns. *A*

White Bird by Clyde Robert Bulla; illustrated by Leonard Weisgard. Crowell, 1966. The moving story of a lonely boy who lives with a Tennessee hermit and finds a white crow for a pet. *I*

The Wounded Wolf by Jean Craighead George; illustrated by John Schoenherr. Harper, 1978. The fox, the snow owl, and the grizzly bear join the death watch of a wounded wolf in the Arctic. Great for reading aloud. *P–I*

CHILDREN'S PROJECTS AND ADVENTURES

About the B'nai Bagels written and illustrated by E. L. Konigsburg. Atheneum, 1969. A member of the B'nai Bagels, a Little League team, tells the story of his mounting problems: his mother is team manager, his brother the coach, and he must prepare for his Bar Mitzvah. *I–A*

Anastasia Krupnik by Lois Lowry; illustrated by Diane de Groat. Houghton, 1979; Bantam paperback. The tale of a ten-year-old who resents the imminent arrival of a baby in the family. *I*

*. . . And Now Miguel by Joseph Krumgold; illustrated by Jean Charlot. Crowell, 1953; Apollo paperback. The middle son in a family of New Mexican sheepherders longs to go to the mountains with the men of the family. *I–A*

*Are You There, God? It's Me, Margaret by Judy Blume. Bradbury, 1970; Dell paperback. A preteen girl's concern with signs of puberty and her private conversations with God. *A*

A Big Fat Enormous Lie by Marjorie Weinman Sharmat; illustrated by David McPhail. Dutton, 1978. "I told a lie," a small boy admits. "A big fat enormous gigantic lie." His anxiety and the pictures grow in proportion. *N–P*

Illustration by David McPhail in *A Big Fat Enormous Lie*

Blubber by Judy Blume. Bradbury, 1974; Dell paperback. The fattest girl in fifth grade is tormented by the other girls until one begins to show sympathy and is then persecuted herself. A realistic and provocative story. *I–A*

Burnish Me Bright by Julia Cunningham; illustrated by Don Freeman. Pantheon, 1970; Dell paperback. A mute orphan boy makes friends with a famous mime, now retired and very old, in a remote village of France. Through this touching friendship the boy is drawn out of his shell of loneliness. *I–A*

Busybody Nora by Johanna Hurwitz; illustrated by Susan Jeschke. Morrow, 1976; Dell paperback. The apartment-life adventures of five-year-old Nora and her younger brother. Also *Nora and Mrs. Mind-Your-Own-Business*, 1977; Dell paperback. *P–I*

The Carp in the Bathtub by Barbara Cohen; illustrated by Joan Halpern. Lothrop, 1972; Dell paperback. First-person story of a little girl's affection for the carp Mama has swimming in the bathtub just before she needs it to make gefilte fish for Passover. *P–I*

The Cat Ate My Gymsuit by Paula Danziger. Delacorte, 1974; Dell paperback. A thirteen-year-old hates being fat, dislikes school, dislikes herself, but a sensitive teacher changes her life. Very amusing and perceptive. *I–A*

Dinky Hocker Shoots Smack! by M. E. Kerr. Harper, 1972; Dell paperback. A junior high girl who is overweight, feels neglected by her parents and unsuccessful with boys makes a strong and hilarious protest. *A*

The Family Under the Bridge by Natalie Savage Carlson; illustrated by Garth Williams. Harper, 1958; Scholastic paperback. Three children with their mother find shelter under one of the bridges of Paris and then win the affection of a hobo who shows them Christmas in the city and finds them a real home. *I*

Far Out the Long Canal by Meindert DeJong; illustrated by Nancy Grossman. Harper, 1964. The two-day adventures of a Dutch boy of Holland who does not learn to skate until he is off on a wild adventure where the ice is thin. *I–A*

Fiona's Bee by Beverly Keller; illustrated by Diane Paterson. Coward, 1975; Dell paperback. How a lonely little girl and her pet bee make friends. *P*

Flight of the Sparrow by Julia Cunningham. Pantheon, 1980. Stirring first-person story of a nine-year-old French waif and her grim struggle with street toughs, relieved by occasional beautiful friendships. *A*

From the Mixed-Up Files of Mrs. Basil E. Frankweiler by E. L. Konigsburg. Atheneum, 1967. The hilarious story of children from Greenwich, Connecticut, who run away from home and live for days in the Metropolitan Museum of Art. *A*

George the Babysitter written and illustrated by Shirley Hughes. Prentice, 1978. How a teenage boy manages a family of three small children while their mother is at work. *N–P*

A Girl Called Al by Constance C. Greene; illustrated by Byron Barton. Viking, 1969; Dell paperback. Life is a series of problems and disappointments until Al finds a friend. Continued in *I Know You, Al,* 1975; Dell, and *Your Old Pal, Al,* 1979. *I*

Go and Hush the Baby by Betsy Byars; illustrated by Emily A. McCully. Viking, 1971. How an older brother devises ways to amuse the baby in the family. *N–P*

Harriet the Spy written and illustrated by Louise Fitzhugh. Harper, 1964; Dell paperback. The only child of well-to-do and preoccupied New Yorkers, Harriet is a self-appointed spy who keeps detailed notebooks of her spying. Continued in *The Long Secret,* 1965; Dell paperback. *I–A*

Henry Huggins by Beverly Cleary; illustrated by Louis Darling. Morrow, 1950; Dell paperback. The adventures of a boy who always gets into funny situations. Also *Henry and Beezus,* 1952, *Henry and Ribsy,* 1954, and *Henry and the Clubhouse,* 1962. *P–I*

The House of Wings by Betsy Byars; illustrated by Daniel Schwartz. Viking, 1972. When Sammy finds himself alone with his grandfather in the dilapidated old house where birds fly inside, he runs away. But the old man's gentle way with a wounded crane wins the boy. *I–A*

How the Children Stopped the Wars by Jan Wahl; illustrated by Mitchell Miller. Farrar, 1969; Avon paperback. An unforgettable story about the absurdity of war. *I–A*

How to Eat Fried Worms by Thomas Rockwell; illustrated by Emily A. McCully. Watts, 1973; Dell paperback. Billy makes a bet that he can eat fifteen worms, one a day, in a fast-paced story with the kind of humor fourth graders love. *I–A*

It's Like This, Cat by Emily Cheney Neville. Harper, 1963. Fourteen-year-old Dave Mitchell, beginning to explore New York on his own, confides in his cat as his closest friend. *A*

Jennifer, Hecate, Macbeth, William McKinley, and Me, Elizabeth written and illustrated by E. L. Konigsburg. Atheneum, 1967. A lonely small girl tells the story of Jennifer, a black friend, who pretends she is a witch and can do magic tricks. *I–A*

Julie of the Wolves by Jean Craighead George; illustrated by John Schoenherr. Harper, 1972. Lost, without food or compass, on the North Slope of Alaska, thirteen-year-old Julie is accepted by a pack of Arctic wolves who help her survive to make her way to her father. *A*

Keep Running, Allen! by Clyde Robert Bulla; illustrated by Satomi Ichikawa. Crowell, 1978. How the youngest of three tries to keep up and surprisingly finds a way to slow them down. *N–P*

Maudie and Me and the Dirty Book by Betty Miles. Knopf, 1978. Sixth-grader Kate reads to first graders a picture book about the birth of puppies and finds herself in trouble with protesting parents. *I–A*

Meet M and M by Pat Ross; illustrated by Marilyn Hafner. Pantheon, 1980. The ups and downs of the friendship of Mandy and Mimi, apartment-house neighbors. *P*

The Moffats by Eleanor Estes; illustrated by Louis Slobodkin. Harcourt, 1941. The Moffats—four children and Mama—have exciting times despite a limited income. Continued in *The Middle Moffat*, 1943. *I–A*

Moon-Watch Summer by Lenore Blegvad; illustrated by Erik Blegvad. Harcourt, 1972. Eleven-year-old Adam, spending the summer on Grandmother's farm, is horrified to find she has no television, but gradually learns there are more exciting ways of being entertained. *I–A*

*My Side of the Mountain written and illustrated by Jean George. Dutton, 1959. The first-person story of a New York City boy who goes to the Catskills to live on the abandoned acres of his great-grandfather. His home is a hollow in the trunk of a hemlock with a six-foot diameter. *A*

Plain Lane Christmas written and illustrated by C. Walter Hodges. Coward, 1978. Residents and shopkeepers of a quaint old street organize to fight threats to their neighborhood. *N–P*

*A Pocketful of Cricket by Rebecca Caudill; illustrated by Evaline Ness. Holt, 1964. A farm boy takes a cricket to school in his pocket. *N–P*

*Ramona the Brave by Beverly Cleary; illustrated by Allan Tiegreen. Morrow, 1975; Dell paperback. First introduced as the pesky little sister in *Henry Huggins,* Ramona, now a very independent first grader, struggles to comply with school ways while being her own spunky self. Also: **Ramona the Pest,* 1968; **Ramona and Her Father,* 1977; and **Ramona and Her Mother,* 1979. *I*

*The Real Me by Betty Miles. Knopf, 1974; Avon paperback. With the backing of her family, Barbara fights sexism in her school and on a paper route. *I*

A Salmon for Simon by Betty Waterton; illustrated by Ann Blades. Atheneum, 1980. A bald eagle drops a salmon in a clam hole beside a Canadian Indian boy. A gentle, thoughtful tale with brilliant watercolors. *I*

*Shadow of a Bull by Maia Wojciechowska; illustrated by Alvin Smith. Atheneum, 1964. The moving story of the son of a great Spanish bullfighter who is expected to fight as his father did. *I–A*

*Tales of a Fourth Grade Nothing by Judy Blume; illustrated by Roy Doty. Dutton, 1972; Dell paperback. Nine-year-old Peter tells of his problems with his attention-getting little brother. Light and humorous. *I–A*

The TV Kid by Betsy Byars; illustrated by Richard Cuffari. Viking, 1976; Scholastic paperback. Satire, pathos, and suspense mark the story of Lennie, the TV addict, whose entire world changes when he is bitten by a rattlesnake. *I*

Veronica Ganz by Marilyn Sachs; illustrated by Louis Glanzman. Doubleday, 1968; Dell paperback. Thirteen-year-old Veronica, tall for her age, bullies the little children and then finds that the smallest boy in the class is really her friend. Continued in *Peter and Veronica,* 1969. *I–A*

A Very Young Dancer by Jill Krementz; photos by the author. Knopf, 1976. A ten-year-old dancer tells of her preparation and performance in the New York City Ballet's *Nutcracker Suite.* Very professional, full of backstage excitement. Also *A Very Young Rider,* 1977, and *A Very Young Gymnast,* 1978. *I*

The Westing Game by Ellen Raskin. Dutton, 1978; Avon paperback. An intriguing and highly complicated guessing game leads sixteen people to play detective so as to qualify for a share in a multimillion-dollar estate. *A*

FANTASY

The Book of Three by Lloyd Alexander. Holt, 1964; Dell paperback. The first of five chronicles of the fantasy Kingdom of Prydain. Also *The Black Cauldron,* 1965, and *The Castle of Llyr,* 1966. *A*

The Borrowers by Mary Norton; illustrated by Beth and Joe Krush. Harcourt, 1953. About the inhabitants of a fascinating miniature society who live by borrowing what they need. Also *The Borrowers Afield,* 1955, and *The Borrowers Afloat,* 1959. *I–A*

The Dark Is Rising by Susan Cooper. Atheneum, 1973. A sequence of five volumes and the title of the second. These are intricate fantasies which combine ancient lore, a magical world, and the contemporary scene. *A*

The Devil's Storybook written and illustrated by Natalie Babbitt. Farrar, 1974. Ten original stories about an all-too-human Devil and his encounters with all sorts of people, a pig, and a goat. *I–A*

Elizabeth Elizabeth by Eileen Dunlop; illustrated by Peter Farmer. Holt, 1977. While visiting in an old house in Scotland, Elizabeth looks in a mirror that takes her into the eighteenth century and transforms her into the Elizabeth who once lived in the same house. A touching and convincing fantasy. *A*

*The Fledgling by Jane Langton. Harper, 1980. Tiny Georgie, who longs to fly, meets a mysterious Canada goose who makes her dream come true. *I–A*

*Half Magic by Edward Eager; illustrated by N. M. Bodecker. Harcourt, 1954. As a result of the half magic created by a strange old coin, Jane, her two sisters, and her brother have unequaled adventures in time and space. Also *Magic or Not?*, 1959. *I–A*

The House on Mayferry Street by Eileen Dunlop; illustrated by Phillida Gili. Holt, 1977. Mysterious whispers and the music of a flute change the lives of the Ramsay family, who live in an old house in Edinburgh. *A*

*The Lion, the Witch and the Wardrobe by C. S. Lewis. Macmillan, 1951. Four children in the country to escape London air raids during World War II have exciting adventures by traveling through the wardrobe in an empty room to the mysterious land of Narnia. Continued in **The Magician's Nephew,* 1970, **The Last Battle,* 1956, and others. *A*

Little Tim and the Brave Sea Captain written and illustrated by Edward Ardizzone. Walck, 1955. A vivid story of life at sea with a five-year-old boy as hero. *P–I*

*Miss Pickerell Goes to Mars by Ellen MacGregor; illustrated by Paul Galdone. McGraw, 1951; Archway paperback. Precise Miss Pickerell, who wouldn't venture on a Ferris wheel, suddenly finds herself whisked off to another planet. Also *Miss Pickerell Goes Undersea. I*

*The Mouse and the Motorcycle by Beverly Cleary; illustrated by Louis Darling. Morrow, 1965; Dell paperback. Ralph, a daredevil mouse, drives the miniature toy motorcycle of a boy staying at the same hotel, and the two become fast friends. Continued in **Runaway Ralph,* 1974; Archway paperback. *I*

Mrs. Beggs and the Wizard written and illustrated by Mercer Mayer. Scholastic paperback, 1980. A wizard takes a room in Mrs. Beggs's boarding house and brings catastrophes galore until Mrs. Beggs gets out her own box of witchery and does him in. *P–I*

The Pig Who Could Conjure the Wind by Shirley Rousseau Murphy; illustrated by Mark Lefkowitz. Atheneum, 1978. How a demon wind changed the lifestyle of the pig who was a witch. *P*

The Pushcart War by Jean Merrill; illustrated by Ronni Solbert. Addison-Wesley, 1964; Dell paperback. Hilarious spoof on life in New York where pushcart peddlers organize to fight trucks with peashooters. *A*

A Question of Time by Dina Anastasio; illustrated by Dale Payson. Dutton, 1978. A convincing mystery about toy-store dolls that look like the townspeople of 1901. *P*

A String in the Harp by Nancy Bond. Atheneum, 1976. An American family living in Wales is torn by the visions which take twelve-year-old Peter into the mystic past of legendary Wales. *A*

Tuppenny by Julia Cunningham. Dutton, 1978; Avon paperback. A mysterious girl, who seems to come from nowhere, changes the lives of all she meets, then vanishes, but leaves a lasting memory. *A*

The Twenty-one Balloons written and illustrated by William Pène du Bois. Viking, 1947; Dell paperback. Fantasy, science, and adventure are in this story of Professor William Waterman Sherman, who starts out in one balloon and is picked up in the Atlantic in the wreckage of twenty balloons. *A*

A Wrinkle in Time by Madeleine L'Engle. Farrar, 1962; Dell paperback. Three youngsters are spirited to a world in outer space by three supernatural beings in intriguing science fiction. *A*

THE SUPERNATURAL

Big Bad Bruce written and illustrated by Bill Peet. Houghton, 1977. A foxy little witch stops the evil deeds of a bear who is a bully. *P*

The Blue-Nosed Witch by Margaret Embry. Holiday, 1956. Blanche, a modern young witch with a nose she can make glow in the dark, joins Halloweeners on a trick-or-treat expedition. *I*

Clyde Monster by Robert L. Crowe; illustrated by Kay Chorao. Dutton, 1976. A child monster is afraid of the dark and the people who might get him at night. *P*

*Ghost in a Four-Room Apartment written and illustrated by Ellen Raskin. Atheneum, 1970. A "two-voice" book—first the ghost and then the narrator—one creating havoc during a family reunion in a small apartment, the other trying to explain who's who. For those who love confusion, noise, and surprises. *P–I*

The Ghost of Tillie Jean Cassaway by Ellen Harvey Showell; illustrated by Stephen Gammel. Four Winds, 1978. A deserted house and an elusive "ghost" girl provide excitement in the Appalachian hills. *A*

Haunted Houses written and illustrated by Larry Kettelkamp. Morrow, 1969. Ten documented ghost stories are analyzed, with explanations plus old photos of two of the ghosts. Also *Spooky Magic*, 1955. *I–A*

*The House With a Clock in Its Walls by John Bellairs; illustrated by Edward Gorey. Dial, 1973; Dell paperback. Lewis discovers his uncle is a real wizard, then dabbles in magic himself—all too successfully—in a ghost story with mounting suspense. Continued in **The Figure in the Shadows*, 1975, and **The Letter, the Witch, and the Ring*, 1976; Dell paperback. *I–A*

*How to Care for Your Monsters written and illustrated by Norman Bridwell. Scholastic paperback, 1972. Hilarious how-to-do-it manual on the care and feeding of monsters, mummies, vampires, and werewolves, and a guide to staging a monster show. *P–I*

*Marco Moonlight by Clyde Robert Bulla; illustrated by Julia Noonan. Crowell, 1976; Dell paperback. Marco's dream of having a brother grows into a nightmare. *P–I*

*Meet the Werewolf by Georgess McHargue; illustrated by Stephen Gammell. Lippincott, 1976. Retelling of popu-

lar tales about werewolves with historical events that may have given such stories credence. Also *Meet the Vampire,* Dell paperback. *I*

Monsters From the Movies by Thomas G. Aylesworth. Lippincott, 1972; Bantam paperback. Familiar beasts and ghouls from movies and TV, with photos. *A*

Monsters, Ghoulies, and Creepy Creatures by Lee Bennett Hopkins; illustrated by Vera Rosenberry. Albert Whitman, 1977. An excellent collection of scary stories and poems. *I*

© 1973 Kay Sproat Chorao in *My Mama Says There Aren't Any Zombies, Ghosts, Vampires, Creatures, Demons, Monsters, Fiends, Goblins, or Things*

My Friend the Monster by Clyde Robert Bulla; illustrated by Michele Chessare. Crowell, 1980. The first time young Prince Hal is out in the world alone he meets a monster who becomes his best friend. *P–I*

My Mama Says There Aren't Any Zombies, Ghosts, Vampires, Creatures, Demons, Monsters, Fiends, Goblins, or

Things by Judith Viorst; illustrated by Kay Chorao. Atheneum, 1973. A small boy's rhythmical account of his mother's reassurance—but "sometimes even Mamas can make mistakes." N–P

Poltergeists: Hauntings and the Haunted by David C. Knight; illustrated with photos and old prints. Lippincott, 1972. Twelve factual reports of activities of poltergeists (noisy ghosts) from the seventeenth century to the present in England and the United States. I–A

Space Monsters From Movies, TV and Books by Seymour Simon. Lippincott, 1977. Exciting material told with humor and aided by photos. Also *Creatures From Lost Worlds*, 1979. A

Tim and Trisha written and illustrated by Otto S. Svend; translated by Joan Tate. Merrimack Book Services, 1977. A little girl meets a troll child and goes home with him to play happily in a beautiful woodland setting. P–I

Vampires and Other Ghosts by Thomas G. Aylesworth; illustrated with old woodcuts and prints. Addison-Wesley, 1972. A nonfiction examination of the lore and mystery behind centuries of myths about vampires, zombies, and animal ghosts throughout the world and throughout history. Also *Werewolves and Other Monsters*, 1971. I–A

Werewolves by Nancy Garden; illustrated with old woodcuts and engravings. Lippincott, 1973; Bantam paperback. Werewolves throughout history as revealed in stories, superstitions, legends; includes ways of dealing with the phenomenon. I–A

Witch, Goblin, and Sometimes Ghost by Sue Alexander; illustrated by Jeanette Winter. Pantheon, 1976. Six ministories about three good friends. Also *More Witch, Goblin, and Ghost Stories*, 1978. P

MYSTERIES

Cam Jansen and the Mystery of the Stolen Diamonds by David A. Adler; illustrated by Susanna Natti. Viking, 1980. A fifth-grade girl detective is unbeatable. Also *Cam Jansen and the Mystery of the U.F.O.*, 1980. P–I

The Case of the Cat's Meow written and illustrated by Crosby Bonsall. Harper, 1965. Four small boys become self-appointed detectives who search for a missing cat. Also *The Case of the Hungry Stranger*, 1963, and *The Case of the Double Cross, 1980. P*

Deadline for McGurk by E. W. Hildick; illustrated by Lisl Weil. Macmillan, 1975; Archway paperback. An action-packed, easy-to-read mystery adventure of a ten-year-old detective and his organization. Also *The Great Rabbit Rip-off, 1977. I*

Einstein Anderson, Science Sleuth by Seymour Simon; illustrated by Fred Winkowski. Viking, 1980. A sixth-grade science whiz teases the reader into unraveling his clues. Also *Einstein Anderson Shocks His Friends. P–I*

Encyclopedia Brown, Boy Detective by Donald J. Sobol; illustrated by Leonard Shortall. Nelson, 1963; Bantam paperback. The first of a series telling of the remarkable cases solved by the boy detective. *A*

The Fireball Mystery by Mary Adrian; illustrated by Reisie Lonette. Hastings, 1977. An easy detective story unfolds as children explore a mysterious island. *P–I*

The House of Dies Drear by Virginia Hamilton; illustrated by Eros Keith. Macmillan, 1968; Dell paperback. When a black family moves into the house of Dies Drear, strange and frightening things begin to happen. Ghosts from the Underground Railroad and a neighborhood hoax add suspense. *A*

How to Write Codes and Send Secret Messages by John Peterson; illustrated by Bernice Myers. Four Winds, 1970; Scholastic paperback. Clear, lively directions for writing and deciphering space codes, hidden word codes, and several alphabet codes. *I*

The Lemonade Trick by Scott Corbett; illustrated by Paul Galdone. Little, Brown, 1960. Two drops of a mysterious chemical added to the lemonade start a series of strange events that are puzzling as well as good reading. Also *The Mailbox Trick, 1961, and The Baseball Trick, 1965. I*

The Mystery in Lochness written and illustrated by Jeanne Bendick. McGraw, 1976. Informal run-down of the facts and speculations about the great creature. *A*

*The Mystery of the Great Swamp by Marjorie A. Zapf; illustrated by Carl Kidwell. Atheneum, 1967. A boy who lives in Okefenokee Swamp explores it by punt, loses his way, and meets exciting adventures. *I–A*

The Mystery of Lincoln Detweiler and the Dog Who Barked Spanish by Jean Robinson; illustrated by Gioia Fiammenghi. Follett, 1977. How Lincoln solved the mystery of thefts and prowlers. *A*

*Nate the Great and the Sticky Case by Marjorie Weinman Sharmat; illustrated by Marc Simont. Coward, 1978; Dell paperback. The famous boy detective finds the lost stegosaurus. Also **Nate the Great and the Phoney Clue*. 1977. *P*

Rooftop Mystery by Joan M. Lexau; illustrated by Syd Hoff. Harper, 1968. Clever detective work solves the mystery of the missing doll. Also *The Homework Caper*, 1966. *P*

Something Queer on Vacation: A Mystery by Elizabeth Levy; illustrated by Mordicai Gerstein. Delacorte, 1980. Two girls eager to win the July 4th sand castle contest track down the villain who keeps wrecking their entry. Lots of conversation and suspense with comic-book art. Also **Something Queer Is Going On*, 1973. *P–I*

HISTORY—FACT AND FICTION

Before 1850

And Then What Happened, Paul Revere? by Jean Fritz; illustrated by Margot Tomes. Coward, 1973. A humorous, fast-paced story, which is historically accurate and at the same time too exciting to put down. Also *Can't You Make Them Behave, King George?* 1977; *What's the Big Idea, Ben Franklin?* 1976, and *Where Do You Think You're Going, Christopher Columbus?* Putnam, 1980. *I*

*The Bears on Hemlock Mountain by Alice Dalgliesh; illustrated by Helen Sewell. Scribner's, 1952. An eight-year-

old sent over Hemlock Mountain to borrow an iron pot is fearful of bears on the trail and finally meets them. *P–I*

Ben and Me written and illustrated by Robert Lawson. Little, Brown, 1939; Dell paperback. The humorous life history of Benjamin Franklin as told by his good mouse Amos. Also *Mr. Revere and I,* the biography of Paul Revere as told by his horse. Dell paperback. *P–I*

The Cabin Faced West by Jean Fritz; illustrated by Feodor Rojankovsky. Coward, 1958. Excellent story of a little girl in the pioneer days of western Pennsylvania. *I–A*

Carry On, Mr. Bowditch by Jean Lee Latham; illustrated by J. O. Cosgrove. Houghton, 1955. Biography of a young boy who mastered the secrets of navigation by himself and became famous in marine history. *A*

The Courage of Sarah Noble by Alice Dalgliesh; illustrated by Leonard Weisgard. Scribner's, 1954. Eight-year-old Sarah goes into the Connecticut wilderness with her father in the early 1700s to take care of him while he builds a house for the family. *P–I*

The Door in the Wall written and illustrated by Marguerite de Angeli. Doubleday, 1949. A ten-year-old, crippled by the plague in thirteenth-century England, gains courage and finally triumphs. *A*

A Gathering of Days: A New England Girl's Journal, 1830–32 by Joan W. Blos. Scribner's, 1979. In two important "growing-up years," Catherine recounts the details of pioneer life, momentous decisions, close tragedy, and the widening of her world. *I–A*

Johnny Tremain by Esther Forbes; illustrated by Lynd Ward. Houghton, 1943; Dell paperback. The moving story of a silversmith's apprentice in Boston at the time of Paul Revere. *A*

Night Journeys by Avi. Pantheon, 1979. A very exciting tale of two runaway indentured servants, age ten and eleven, in Pennsylvania in 1767, and the risks others take to save them. *I–A*

Ox-Cart Man by Donald Hall; illustrated by Barbara Cooney. Viking, 1979. Rhythmical account of family life in early nineteenth-century. New England—growing and tending sheep, spinning, weaving, marketing, and the renewal of the cycle. *P*

Pearl in the Egg by Dorothy Van Woerkon; illustrated by Joe Lasker. Crowell, 1980. Eleven-year-old Pearl, who runs away to escape a life of serfdom in thirteenth century England, joins a troupe of minstrels and has an exciting and heartwarming career. *I–A*

*Poor Richard in France by F. N. Monjo; illustrated by Brinton Turkle. Holt, 1973; Dell paperback. Fictionalized story told by seven-year-old Benny, grandson of Benjamin Franklin, who went with his grandfather to France where they lived for two years. *P–I*

Tituba of Salem Village by Ann Petry. Crowell, 1964. There is beautiful detail and characterization, as well as mounting suspense, in this story of a black slave who is slowly drawn into the Salem witchcraft trials. *A*

*The Witch of Blackbird Pond by Elizabeth Speare. Houghton, 1958; Dell paperback. A girl from Barbados, visiting in the Connecticut colony, befriends an old woman accused of witchcraft and is caught in the hysteria of the great witch hunt. *A*

PIONEERS WESTWARD

By the Great Horn Spoon! by Sid Fleischman; illustrated by Eric Von Schmidt. Little, Brown, 1963. Jack Flagg, twelve, stows away on a ship bound for California and the Gold Rush, with Praiseworthy, a dignified butler, as his companion and master strategist. *I–A*

Chancy and the Grand Rascal by Sid Fleischman; illustrated by Eric Von Schmidt. Little, Brown, 1966. Chancy and his Uncle Will, the grand rascal, have adventures galore on the Ohio River. Good details about pioneer life. *I–A*

*Little House on the Prairie by Laura Ingalls Wilder; illustrated by Garth Williams. Harper, 1953. Autobiographical story of a pioneer family in the 1870s. Continued in **Farmer Boy*, 1953, **On the Banks of Plum Creek*, 1953, **By the Shores of Silver Lake*, 1953, and others. *I*

Mr. Mysterious & Company by Sid Fleischman; illustrated by Eric Von Schmidt. Little, Brown, 1962. A traveling musician, who is going to California in a brightly covered wagon with his wife and three children, puts on a magic show at each frontier town. *I*

Old Blue by Sybil Hancock; illustrated by Erick Ingraham. Putnam, 1980. Davy's first cattle drive provides thrills galore. *P*

*Old Yeller by Fred Gipson; illustrated by Carl Burger. Harper, 1956. A stray dog attaches himself to a family in the Texas hill country in the 1860s and defends all against wild animals and every danger. *A*

Riding the Pony Express by Clyde Robert Bulla. Crowell, 1948. The son of a Pony Express rider has to pinch-hit for his father in a crisis. Also **Down the Mississippi, 1954;* Scholastic paperback, and **Ghost Town Treasure, 1958;* Scholastic paperback. *I*

Wagon Wheels by Barbara Brenner; illustrated by Don Bolognese. Harper, 1978. An easy-to-read story of pioneer life, helpful Indians, and black settlers. *P–I*

ABOUT THE CIVIL WAR

*Abe Lincoln Gets His Chance by Frances Cavanah; illustrated by Don Sibley. Scholastic paperback. A warm, fictionalized story of Lincoln's life before becoming President. *I*

*Across Five Aprils by Irene Hunt. Follett, 1964; Grossett paperback. Moving story of nine-year-old Jethro, who becomes head of the family in rural Illinois during the five springs of the Civil War. *A*

Brady by Jean Fritz; illustrated by Lynd Ward. Coward, 1960. The story of a boy in pre-Civil War days who makes up his mind on the slavery issue and helps his father in the Underground Railroad. *I–A*

The Drinking Gourd by F. N. Monjo; illustrated by Fred Brenner. Harper, 1969. The simple, dramatic story of a New England boy who helps save a slave family traveling north by Underground Railroad during the Civil War. *P–I*

Harriet Tubman: Conductor on the Underground Railroad by Ann Petry. Crowell, 1955; Archway paperback. About the black leader, born a slave, who escaped by the Underground Railroad and led 300 others to safety. *A*

Me and Willie and Pa: The Story of Abe Lincoln and His Son Tad by F. N. Monjo; illustrated by Douglas Gorsline. Simon and Schuster, 1973. The story of Abe Lincoln's four years in the White House as told by young Tad Lincoln. Also *Grand Papa and Ellen Aroon. P–I*

ABOUT WORLD WAR II

The Ark by Margot Benary-Isbert. Harcourt, 1953. A post-war German family in a bombed-out city makes a new beginning in West Germany. *A*

The Endless Steppe: Growing Up in Siberia by Esther Hautzig. Crowell, 1968; Scholastic paperback. The author tells of her five years of exile in Siberia, life in cramped and desolate quarters, and forced labor in fields or mines. *A*

The Little Fishes by Erik Christian Haugaard; illustrated by M. Johnson. Houghton, 1967. Homeless children in World War II Italy must wander, beg, and steal to survive, but they always dream of better days when there will be peace. *A*

North to Freedom by Anne Holm. Translated from the Danish. Harcourt, 1965. A boy who escapes from a concentration camp makes his way across Europe and slowly learns that truth and friendship still exist in the world. *A*

A Pocket Full of Seeds by Marilyn Sachs; illustrated by Ben F. Stahl. Doubleday, 1973. Convincing story of a Jewish girl in Germany during World War II whose family think that Nazi persecution can never happen to them. *I–A*

Snow Treasure by Marie McSwigan. Dutton, 1942; Scholastic paperback. How Norwegian children during the Nazi occupation got blocks of gold out of the country. *A*

Summer of My German Soldier by Bette Green. Dial, 1973; Bantam paperback. Twelve-year-old Patty, daughter of constantly reprimanding Jewish parents in Arkansas during World War II, tells the story of protecting a German POW, and being sent to reform school. *A*

Twenty and Ten by Claire Huchet Bishop. Viking, 1952; Penguin paperback. Twenty French children risk everything during World War II to shelter ten Jewish refugee children. *I–A*

The Upstairs Room by Johanna Reiss. Crowell, 1972; Bantam paperback. Very moving story of two Jewish girls who were hidden for more than two years in an upstairs room by a Gentile farm family in Holland during World War II. *A*

PROBLEMS CHILDREN FACE

PHYSICAL AND MENTAL HANDICAPS

David in Silence by Veronica Robinson; illustrated by Victor Ambrus. Lippincott, 1965. A deaf boy meets varied reactions as he tries to share the usual activities of the other boys. *A*

Me Too by Vera and Bill Cleaver. Lippincott, 1973; New American Library paperback. Lydia determines to teach her retarded twin sister to speak and act like a normal person, but meets frustration at every turn. *I–A*

Mine for Keeps by Jean Little. Little, Brown, 1962; Archway paperback. When Sally comes to live at home after five years at a cerebral palsy center, she has to make many adjustments. Her pet dog, "mine for keeps," helps her win security and friends. *I–A*

My Brother Steven Is Retarded by Harriet Langsam Sobol; photos by Patricia Agre. Macmillan, 1977. An eleven-year-old tells of her retarded older brother with rare understanding and compassion. *I*

The Summer of the Swans by Betsy Byars; illustrated by Ted CoConis. Viking, 1970; Avon paperback. Eighth-grader Sara, shy and sensitive, tries to protect her younger brother, who is retarded. *A*

Take Wing by Jean Little; illustrated by Jerry Lazare. Little, Brown, 1968. Laurel struggles to make friends with

other children while protecting her brother, who is mentally retarded, although others in the family fail to acknowledge this. A very moving story. *A*

Where the Lilies Bloom by Vera and Bill Cleaver; illustrated by Jim Spanfeller. Lippincott, 1969; New American
Library paperback. First-person story of a fourteen-year-old
girl of Appalachia who struggles to keep the fatherless
family together. *A*

FAMILY TENSIONS

The Bears' House by Marilyn Sachs; illustrated by Louis
Glanzman. Doubleday, 1971. An unhappy nine-year-old
clings to her baby sister and the Bears' House in her
schoolroom in her retreat from her impoverished and fatherless family. *I–A*

Can You Sue Your Parents for Malpractice? by Paula
Danziger. Delacorte, 1979. A humorous story of family
tensions and distress. *I–A*

Ellen Grae by Vera and Bill Cleaver; illustrated by Ellen
Raskin. Lippincott, 1967; New American Library paperback.
Eleven-year-old Ellen Grae, whose parents are divorced,
swings from the telling of endless tall tales to days of
silence and deep anxiety. Followed by *Grover,* 1970; New
American Library paperback. *A*

Emily and the Klunky Baby and the Next-Door Dog by
Joan M. Lexau; illustrated by Martha Alexander. Dial, 1972.
A little girl whose parents are divorced decides to run away
to Daddy. *P–I*

Freaky Friday by Mary Rodgers. Harper, 1972. A
thirteen-year-old awakes one morning to find she is her
own mother and must cope with the tricky and freaky
problems which are her mother's daily diet. *A*

The Great Gilly Hopkins by Katherine Paterson. Crowell,
1978; Avon paperback. The convincing story of a tough
and rebellious foster child who gradually learns to accept
love and to give it. *I–A*

The Grizzly by Annabel and Edgar Johnson; illustrated
by Gilbert Riswold. Harper, 1964; Scholastic paperback.

Eleven-year-old David dreads a weekend camping expedition with his father, a rigid get-tough perfectionist, whom he barely knows. When a grizzly bear threatens, the boy sees the father in a new light, and the relationship is strengthened. *A*

"Hey, What's Wrong With This One?" by Maia Wojcie-chowska; illustrated by Joan Sandin. Harper, 1969. Three scrapping small boys help their father pick out a new wife. *I*

*The Hundred Dresses by Eleanor Estes; illustrated by Louis Slobodkin. Harcourt, 1944. A little Polish girl, teased by her classmates because she always wears the same dress, finally wins approval. *I*

*It's Not the End of the World by Judy Blume. Bradbury, 1972; Bantam paperback. A twelve-year-old recounts the discord and mounting tension among three children and their parents for whom divorce is inevitable. *I–A*

Judy's Journey written and illustrated by Lois Lenski. Lippincott, 1947. Judy is the daughter of an Alabama share-cropper who becomes a migratory worker and follows the crops. Also **Strawberry Girl,* a story laid in Florida cracker country, Dell paperback. *I*

A Look at Divorce by Margaret S. Pursell; photos by Maria S. Forrai. Lerner, 1976. (Lerner Awareness Books). Clear black-and-white photos and simple text show causes of divorce, possible outcomes, and the child's adjustment. Factual, straightforward help for the reader. Others in the series: *Alcoholism, Adoption, Birth, Death, Physical Handicaps, Aging. I–A*

Me Day by Joan M. Lexau; illustrated by Robert Weaver. Dial, 1971. A small boy whose parents are divorced is disappointed when there is no birthday letter from his father. *P–I*

*Mommies at Work by Eve Merriam; illustrated by Beni Montresor. Scholastic paperback, 1973. About "mommies" at work, at home, in offices, on ranches, in stores and banks—all told in simple rhythmical lines. *N–P*

*My Dad Lives in a Downtown Hotel by Peggy Mann; illustrated by Richard Cuffari. Doubleday, 1973; Avon pa-

perback. Story of a ten-year-old's reaction to his parents' divorce. *I*

The Night Swimmers by Betsy Byars; illustrated by Troy Howell. Delacorte, 1980. With false bravado, Retta struggles to provide for two younger brothers who need her and resent her. Also *The Pinballs,* Harper, 1977; Scholastic paperback. *I–A*

Nobody's Family Is Going to Change by Louise Fitzhugh. Farrar, 1974; Dell paperback. Two children in a black family are frustrated by their father's expectations for them. *I–A*

Queenie Peavy by Robert Burch; illustrated by Jerry Lazare. Viking, 1966. A thirteen-year-old Georgia girl in the Great Depression is taunted because her father is in prison. She fights back, then learns to understand herself. Queenie is a strong character who is not easily forgotten. *A*

The Terrible Thing That Happened at Our House by Marge Blaine; illustrated by John C. Wallner. Parents, 1975; Scholastic paperback. When Mother gets a job, the children think a real catastrophe has hit the family until they work out a plan of cooperation. *P–I*

Then Again, Maybe I Won't by Judy Blume. Bradbury, 1971; Dell paperback. A thirteen-year-old boy whose family moves into a more affluent neighborhood is worried by his own pubertal development, a young shoplifter among his acquaintances, and the changes that money has made in his family's sense of values. *A*

ETHNIC GROUPS

All Us Come Cross the Water by Lucille Clifton; illustrated by John Steptoe. Holt, 1973. The first-person story of a small black city boy, who is plagued by the question "Where we from?" From an old man he learns that all black Americans have their roots in Africa and are one people. *P*

Brother Mouky and the Falling Sun written and illustrated by Karen Whiteside. Harper, 1980. A black city boy finds a way to calm his angry feelings toward his brother and forgive him. *P–I*

Dragonwings by Laurence Yep. Harper, 1975. First-person story of a Chinese boy, living in San Francisco during the great earthquake, whose father's dream was to build and fly an airplane. *I–A*

Everett Anderson's 1-2-3 by Lucille Clifton; illustrated by Ann Grifalconi. Holt, 1977. In free-rolling verse, a joyful, black six-year-old tells of his life in a housing development. Also *Everett Anderson's Nine Month Long. N–P*

From Lew Alcindor to Kareem Abdul-Jabbar by James Haskins. Lothrop, 1978. The extraordinary story of the lonely black boy who became one of the greatest basketball players of all time. *A*

© 1980 Ashley Bryan in *Beat the Story-Drum, Pum-Pum*

Henner's Lydia written and illustrated by Marguerite de Angeli. Doubleday, 1936. About a Pennsylvania German girl and her hooked rug. More Pennsylvania German stories: *Skippack School,* 1939, and *Yonie Wondernose,* 1944. *I*

Island of the Blue Dolphins by Scott O'Dell. Houghton, 1960; Dell paperback. The haunting story, based on fact, of an Indian girl who is forced to spend eighteen years alone on an island off the coast of California. *A*

The Jazz Man by Mary Hays Weik; illustrated by Ann Grifalconi. Atheneum, 1966. A lame black boy who seldom leaves his Harlem tenement is fascinated by the Jazz Man whose music fills the narrow court. *A*

Malcolm X by Arnold Adoff; illustrated by John Wilson. Crowell, 1970. A brief, honest portrayal of the man who was a forceful spokesman for American blacks before his assassination in 1965. *A*

Martin Luther King, Jr.: Man of Peace written by Lillie Patterson; illustrated by Victor Mays. Garrard, 1969. Easy-to-read biography with appealing illustrations. *P*

Martin Luther King: The Peaceful Warrior by Ed Clayton; illustrated by David Hodges. Prentice, 1964; Archway paperback. A biography of the great black leader in the revolution of nonviolence. *I–A*

Roll of Thunder, Hear My Cry by Mildred D. Taylor; illustrated by Jerry Pinkney. Dial, 1976; Bantam paperback. Deeply moving story of a black Mississippi family during the Depression. Also, *Let the Circle Be Unbroken*. Dial, 1981. *I–A*

Roosevelt Grady by Louisa R. Shotwell; illustrated by Peter Burchard. Philomel, 1963; Dell paperback. Nine-year-old Roosevelt, the son of black migrant workers, longs for a place to "stay put." *I–A*

Sing Down the Moon by Scott O'Dell. Houghton, 1970; Dell paperback. The haunting story of the Long Walk of the Navajos and their degradation at the hands of the Spaniards and then Kit Carson and his men. *I–A*

Sounder by William H. Armstrong; illustrated by James Barkley. Harper, 1969. The bitter story of a black share-cropper who steals food for his family and is sent to jail. A stark tragedy which was the basis for a movie. *I–A*

The Street of the Flower Boxes by Peggy Mann; illustrated by Peter Burchard. Archway paperback. Tough black and Puerto Rican boys pull up flowers planted by newcomers to their block, but soon they lead a campaign to beautify West 94th Street. *P–I*

Tough Tiffany by Belinda Hurmence. Doubleday, 1980. The youngest in a poor black family tries to be tough but grows increasingly sensitive to the ups and downs of her life. *I–A*

The Treasure of Topo-el-Bampo by Scott O'Dell; illustrated by Lynd Ward. Houghton, 1972. In Topo-el-Bampo, the poorest village in Mexico 200 years ago, two burros are sold to silver mines, but return to save the village from starvation. *I*

Willie Blows a Mean Horn by Ianthe Thomas; illustrated by Ann Toulmin-Rothe. Harper, 1981. The small son of Willie, "the Jazz King," watches a nightclub performance and dreams that someday he, too, "will play a lullaby to the wind." *P*

Zeely by Virginia Hamilton; illustrated by Symeon Shimin. Macmillan, 1967; Dell paperback. Zeely, six-and-a-half feet tall and as black as ebony, becomes a queen in the eyes of a little black girl from the city. *A*

OLD AGE AND DEATH

Annie and the Old One by Miska Miles; illustrated by Peter Parnall. Little, Brown, 1971. A little Navajo girl in a sheep-raising family tries to postpone her grandmother's death in this beautiful story. *P–I*

Bridge to Terabithia by Katherine Paterson. Crowell, 1977; Avon paperback. The touching story of the mutually enriching friendship of two fifth graders, their imaginative play, and the tragedy which leaves only one to carry on. *A*

A Figure of Speech by Norma Fox Mazer. Delacorte, 1973; Dell paperback. Jenny struggles to protect her eighty-three-year-old grandfather from the ridicule and abuse of the rest of the family. *I–A*

Grandma Didn't Wave Back by Rose Blue; illustrated by Ted Lewin. Watts, 1972. Debbie sees her grandmother slip into senility in a tender, sensitive story. *I–A*

The Hundred Penny Box by Sharon Bell Mathis; illustrated by Leo and Diane Dillon. Viking, 1975. A tender story about a boy's love for his 100-year-old great-great-aunt. A strong picture of family loyalty and continuity. *I–A*

Maxie by Mildred Kantrowitz; illustrated by Emily A. McCully. Four Winds, 1970. The old lady living on the top floor of the apartment house has a noisy routine that awakens all her neighbors until one morning she stays quietly in bed. A happy and touching ending. *P–I*

*Nana Upstairs & Nana Downstairs written and illustrated by Tomie de Paola. Putnam, 1973; Penguin paperback. This story is about a child's love for grandmother and great-grandmother and the struggle to understand and accept death. *N–P*

*A Summer to Die by Lois Lowry; illustrated by Jenni Oliver. Houghton, 1977; Bantam paperback. Slowly Meg realizes that the sister she admires and has been a little jealous of is dying. *A*

*A Taste of Blackberries by Doris Buchanan Smith; illustrated by Charles Robinson. Crowell, 1973; Scholastic paperback. First-person story of a young boy whose closest pal dies from a bee sting while the other children are scraping Japanese beetles off grape leaves. *I*

*The Tenth Good Thing About Barney by Judith Viorst; illustrated by Erik Blegvad. Atheneum, 1971. Exquisite first-person story of a small boy who seeks to understand and reconcile himself to the death of Barney, his pet cat. *P*

*There Are Two Kinds of Terrible by Peggy Mann; illustrated by Richard Cuffari. Doubleday, 1977; Avon paperback. Robbie struggles to pull himself together after the death of the person he loves most. *I–A*

*A Treasure Hunt by Christopher Wilson; illustrated by Dagmar Wilson. National Institute on Aging, 1980. Supt. of Documents, Government Printing Office, Washington, DC 20402. A charming story that shatters the stereotyped view of older people. *P–I*

SCIENCE AND NATURE

Ecology

All Upon a Stone by Jean George; illustrated by Don Bolognese. Crowell, 1971. An exquisite nature study of the tiny community in which a mole cricket tunnels, surfaces, swims, and meets others of his species—all upon a stone. *P–I*

Around the House That Jack Built: A Tale of Ecology by Roz Abisch; illustrated by Boche Kaplan. Parents, 1972. With the old nursery rhyme as a pattern, this rhyming tale reports on the ecological situation in the world today. *P–I*

The Beaver Pond by Alvin Tresselt; illustrated by Roger Duvoisin. Lothrop, 1970. Exquisitely illustrated story of the making of a beaver pond, how it silts up and how the area returns to stream and meadow. *P–I*

*The Only Earth We Have by Laurence Pringle; photos and diagrams. Macmillan, 1969. How man is plundering the earth's resources and what can be done to protect and preserve the only earth we have. *I*

*Save the Earth! by Betty Miles; illustrated with photos and drawings by Claire A. Nivola. Knopf, 1974. Information about land, air, and water pollution with provocative questions and projects to dramatize the urgency of the ecology crisis. *I*

The Seal and the Slick written and illustrated by Don Freeman. Viking, 1974. A beautiful plea to keep offshore waters clean. *P–I*

*Who Really Killed Cock Robin? An Ecological Mystery by Jean Craighead George. Dutton, 1971. A compelling mystery that deals with the cycles of nature and the problems of modern living. *I–A*

Animals and Plants

*All Kind of Babies by Millicent E. Selsam; illustrated by Symeon Shimin. Scholastic paperback, 1967. Beautifully illustrated account of baby animals—some like their parents

and some quite different. The evolution of tadpole to frog and caterpillar to butterfly is particularly interesting. *P–I*

Alligator by Evelyn Shaw; illustrated by Frances Zweifel. Harper, 1972. Easy-to-read life story of the alligator of the Southeast—how she lays her eggs, guards the nest, fights off predators, and guides her young. *P–I*

*Animal Fact/Animal Fable by Seymour Simon; illustrated by Diane de Groat. Crown, 1979. Common beliefs about animals (an owl is a wise bird, for example) are explained as fact or fable in an intriguing guessing-game style with exquisite illustrations. *P–I*

Bats: Wings in the Night by Patricia Lauber; illustrated with photos. Random, 1968. Fascinating account of various kinds of bats and how they live—from one the size of a hummingbird to the largest with a wingspread of six feet. *I–A*

Digging Up Dinosaurs written and illustrated by Aliki. Crowell, 1981. Fascinating account of locating and digging out the dinosaur bones later assembled in a museum. Amusing cartoon-strip commentary supplements excellent text. *P*

Houses From the Sea by Alice E. Goudey; illustrated by Adrienne Adams. Scribner's, 1959. Rhythmical text and exquisite illustrations tell of finding sea shells and identifying them. Also *The Day We Saw the Sun Come Up. P*

*How Kittens Grow by Millicent E. Selsam; photos by Esther Bubley. Four Winds, 1975; Scholastic paperback. Four adorable kittens are shown at every stage of growth from birth to eight weeks of age. Also **How Puppies Grow,* 1972. *P*

*It's Nesting Time by Roma Gans; illustrated by Kazue Mizumura. Crowell, 1964. How different birds build their nests. Familiar birds such as the robin, blue jay, mourning dove, meadow lark, etc. are included. *P*

*Junior Science Book of Penguins by Patricia Lauber. Garrard, 1968; Scholastic paperback. Photos and appealing text give scientific information about penguins and their way of life. *P–I*

Land of the Giant Tortoise: The Story of the Galapagos by Millicent E. Selsam; photos by Les Line and Millicent E. Selsam. Four Winds, 1977. Fascinating report of the plants and animals of these volcanic islands. *I*

My Puppy Is Born by Joanna Cole; photos by Jerome Wexler. Morrow, 1973. Photo story of the birth and infancy of a miniature dachshund with a few lines of explanation for each picture. *P–I*

A Snake-Lover's Diary written and illustrated by Barbara Brenner. Addison-Wesley, 1970. A young boy's report of collecting and housing snakes from April to September. *I–A*

Tarantulas: The Biggest Spiders by Alexander L. Crosby; photographs and drawings. Walker, 1981. A vivid report of the way of life of the giant spider that can be vanquished by a tiny wasp. *P–I*

Turtle Pond by Berniece Freschet; illustrated by Donald Carrick. Scribner's, 1971. How a mother turtle lays her eggs, how the young turtles hatch, and make their way to the pond despite various marauders. Exquisite full-color watercolor illustrations. *I*

The Web in the Grass by Berniece Freschet; illustrated by Roger Duvoisin. Scribner's, 1972. Life cycle story of the spider who spins her web, evades her enemies, traps her food, and lays her eggs—all beautifully illustrated with colorful collages. *P*

The Wentletrap Trap by Jean Craighead George; illustrated by Symeon Shimin. Dutton, 1978. Moving story of a Bimini Island boy searching for a rare sea shell as proof that he is grown-up. Wonderful family relationships and natural science details. *N–P*

What Is That Alligator Saying? by Ruth Belov Gross; illustrated by John Hawkinson. Hastings, 1972. A beginning book on animal communication—how various animals communicate and what they communicate about. *P*

Pregnancy and Childbirth

A Baby Is Born, the Story of How Life Begins by Milton Levine and Jean H. Seligmann. Western, 1966. A clear explanation with beautiful illustrations. *I*

Inside Mom: An Illustrated Account of Conception, Pregnancy, and Childbirth by Sylvia Caveney and Simon Stern; illustrated by Salvatore Raciti plus photos. St. Martin's, 1977. Straightforward information on all aspects of the birth cycle. *I–A*

New Baby Comes by Julian May; illustrated by Brendan Lynch. Creative Education Inc., 1970. With simple text and clear illustrations, the growth of the fetus until birth is shown. *P–I*

Watching the New Baby by Joan Samson; photos by Gary Gladstone. Atheneum, 1974. Discussion of fetal development, through growth and development of an infant. *N–P–I*

The Wonderful Story of How You Were Born by Sidonie Matsner Gruenberg; illustrated by Symeon Shimin. Doubleday, 1970. The facts of human reproduction with warm sensitive illustrations. Too advanced for most children to read, but excellent to read aloud with them. *A*

The Sun, the Moon and Outer Space

A Book of Moon Rockets for You by Franklyn M. Branley; illustrated by Leonard Kessler. Crowell, 1970. What moon rockets are and how they were used in planning man's first trips to the moon, with photos taken on the first lunar probes. Also, *A Book of Flying Saucers for You*, 1972. *I–A*

Eclipse: Darkness in Daytime by Franklyn M. Branley; illustrated by Donald Crews. Crowell, 1973. Why eclipses happen and how to watch safely. *N–P*

First Travel Guide to the Moon by Rhonda Blumberg; illustrated by Roy Doty. Four Winds, 1980. What to pack, how to go, and what to see when you get there. An imaginative adventure based on scientific fact. *I*

How Did We Find Out About Black Holes? by Isaac Asimov; illustrations by David Wool. Walker, 1978. Information and conjecture about collapsed stars or "black holes." *A*

Journey to the Moon written and illustrated by Erich Fuchs. Delacorte, 1970. Brilliant art and clear, brief text tell of the Apollo II mission. *I–A*

Long View Into Space by Seymour Simon; photographs. Crown, 1979. The planets, the solar system and beyond, in striking photographs and brief, easy-to-read descriptions. *I–A*

Mars by Dinah Moche; illustrated. Watts, 1978. Easy-to-read facts about the Viking space missions and their report on Mars. *P–I*

The Planets in Our Solar System by Franklyn M. Branley; illustrated by Don Madden. Crowell, 1981. Up-to-date introduction to our solar system and its nine planets, plus directions for making models to show distance and size of the planets. *N–P*

THE WEATHER

Junior Science Book of Rain, Hail, Sleet and Snow by Nancy Larrick; illustrated by Weda Yap. Garrard, 1961. Simple facts answer the common questions about weather and how it works. *P–I*

Lightning and Thunder by Herbert S. Zim. Morrow, 1952. An explanation of lightning and thunder with suggested activities to help understand static electricity. *I*

Nature's Weather Forecasters by Helen Roney Sattler; illustrations. Elsevier-Nelson, 1978. How to observe and interpret signs of weather change. *A*

Storm at the Jetty written and illustrated by Leonard Everett Fisher. Viking, 1981. A young boy watches the drama of the coastline as he sits on the jetty near his home. Dramatic text and illustrations. *I*

The Storm Book by Charlotte Zolotow; illustrated by Margaret Bloy Graham. Harper, 1952. Poetic prose and exquisite pictures describe a summer storm sweeping over the city, the countryside, and the seashore. *P*

What's Happening to Our Climate? by Malcolm E. Weiss; illustrated by Paul Plumer. Messner, 1978. Theories to explain the changing weather conditions through the centuries. *I*

FUN WITH MAGIC

*Funny Magic: Easy Tricks for the Young Magician by Rose Wyler and Gerald Ames; illustrated by Talivaldis Stubis. Four Winds, 1972; Scholastic paperback. A delightful collection of simple sleight of hand tricks to be done by one child, sometimes two, and requiring only the simplest materials. Also **Magic Secrets,* 1971; Scholastic. *P–I*

*Give a Magic Show by Burton and Rita Marks; illustrated by Don Madden. Lothrop, 1977; Scholastic paperback. Diagrams, humorous cartoons and concise directions for putting on a successful performance. *I*

RIDDLES, JOKES, AND NONSENSE

*Ballpoint Bananas and Other Jokes for Kids compiled by Charles Keller; illustrated by David Barrios. Prentice, 1973. Zany rhymes and riddles with amusing illustrations. *I*

Five Men Under One Umbrella: And Other Ready-to-Read Riddles collected and illustrated by Joseph Low. Macmillan, 1975. Each riddle is on a right-hand page; turn the page and you have the answer. Also *Mad Wet Hen and Other Riddles.* Greenwillow, 1977. *P*

*Give Up? Cartoon Riddle Rhymes by William Cole; illustrated by Mike Thaler. Watts, 1978; Avon paperback. Riddles and rhyming answers. *P*

*Silly Questions and Funny Answers written and illustrated by William Wiesner. Scholastic paperback, 1974. Fine collection of more than sixty riddles for the very young. *P*

Stoo Hample's Silly Joke Book. Delacorte, 1978. Cartoons, jokes and riddles in easy-to-read format. *P*

Syd Hoff's Best Jokes Ever illustrated by Syd Hoff. Putnam, 1978. Puns and jokes that are easy to read. *P–I*

Ten Copycats in a Boat and Other Riddles by Alvin Schwartz; illustrated by Marc Simont. Harper, 1980. Twenty-five rib-ticklers. A sure winner. *P*

This Can Lick a Lollipop by Joel Rothman and Argentina Palacios; illustrated with photos. Doubleday, 1979. Each page poses a body riddle in rhyme which is answered on the next page. Text in both English and Spanish. *P–I*

Tomfoolery: Trickery and Foolery with Words compiled by Alvin Schwartz; illustrated by Glen Rounds. Lippincott, 1973. Tricks, jokes, nonsense tales, and puns with folksy humor. *I*

What Do You Say, Dear? by Sesyle Joslin; illustrated by Maurice Sendak. Addison-Wesley, 1958. Comical presentation of simple rules of etiquette. "You are walking downtown backwards and bump into a crocodile. What do you say, dear?" (Excuse me.) Also *What Do You Do, Dear?* 1961. *P–I*

POETRY FOR EVERYONE

INDIVIDUAL POETS

Bodecker, N. M. *Hurry, Hurry, Mary Dear! and Other Nonsense Poems,* illustrated by the poet. Atheneum, 1976. Brief, witty, very appealing. Also **Let's Marry Said the Cherry,* 1974. *I–A*

Ciardi, John. *The Man Who Sang the Sillies,* illustrated by Edward Gorey. Lippincott, 1961. Humorous poems that range from gentle nonsense to the ridiculous. Also *You Read to Me, I'll Read to You.* Lippincott, 1962. *P–I*

de Gasztold, Carmen Bernos, **Prayers from the Ark* and *The Creatures Choir* (one vol.), translated by Rumer Godden, illustrated by Jean Primrose. Penguin paperback, 1968. Animals offer their prayers with wit, gentle irony, and a certain pathos that appeals to children. *P–I–A*

Fisher, Aileen. *Cricket in a Thicket,* illustrated by Feodor Rojankovsky; Scribner's, 1963. *Feathered Ones and Furry,* illustrated by Eric Carle; Crowell, 1979. *Going Barefoot,* illustrated by Adrienne Adams; Crowell, 1960. *Listen, Rabbit,* illustrated by Symeon Shimin; Crowell, 1964. Delightful verses about insects, rabbits, chipmunks and a child's response to nature. *P–I*

Frost, Robert. *You Come Too,* illustrated by Thomas W. Nason. Holt, 1959. Fifty-two favorite poems selected for young readers. *A*

Giovanni, Nikki. *Spin a Soft Black Song,* illustrated by Charles Bible. Hill and Wang, 1971. A black poet and black artist tell of childhood experiences with the freshness and candor of all children. *P–I*

Greenfield, Eloise. *Honey, I Love: And Other Love Poems,* illustrated by Diane and Leo Dillon. Crowell, 1978. Sixteen love poems straight from the heart of a small child. *P–I*

Holman, Felice. *At the Top of My Voice and Other Poems,* illustrated by Edward Gorey. Scribner's, 1970. Charming, often humorous, poems about children's experiences. *P–I*

Kennedy, X. J. *One Winter Night in August and Other Nonsense Jingles,* illustrated by David McPhail. Atheneum, 1975. Over fifty humorous poems, absurd and freewheeling. Also, *The Phantom Ice Cream Man,* 1979. *I–A*

Kuskin, Karla. *Dogs & Dragons, Trees & Dreams.* Harper, 1980. Also *Near the Window Tree: Poems and Notes,* illustrated by the poet, 1975. Gay and whimsical poems appealing to the very young. *N–P*

Lee, Dennis. *Alligator Pie,* illustrated by Frank Newfield. Houghton, 1975. Way-out wacky rhyming verses. Also *Garbage Delight,* 1978. *I*

Livingston, Myra Cohn. *The Malibu and Other Poems,* illustrated by James Spanfeller. Atheneum, 1972. *O Sliver of Liver and Other Poems,* 1979. Sparkling poems which reflect the moods, situations, and viewpoints of today. *I–A*

McCord, David. *One at a Time: His Collected Poems for the Young,* illustrated by Henry B. Kane; Little, Brown, 1977. *Speak Up: More Rhymes of the Never Was and Always Is,* 1980. Poems that sing out with crisp lines, wonderful humor, and a vigor that is exciting. *P–I*

Merriam, Eve. *There Is No Rhyme for Silver;* Atheneum, 1962. *It Doesn't Always Have to Rhyme,* 1964. *Rainbow Writing,* 1976. Modern poetry that is both amusing and provocative. *I–A*

© 1974 N. M. Bodecker in *Let's Marry Said the Cherry*

Milne, A. A. *When We Were Very Young*, illustrated by
E. H. Shepard. Dutton, 1924; Dell paperback. A delightful
collection of poems written for the poet's son about his fun
and fantasy. Continued in *Now We Are Six*. Dutton, 1927;
Dell paperback. *N–P*

Moore, Lilian. *I Feel the Same Way*, illustrated by Robert
Quackenbush. Atheneum, 1967. The secret feelings of a
young child. Also *Think of Shadows*. Atheneum, 1980. *I*

O'Neill, Mary. *Hailstones and Halibut Bones*, illustrated
by Leonard Weisgard. Doubleday, 1961. Poems about colors. *P–I*

Prelutsky, Jack. *The Headless Horseman Rides Tonight:
More Poems to Trouble Your Sleep*, illustrated by Arnold

Lobel. Greenwillow, 1980. Twelve haunting poems about such creatures as a mummy, a banshee, a poltergeist, and the abominable snowman. Also *Nightmares: Poems to Trouble Your Sleep.* A

Sandburg, Carl. *Early Moon,* illustrated by James Daugherty; Harcourt, 1930. *Wind Song,* illustrated by William A. Smith; 1960. Two splendid collections which sparkle with wisdom, beauty, humor, and vibrant feeling for life. *I–A*

Silverstein, Shel. *Where the Sidewalk Ends: Poems and Drawings.* Harper, 1974. Hilarious poems make this the children's favorite. Also *A Light in the Attic,* 1981. *P–I–A*

Watson, Clyde. *Father Fox's Pennyrhymes,* illustrated by Wendy Watson. Crowell, 1971; Scholastic paperback. Father Fox in stout overalls sings exuberant nursery rhymes set in rural New England. *N–P*

POETRY ANTHOLOGIES

City in All Directions, edited by Arnold Adoff; illustrated by Donald Carrick. Macmillan, 1969. Modern poems about the city by poets of many countries. *I–A*

The Earth Is Sore: Native Americans on Nature, adapted and illustrated by Aline Amon. Atheneum, 1981. Poems and poetic statements by American Indians reflecting their love of nature and identification with the earth and sky. *I–A*

First Voices, edited by Geoffrey Summerfield. Books 1, 2, 3, and 4. Knopf, 1970. Four fascinating collections of new and old poetry, with some by children, plus photos. *I–A*

Go With the Poem, selected by Lilian Moore. McGraw, 1979. A rich and varied collection of ninety poems which are contemporary in spirit. *I–A*

Hosannah the Home Run! Poems About Sports, selected by Alice Fleming; illustrated with photos. Little, Brown, 1972. Thirty-four poems about sports which reveal humor, exciting moments, and quiet satisfaction. *I–A*

How to Eat a Poem & Other Morsels: Food Poems for Children, selected by Rose H. Agree; illustrated by Peggy Wilson. Pantheon, 1967. A veritable smorgasbord of verses, mostly humorous, about all sorts of foods and those who love them. *I–A*

I Am the Cat, selected by Lee Bennett Hopkins; illustrated by Linda Rochester Richards. Harcourt, 1981. Twenty-four poems and pictures make this a cat lover's dream book. *P–I*

*I Am the Darker Brother, edited by Arnold Adoff; illustrated by Benny Andrews. Macmillan, 1968. Modern poems by black Americans. Also *Black Out Loud,* 1970. *A*

*Oh, What Nonsense!, edited by William Cole; illustrated by Tomi Ungerer. Viking, 1966; Penguin paperback. Fifty rib-ticklers, old and new. Also *Oh, How Silly!* 1970, and *Oh, That's Ridiculous!* 1972. *P–I*

On City Streets, edited by Nancy Larrick; illustrated with photos by David Sagarin. Evans, 1968. Poetry about city scenes and city people of today. Also *I Heard a Scream in the Street,* 1970. *A*

On Our Way: Poems of Pride and Love, selected by Lee Bennett Hopkins; illustrated with photos by David Parks. Knopf, 1974. Twenty-two poems by poets proud of their blackness and confident of the future. *I–A*

Poetry for Holidays, selected by Nancy Larrick; illustrated by Kelly Oechsli. Garrard, 1966. Fifty-seven favorite poems sing of the important holidays. Also **More Poetry for Holidays,* 1973, Scholastic paperback. *P–I*

The Poetry Troupe: An Anthology of Poems to Read Aloud, compiled by Isabel Wilner. Scribner's, 1977. Poems that invite participation through chanting, impromptu choral reading, and dramatization. *P–I*

Room for Me and a Mountain Lion: Poems of Open Space, selected by Nancy Larrick; illustrated with photos. Evans, 1974. Poems that speak of the joy and freedom of open space. Also *Crazy to Be Alive in Such a Strange World,* 1977. *I–A*

Tambourines! Tambourines to Glory! Prayers for Children, selected by Nancy Larrick. Westminster, 1982. Prayers from many periods and many cultures voice an exultant faith. *P–I–A*

They've Discovered a Head in the Box for the Bread and Other Laughable Limericks, collected by John E. Brewton and Lorraine A. Blackburn; illustrated by Fernando Krahn. Crowell, 1978. 200 hilarious limericks—touching, scary, tricky. *I*

When the Dark Comes Dancing: The Bedtime Poetry Book, compiled by Nancy Larrick; illustrated by John Wallner. Philomel, 1982. A beautifully illustrated collection of poems and lullabies to read or sing at bedtime, with notes for parents. *N–P*

SONG BOOKS

American Folk Songs for Children, edited by Ruth Seeger; illustrated by Barbara Cooney. Doubleday, 1948. An inviting songbook for the entire famiy. *N–P–I–A*

The Baby's Song Book, selected and arranged by Elizabeth Poston; illustrated by William Stobbs. Crowell, 1972. Eighty of the traditional nursery songs with piano arrangements and beautiful illustrations in full color. *N–P*

*Eye Winker, Tom Tinker, Chin Chopper: A Collection of Musical Fingerplays, collected by Tom Glazer; illustrated by Ron Himler. Doubleday, 1973. A happy collection of fingerplays with piano arrangements, guitar chords, and humorous illustrations. *N–P*

' *The Fireside Book of Children's Songs,* collected and edited by Marie Winn; music by Allan Miller; illustrated by John Alcorn. Simon & Schuster, 1966. More than 100 of the most beautiful and the funniest songs. *N–P–I*

The Fireside Book of Folk Songs, selected by Margaret Boni; illustrated by Alice and Martin Provensen. Simon & Schuster, 1947. 150 work songs, dances, nursery rhymes, marches, ballads, and spirituals. Also **The Fireside Book of Favorite American Songs,* 1963. *N–P–I–A*

Frog Went A-Courtin', retold by John Langstaff and Feodor Rojankovsky; illustrated by Feodor Rojankovsky. Harcourt, 1955. The old familiar ballad with beautifully detailed illustrations, plus music. Also *Over in the Meadow*, 1975. *N–P–I*

The Great Song Book, edited by Timothy John; illustrated by Tomi Ungerer. Doubleday, 1978. Over sixty of the best-loved songs, with music and full-color illustrations. *N–P–I–A*

Lullabies and Night Songs, edited by William Engvick; music by Alec Wilder; illustrated by Maurice Sendak. Harper, 1965. Forty-eight lullabies and songs with simple new melodies and arrangements by a modern composer, plus color illustrations. *N–P*

Sing Together Children, edited by Frances M. Andrews. World Around Songs, Rt. 5, Box 398, Burnsville, NC 28714. Words with melody for 125 old favorites, singing games, folk songs from around the world, holiday songs—all in a tiny eighty-page paperback. *N–P–I–A*

PUBLISHERS WHOSE BOOKS APPEAR IN THIS CHAPTER

Addison-Wesley Publishing Co., Inc. Reading, MA 01867
Apollo Editions. *See* Harper & Row
Archway Paperbacks, c/o Pocket Books, 1230 Ave. of the
    Americas, New York, NY 10020
Atheneum Publishers, 597 Fifth Ave., New York, NY 10017
The Atlantic Monthly Press, 8 Arlington St., Boston, MA
    02116
Avon Books, 959 Eighth Ave., New York, NY 10019

Bantam Books, Inc., 666 Fifth Ave., New York, NY 10103
Bradbury Press, Inc., 2 Overhill Rd., Scarsdale, NY 10583

Coward, McCann & Geoghegan, Inc., 200 Madison Ave.,
    New York, NY 10016
Creative Education, Inc., Box 227, 123 S. Broad St., Man-
    kato, MN 56001
Crowell Junior Books. *See* Harper & Row
Crown Publishers, Inc., One Park Ave., New York, NY
    10016

Delacorte Press, One Dag Hammarskjold Plaza, New York,
    NY 10017

Dell Publishing Co., Inc., One Dag Hammarskjold Plaza, New York, NY 10017

The Dial Press, One Dag Hammarskjold Plaza, New York, NY 10017

Doubleday & Co., Inc., 245 Park Ave., New York, NY 10167

Dover Publications, Inc., 180 Varick St., New York, NY 10014

E. P. Dutton, Inc., 2 Park Ave., New York, NY 10016

M. Evans & Co., 216 E. 49 St., New York, NY 10017

Farrar, Straus & Giroux, 19 Union Square W., New York, NY 10003

Follett Publishing Co., 1010 W. Washington Blvd., Chicago, IL 60607

Four Winds Press. Division of Scholastic Book Services

Garrard Publishing Co., 1607 N. Market St., Champaign, IL 61820

Greenwillow Books, 105 Madison Ave., New York, NY 10016

Grosset & Dunlap, Inc., A member of The Putnam Publishing Group. 200 Madison Ave., New York, NY 10016

Harcourt Brace Jovanovich, Inc., 757 Third Ave., New York, NY 10017

Harper & Row, Publishers, Inc., 10 E. 53 St., New York, NY 10022

Hastings House, Publishers, Inc., 10 E. 40 St., New York, NY 10016

Hill & Wang, Inc. Division of Farrar, Straus & Giroux

Holiday House, Inc., 18 E. 53 St., New York, NY 10022

Holt, Rinehart & Winston, 521 Fifth Ave., New York, NY 10175

Houghton Mifflin Co., 2 Park Street, Boston, MA 02107

Alfred A. Knopf, Inc., 201 E. 50 St., New York, NY 10022

Lerner Publications Co., 241 First Ave. North, Minneapolis, MN 55401

Lippincott Junior Books. *See* Harper & Row

Little, Brown & Co., 34 Beacon St., Boston, MA 02106

Lothrop, Lee & Shepard Books, 105 Madison Ave., New York, NY 10016

McGraw-Hill Book Co., 1221 Ave. of the Americas, New York, NY 10020

Macmillan Publishing Co., Inc., 866 Third Ave., New York, NY 10022

Merrimack Book Services, Inc., 55 Union St., Lawrence, MA 01843

Julian Messner. Division of Simon & Schuster.

William Morrow & Co., 105 Madison Ave., New York, NY 10016

Thomas Nelson, Inc., P.O. Box 141000, Nashville, TN 37214

The New American Library, Inc., 1633 Broadway, New York, NY 10019

Pantheon Books, 201 E. 50 St., New York, NY 10022

Parents Magazine Press, 685 Third Ave., New York, NY 10017

Parnassus Press, Wayside Rd., Burlington, MA 01803

Penguin Books, 625 Madison Ave., New York, NY 10022

S. G. Phillips, Inc., 305 W. 86 St., New York, NY 10024

Philomel Books, 200 Madison Ave., New York, NY 10016

Prentice-Hall, Inc., Englewood Cliffs, NJ 07632

G. P. Putnam's Sons, 200 Madison Ave., New York, NY 10016

Rand McNally & Co., Box 7600, Chicago, IL 60680

Random House, Inc., 201 E. 50 St., New York, NY 10022

St. Martin's Press Inc., 175 Fifth Ave., New York, NY 10010

Scholastic Book Services, 50 W. 44 St., New York, NY 10036

Charles Scribner's Sons, 597 Fifth Ave., New York, NY 10017

Simon & Schuster, 1230 Ave. of the Americas, New York, NY 10020

Vanguard Press, Inc., 424 Madison Ave., New York, NY 10017

The Viking Press, 625 Madison Ave., New York, NY 10022

Henry Z. Walck, Inc., c/o David McKay Co., Inc., 2 Park Ave., New York, NY 10016

Walker & Co., 720 Fifth Ave., New York, NY 10019

Frederick Warne & Co., Inc., 2 Park Ave., New York, NY 10016

Franklin Watts, Inc., 730 Fifth Ave., New York, NY 10019

Western Publishing Co., Inc., 850 Third Ave., New York, NY 10022

The Westminster Press, 925 Chestnut St., Philadelphia, PA 19107

Albert Whitman & Co., 560 W. Lake St., Chicago, IL 60606

Windmill Books Inc., *See* Simon & Schuster

World Around Songs, Rt. 5, Box 398, Burnsville, NC 28714

17

Magazines for Children

The child who receives a magazine through the mail is almost invariably pleased and proud. Receiving mail is one sign of being grown-up and responsible, both welcome attributes to a child. Furthermore, the magazine comes again and again so it is something to look forward to, a bearer of new treats and treasures.

Perhaps a relative or family friend would welcome information about a gift subscription to your child. It would surely bring periodic delight and repeated remembrance of a special person or occasion.

The child's positive response to a new magazine is more apt to develop if a parent or older sibling introduces the highlights when the first issue arrives. Together you can explore the lead articles or stories as well as the features to look for in each issue.

Preschool children and those just beginning to read will welcome your reading parts aloud. All ages will become more interested if there is someone with whom to share choice items, explore the illustrations, and raise questions.

Few magazines for children approach the literary and artistic quality of the best children's books. Several are marred by tawdry artwork that suggests comic books or Saturday morning TV cartoons. Some give extensive space to advertising of plastic toys and gadgets that can only be called junk.

Fortunately there are good magazines with child appeal which can broaden a child's outlook and sense of values while providing good entertainment. The following should be considered (prices are subject to change):

Boys' Life (for age 10 and up) published by the Boy Scouts of America. Fiction, nonfiction, book reviews, cartoon features, sports, hobbies, scouting, projects and programs. *Subscription*: $8.40 a year for nonscouts (12 issues), $4.20 a year for scouts. Boys' Life, Box 61030, Dallas/Ft. Worth Airport, TX 75261.

Children's Digest (ages 8–12) published by Parents Magazine Enterprises, Inc. Stories, poems, science features, nature information, book reviews, and songs. *Subscription*: $10.95 a year (9 issues); Benjamin Franklin Literary & Medical Society Inc., Box 567B, 1100 Waterway Blvd., Indianapolis, IN 46206.

Cobblestone: The History Magazine for Young People (ages 8–13). American history comes alive through articles, maps, illustrations, songs, poems, puzzles, crafts and activities. Each issue focuses on one theme: "The First Transcontinental Railroad," for example, or "The Lewis and Clark Expedition," or "John James Audubon." *Subscription*: $16.50 a year (12 issues). Cobblestone Publishing, 28 Main Street, Peterborough, NH 03458.

Cricket (ages 8–12). This is by far the most artistic and literary magazine for children. The editorial board includes distinguished leaders in the field of children's literature, including authors and illustrators who are among the most talented prize-winners. *Cricket* carries stories, poetry, book reviews, informational articles, and a potpourri of how-to-do-its, puzzles, and humor, as well as contributions by children. "A Word for Parents" is a valuable four-page monthly insert. *Subscription*: $15.00 a year (12 issues); Cricket, P.O. Box 2670, Boulder, CO 80322.

Ebony Jr.! (ages 6–12). Fiction, nonfiction, poetry, current events, profiles of outstanding peers, black history, games, crafts, recipes, humor, children's contributions—all presented with a strong accent on the positive. *Subscription*: $8.00 a year (12 issues). Johnson Publishing Co., 820 S. Michigan Ave., Chicago, IL 60605. "Guide for the Use of *Ebony Jr.!*" suggests additional exercises to follow up featured material (accompanies each issue for additional $2.00 a year.)

Highlights for Children (ages 4–12). Fiction, nonfiction, science projects and experiments, craft projects, games, puzzles, hidden pictures, "emphasis on values instead of violence." *Subscription*: $14.95 a year (11 issues). Highlights for Children, P.O. Box 269, 2300 W. Fifth Ave., Columbus, OH 43216.

Humpty Dumpty's Magazine for Little Children (ages 4–8). Read-aloud stories, poems, coloring-book page, science features, and songs. *Subscription*: $8.95 a year (10 issues). Humpty Dumpty's Subscription Office, Children's Better Health Publications, P.O. Box 567B, Indianapolis, IN 46206.

National Geographic World (ages 8–12). Full-color pictures, miniarticles, far-out facts, how-tos, and more. *Subscription*: $7.95 a year (12 issues). National Geographic World, Dept. 00880, 17th and M Sts. NW, Washington, DC 20036.

Owl: The Outdoor and Wildlife Discovery Magazine for Children (ages 7–12). A beautifully illustrated nature magazine from Canada. Full-color photographs and paintings illustrate an interesting assortment of articles, picture stories, puzzles, games, and experiments. *Subscription in the U.S.*: $10.00 a year (10 issues). Scholastic Home Periodicals, P.O. Box 1925, Marion, OH 43302.

Ranger Rick's Nature Magazine (ages 5–12). Nonfiction, some fiction, riddles, puzzles, book reviews—all about nature, with gorgeous full-color photos. Sponsored by the National Wildlife Federation. *Subscription* (only through membership dues): $10.50 a year (12 issues) to Ranger Rick's Nature Magazine, National Wildlife Federation, 1412 16th Street NW, Washington, DC 20036.

Scienceland (ages 5–8). Dramatically beautiful science magazine. Each issue features one topic, such as plants, animals, friction, motion, or lenses, plus science craft or play. *Subscription*: $24.00 a year (8 issues). Scienceland, Suite 2102, 501 Fifth Ave., New York, NY 10017.

Many children are keenly interested in the content of family magazines such as the following:

Animal Kingdom. Bimonthly. New York Zoological Society (Bronx Zoo), 185 St. and Southern Blvd., New York, NY 10460.

Arizona Highways. Monthly. Arizona State Highway Dept., 2039 W. Lewis Ave., Phoenix, AZ 85009.

Audubon Magazine. Bimonthly. National Audubon Society, 950 Third Ave., New York, NY 10022.

Baseball Digest. Monthly. Century Publishing Co., 1708 2nd St., Highland Park, IL 60035.

Beaver. Quarterly. North Hudson's Bay Co., Hudson's Bay House, 77 Main St., Winnipeg, Manitoba, Canada, R3C241.

Car and Driver. Monthly. Ziff-Davis Publishing Co., One Park Ave., New York, NY 10016.

Football Digest. Monthly. Century Publishing Co., 1020 Church St., Evanston, IL 60201.

National Geographic. Monthly. National Geographic Society, 1145 17th St., Washington, DC 20036.

National Wildlife. Bimonthly. National Wildlife Federation, 225 E. Michigan, Milwaukee, WI 53202.

Natural History. Monthly. American Museum of Natural History, Central Park West at 79 St., New York, NY 10024.

Popular Science. Monthly. Popular Science Co., Sub. Dept., Boulder, CO 80302.

Smithsonian. Monthly. Smithsonian Institution National Association, Arts and Industries Bldg., 900 Jefferson Drive S.W., Washington, DC 20560.

Sports Illustrated. Weekly. Time, Inc., 1271 Ave. of the Americas, New York, NY 10020.

Zoonooz. Monthly. Zoological Society of San Diego, Inc., Box 551, San Diego, CA 92112.

IV

ESPECIALLY FOR PARENTS

18
Books and Magazines About Children's Reading

BOOKS

Babies Need Books by Dorothy Butler. Atheneum Publishers, 1980. This is a convincing argument for using books with children from birth. The author names specific books, suggests when and how to use them, and relates her reasons to the developmental stages of a child's growth. Very informal, warm, compelling. First published in New Zealand, this volume lists many British books along with some published in the U.S.

*Books, Children & Men by Paul Hazard, translated by Marguerite Mitchell. The Horn Book, 1944. A distinguished French scholar surveys children's books with gaiety and gusto, giving pertinent comments on children's choices and the importance of imagination and fancy.

Choosing Books for Children: A Commonsense Guide by Betsy Hearne. Delacorte Press, 1981. A very practical guide which is a joy to read and learn from.

Cushla and Her Books by Dorothy Butler. The Horn Book, 1980. The inspiring true story of a tiny New Zealand girl with multiple physical handicaps who flowered physically and intellectually with the constant stimulation of books from the time she was four months old.

---

*Available in paperback.

Illustrations in Children's Books by Patricia Cianciolo. William C. Brown, 1976. How to appraise illustrations in children's books, styles of art, artists' media and techniques, and an excellent annotated list of illustrated children's books, well indexed.

The Learning Child: Guidelines for Parents and Teachers by Dorothy H. Cohen. Random, 1972. A forward-looking and creative teacher discusses three periods of childhood growth: the five-year-olds, the six- and seven-year-olds, and the eight- to eleven-year-olds, giving the critical home and school problems of each, and the most important aspects of child growth and learning. Particular emphasis is given to moral growth and personal integrity.

The Pleasure of Their Company: How to Have More Fun With Your Children by the Bank Street College. Bank Street College Bookstore, 610 W. 112 St., New York, NY 10025. Written by more than twenty experts from the Bank Street faculty, this is a treasury of suggestions grouped to fit into the pattern of a child's life: play and toys, books and reading, TV, creative arts, special relationships, changes in family life, etc. All focus on the joy of living constructively with children.

Raising Readers: A Guide to Sharing Literature with Young Children by Linda Leonard Lamme with Vivian Cox, Jane Matanzo, and Miken Olson. Walker and Co., 1980. Detailed suggestions for introducing recommended books to infants, toddlers, prereaders, and beginning readers.

Reading Begins at Home: Preparing Children for Reading Before They Go to School by Dorothy Butler and Marie Clay, illustrated by Peter Dent. Heinemann Educational Books, 4 Front St., Exeter, NH 03833. U.S. edition 1982. From New Zealand comes this invaluable little book of easy and informal ways to introduce young children to written language and reading.

Teaching Young Children to Read at Home by Wood Smethurst. McGraw-Hill, 1975. A warm and sensible guide for parents who want to introduce their preschool children to reading.

Using Literature with Young Children by Betty Coody. William C. Brown, 1979. An introduction to some of the best books for children (ages one to eight) with explicit directions for getting children involved with books at home and at school through reading aloud, storytelling, dramatization, children's creative writing, etc. Excellent annotated lists of books.

MAGAZINES

The Calendar. Quarterly featuring news about children's books, as well as special events, articles, awards, and available materials related to children's books. For sample copy and information, write The Children's Book Council, Inc., 67 Irving Place, NY 10003.

Gifted Children Newsletter. 16-page magazine for parents which is packed with stimulating information and practical suggestions, along with a 4-page "Spin-Off" of puzzles, tricks, games, and challenges for children. 1255 Portland Place, Boulder, CO 80323.

The Horn Book. Reviews of children's books and outstanding articles by authors and illustrators of children's books, librarians, and parents. Bimonthly. The Horn Book, Park Square Bldg., 31 St. James Ave., Boston, MA 02116.

News for Parents From the International Reading Association (2 pages). Lively, concise suggestions for home activities, appealing books, and sources of materials. Published three times a year for the use of IRA members. Available through local IRA Councils or the International Reading Association, Box 8139, 800 Barksdale Rd., Newark, DE 19711.

Parents' Choice. A stimulating review of children's media— books, television, movies, music, records, toys, and games. Parents' Choice Foundation, Box 185, Waban, MA 02168.

Index